Trout Streams of Michigan

Guide Mike Bachelder with a stormy day brown trout

Trout Streams of Michigan

A Fly-Angler's Guide

Bob Linsenman and
Steve Nevala

Foreword by Ernest Schwiebert

2ND EDITION

Backcountry Guides
Woodstock, Vermont

An Invitation to the Reader

With time, access points may change, and road numbers, signs, and landmarks referred to in this book may be altered. If you find that such changes have occurred near the waters described in this book, please let the author and publisher know, so that corrections can be made in future editions. Other comments and suggestions are also welcome. Address all correspondence to:

Fishing Editor
Backcountry Guides
P.O. Box 748
Woodstock, VT 05091

Library of Congress Cataloging-in-Publication Data

Linsenman, Bob.
  Trout streams of Michigan : a fly-angler's guide / Bob Linsenman and Steve Nevala ; foreword by Ernest Schwiebert.—2nd ed.
    p. cm.
  Rev. ed of: Michigan trout streams, c1993.
  ISBN 0-88150-489-0 (alk. paper)
    Trout fishing—Michigan—Guidebooks. 2. Fly fishing—Michigan—Guidebooks. 3. Michigan—Guidebooks. I. Nevala, Steve. II. Linsenman, Bob. Michigan Trout Streams. III. Title.
SH688.U6 L56 2001
799.1'757'09774—dc21

                                        00-068192

Published by Backcountry Guides, a division of The Countryman Press, P.O. Box 748, Woodstock, Vermont 05091

Distributed by W.W. Norton & Company, Inc., 500 Fifth Avenue, New York, NY 10110

Cover and text design by Bodenweber Design
Cover photograph by Bob Linsenman
Maps by Richard Widhu, © 2001 The Countryman Press

Printed in the United States of America

10 9 8 7 6 5 4

To the Blazing Waders

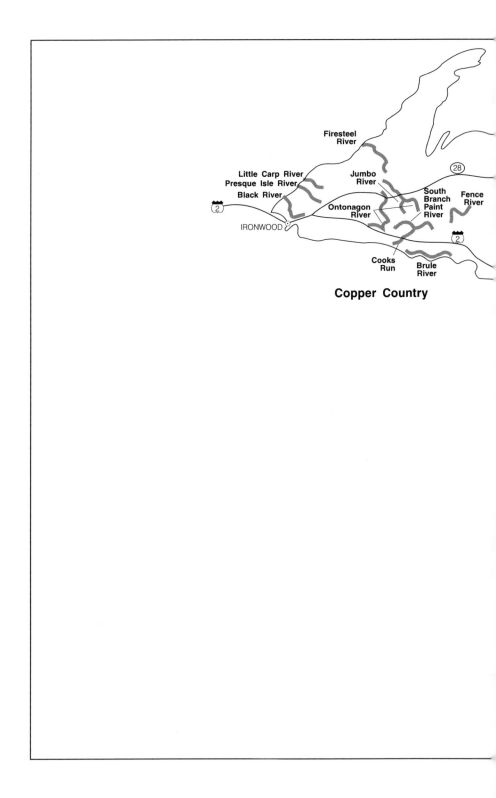

Copper Country

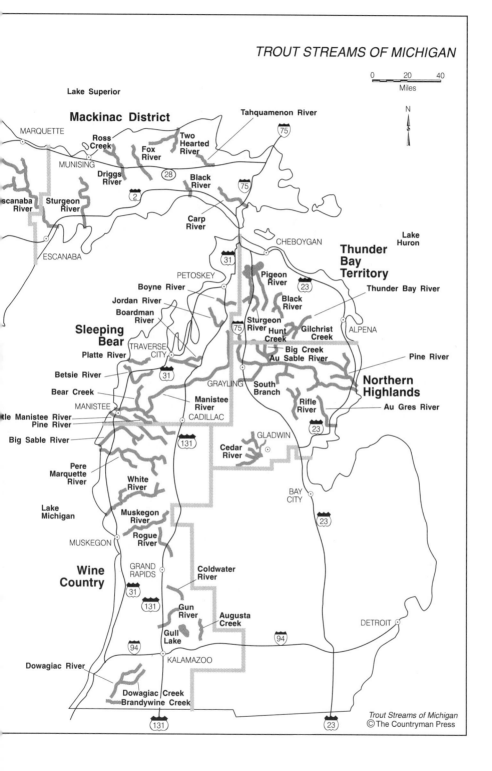

TROUT STREAMS OF MICHIGAN

0   20   40
Miles

N

Lake Superior

Mackinac District

Tahquamenon River

75

MARQUETTE

Ross
Creek

Two
Hearted
River

Fox
River

MUNISING

28

Driggs
River

Black
River

75

2

scanaba
River

Sturgeon
River

Carp
River

ESCANABA

CHEBOYGAN

Lake
Huron

Thunder
Bay
Territory

31

PETOSKEY

Pigeon
River

23

Boyne River

Thunder Bay River

Jordan River

Black
River

Boardman
River

Sleeping
Bear

75

Sturgeon
River

Hunt
Creek

Gilchrist
Creek

ALPENA

Platte River

TRAVERSE
CITY

Big Creek
Au Sable River

Pine River

Betsie River

31

GRAYLING

South
Branch

Northern
Highlands

Bear Creek

Manistee
River

Rifle
River

Au Gres River

MANISTEE

tle Manistee River
Pine River

CADILLAC

23

Big Sable River

131

GLADWIN

Pere
Marquette
River

Cedar
River

White
River

BAY
CITY

Lake
Michigan

Muskegon
River

23

MUSKEGON

Rogue
River

Wine
Country

GRAND
RAPIDS

Coldwater
River

31

131

Gun
River

Augusta
Creek

Gull
Lake

94

DETROIT

94

KALAMAZOO

Dowagiac River

Dowagiac Creek
Brandywine Creek

131

23

Trout Streams of Michigan
© The Countryman Press

Working a long run on big water

Contents

Browsing through *Trout Streams of Michigan* is particularly rewarding for me, since it was Michigan and its rivers that started an obsession with trout fishing that has possessed me since boyhood.

Except for a brief time at the University of Michigan, we lived in the Chicago region, where my father was a college professor and summer vacations were spent fishing farther north. I remember a hot afternoon in a riverfront park at Ann Arbor. My parents had recently returned from Europe aboard the steamship *Normandie,* and had brought me a toy replica of that famous French liner.

It was a simple toy, little more than a basswood block shaped into a tiny hull, with a superstructure and tiny wooden pegs for its stacks. It was painted red and white, and measured about 3 inches. I carried the toy boat everywhere, and I was playing with it in the shallows on that August afternoon. Children are careless, and I lost the boat to the river. It circled and drifted off into deeper water downstream, passing aimlessly under the big willows, bobbing in sunlight and shadow. I stood wailing on the path beside the river. The toy suddenly disappeared in a big splash.

"Something ate my boat!" I protested shrilly.

It was probably a smallmouth bass, since the river still flowed over a clean pea-gravel bottom fifty years ago, and its splash had startled me. My mother later joked that my obsession with fishing was rooted in childish efforts to get even.

Trout fishing soon filled both dreams and daydreams through my boyhood years. It was Michigan that surrendered my first trout, on a brushy little stream near Arcadia. Sometimes we rented a cottage on a small Michigan lake, and sometimes we camped along the streams. Nobody objected to such trespassing in those years. I later took my first fly-caught trout on the Pere Marquette, in a sweeping bend near its Forks Bridge, and my first dry-fly fish was a 10-inch brown from the Little Manistee.

Trout Streams of Michigan is a thoroughly detailed guidebook to some of the finest fly-fishing found east of the Rocky Mountains, and its descriptions of those rivers trigger a cornucopia of happy echoes over the past half century. Its table of contents holds memories of Michigan too, from the wild cedar-bog headwaters of the Ontonagon at Watersmeet to the pastoral orchards along Dowagiac Creek, where the craftsmen at Heddon once supplied everything from beautifully milled split bamboo to bass plugs. Some memories begin shortly before the Second World War, while other memories of Michigan are still quite fresh in my mind.

Bear Creek and the Betsie were part of those childhood summers at Arcadia, shortly before the Second World War. We were fishing with grasshoppers there, capturing them with white mosquito netting on the softball field, walking them up behind third base when the dew was still thick in the grass. Stalking trout in the jackpine headwaters of these Michigan rivers was a lesson in patience and stealth. There are no more critical skills in trout fishing. The Dowagiac served as our refuge during the war years, when both gasoline and tires were tightly controlled with ration stamps, and we spent some happy hours below the dam at North Niles. It is still a surprisingly productive fishery.

Sometimes we collected ration stamps, patiently hoarding them in a glass pitcher, until we had enough to travel farther north to White Cloud and Baldwin for Opening Day. We patiently explored the trout streams there: the gentle White near Hesperia, the serpentine middle reaches of the Pere Marquette, and its tributaries from the Little South to the brushy little Baldwin. Sometimes we rented cottages at Big Star Lake and Wolf Lake, mounting expeditions farther north to fish the Pentwater, Big Sable, Pine, and Little Manistee. There was a weekend with friends at Fife Lake, where we fished the Big Manistee near Kalkaska.

The Holy Water on the Au Sable below Grayling was a pilgrimage mounted to celebrate the German surrender at Rheims, and I fished like a gypsy through the summers that followed the treaty signed aboard the battleship *Missouri* in Tokyo Bay. There were solitary trips to fish Au Sable tributaries such as the North Branch and South Branch, camping alone for weeks. Other seasons in later years found me fishing from the Gates Lodge, Fellows Cottage, Nash Camp, Priest Cabin, Thunderbird, and the beautiful Averill place called Trafeh. The shallow swift-flowing reach called the Holy Water, between Stephan Bridge and the canoe landing at Wakeley, is perhaps the most famous trout water in the Great Lakes country.

There were other solitary expeditions while my father was off in Europe with the Foreign Service, and I explored other rivers farther north. There was still fine brook trout fishing on the Ontonagon in the Upper Peninsula, particularly in the reaches between its Sparrow Rapids and Onion Falls. Other faculty members traveled north to fish there each season. There are memories of the pretty log-choked headwaters of the Sturgeon near Wolverine, with its thick beds of bog marigolds in the spring, and its sister called the

Pigeon in the forests at Pigeon Bridge. Elk still find shelter in these Michigan woods beyond Gaylord, and the tea-colored Black is still the best brook trout fishery south of the Straits of Mackinac. The Jordan is surprisingly wild and beautiful, particularly in its headwaters at Dead Man's Hill and Pinney Bridge, and I learned to wait patiently for twilight spinner swarms on the Boyne near Cherry Hill Road. The Boardman is still swift and trout-filled near Mayfield, where old Leonard Halladay patiently dressed his popular spentwing Adams during those boyhood years.

Although Ernest Hemingway spent his boyhood summers at Walloon Lake and Horton Bay, his serious fishing was focused on trout rivers such as the Bear, Sturgeon, Pigeon, and Black. Hemingway loved these Michigan trout streams, and was late for his wedding at Horton Bay because fishing was too good on the Sturgeon, but the famous story "Big Two-Hearted River" has tied him forever to that wild tea-colored tributary on Lake Superior.

Carlos Heard Baker is perhaps our most knowledgeable Hemingway scholar, and Baker was a teacher of mine at Princeton. Baker and several other Hemingway scholars have proved that Hemingway was describing the Fox in his famous story, in the jackpine country above Seney. Both the logging camp and its surrounding forests were lost to a terrible fire shortly before the First World War, and there is little left of the earlier Seney, except for the foundations hidden in the saplings and trees.

Like countless other literary pilgrims, I once traveled north to search out benchmarks found in "Big Two-Hearted River." The little Fox is still a prime brook trout fishery. It is clear that both the Fox and Seney were the actual settings for the Hemingway story, much to the consternation of literal-minded graduate students, while the Big Two-Hearted River itself lies beyond the Tahquamenon and flows into Lake Superior. The Two-Hearted is steeped in tannic seepages from its headwater bogs and beaver colonies, with a dark ledgerock bottom in its middle reaches. Except for its spring steelhead runs from Superior, its fishing is no match for its north country sisters, the Fox and Tahquamenon and Driggs. Hemingway borrowed the Big Two-Hearted River because he simply liked the poetic metaphors he heard in its Ojibway name.

Trout Streams of Michigan is a painstakingly detailed guidebook to these classic Michigan watersheds, describing both their landmarks and their sport. Some fishermen will argue that its authors have revealed too much information about their favorite streams, but few secrets are still secrets, and a fishery desperately needs a regiment of friends when it is threatened by highways and development and dams. *Trout Streams of Michigan* is unfailingly generous with its knowledge—and such generosity must not be abused.

—Ernest Schwiebert

ACKNOWLEDGMENTS

The authors extend specific thanks and warm wishes for their assistance on the first edition to Hugh Beaman, Walt Bishop, Jeff Bower, Ron Brillinger, Adam Copeland, David Conrad, Jim Johnson, Rusty Gates, Marc Linsenman, Den Nevala, Steve Pensinger, Bill and Carol Powell, Sandy Rolstad, Jim Scott, Troy Scott, Ernest Schwiebert, Glenn and Steve Snook, Bob Willacker, the fisheries professionals of the Michigan Department of Natural Resources, particularly Jim Dexter and Steve Swan, the helpful folks who work at the fly shops mentioned in appendix B, and our families for their patient if bemused support throughout the course of ongoing treatment for terminal trout mania, and last, Carl Taylor and the staff of Backcountry Guides.

Our warmest thanks to all those who facilitated our work on this new second edition, specifically Mike Bachelder, Glen Blackwood, Bob Braendle, Jim Dexter, Rick Ebert, Kelly Galloup, Dawn Kemp, Kelly Neuman, Mike Moreau, John Ramsay, Pete Schantz, Ray Schmidt, Steve Sendek, Matt and Laurie Supinski, and our editor at The Countryman Press, Ann Kraybill.

When *Michigan Trout Streams: A Fly-Angler's Guide* was first published in 1993 we thought we had done a pretty thorough job in creating a useful tool. A better understanding of the fishing opportunities available on the state's premier waters (Part One: "Crown Jewels") and an appreciation of the rewards of exploration of lesser-known streams (Part Two: "Veiled Treasures") were our two main objectives.

We certainly hoped that our work would be accepted by the angling community, but did not anticipate the degree of popularity it has achieved. We see dog-eared, coffee-stained copies on the dashboards of vehicles all over Michigan; often they are parked at our favorite "lesser known" spots and sport license plates from as far away as Florida and California. This is good.

More and more anglers are moving away from a few widely popular access points to less-frequented stretches of the "Crown Jewel" rivers as well as to the streams covered in "Veiled Treasures." Subsequently, angling experiences are enriched with knowledge of "new" water, a degree of solitude, and better fishing. Folks are exploring more and liking it.

The book may well have continued to sell at a steady pace for a few more years, but things have changed since 1993, calling for an update. The Muskegon River has emerged and has solidified its position as a blue-ribbon fishery of national rank. The fly-angling in the Hodenpyle stretch and below Tippy Dam on the Manistee has improved wildly. The stream trout fishing for browns and rainbows below McKinley on the Au Sable is now producing large fish consistently. We have added coverage of more rivers with superb angling and have updated access points, text, and notes for the remaining rivers as we felt appropriate and to the best of our ability. Additionally, we've double-checked for new developments in areas such as "riparian rights" issues (no change, unfortunately) that might affect our sport.

In 2000 Michigan adopted new regulations for trout streams and lakes that will surely have a positive impact on the quality of our angling. In essence, all trout streams fall into "classes," with each class having specific restrictions relative to size, limit, and type of angling (all, artificial, fly only, and so on). The Michigan Department of Natural Resources (MDNR) through its cold-water fisheries biologists and citizen-user input, has developed the regulations based on each river's unique characteristics. Most important, the new rules reduce harvest, increase size limits, and provide a higher level of protection to the resource. Make sure you get a current copy of the regulations (available wherever you buy a fishing license) and refer to it for each body of water you intend to fish.

Michigan is one of the great trout-angling regions on the continent. We have tiny brooks; large, brawling rivers; and everything in between. We have brookies, rainbows, splake, lakers, browns, Atlantic and Pacific salmon, and magnificent steelhead. We have stocked fish and wild fish in every water type of every size. And we have people—lots of people. Residents and tourists use the water heavily and it is important for all of us to respect each other's privacy and space. Give the other angler as much room as possible. Smile and say "Hi." Explore, catch, release, and enjoy.

The name Michigan is based on a Native American word, *michi-gama,* which means "great lake." The Indians named it well. Michigan has 11,169 inland lakes, 38,575 square miles of Great Lakes, and 36,350 miles of rivers and streams. More than 20 percent of the world's freshwater supply flows through the state, enough to flood the 48 contiguous states to a depth of 10 feet. Michigan has more than 3,000 miles of beaches and more waterfront than the entire Atlantic seaboard. That is a lot of water, and a great deal of it is very cold.

Brook trout (the state fish), brown trout, rainbow trout, splake, salmon, and (very) limited numbers of reintroduced grayling populate these cold waters, from the wilderness flows of the cedar swamps and jagged coastlines of Lake Superior to recovering streams, such as Paint Creek, near Detroit's urban sprawl. Highly oxygenated, fertile, and cold, Michigan's 1,500-plus designated trout streams are largely sustained by natural reproduction. Enlightened cold-water conservation attitudes are placing a premium on wild fish and catch-and-release, and the long-term prospects for Michigan's wild-trout fishery are bright.

This book is meant to serve as a starting point, as an encouragement to explore the state's stream-trout resources. With so much water, so many miles of rich and fertile trout streams, it is possible to spread the pressure and increase the quality of our angling experiences. With this foremost in mind, we have attempted to provide introductions to productive areas on both famous and lesser-known rivers throughout the state. Thus, the text is divided into two parts. The rivers in part one—the Au Sable, the Pere Marquette, the Manistee, and the others—are deservedly famous. You have probably read about them more than once and perhaps even watched videos detailing their charms. The streams in part two are more veiled treasures. They do not receive national print-media attention, but do provide high-quality fly-fishing (without the crowds). You will notice that only southeastern Michigan is not represented in this book. That is because it is not an area that supports wild trout to any reasonable or measurable degree. Paint Creek, from Lake Orion to Rochester, is perhaps the area's best trout stream for the fly-angler, and although it is improving, thanks to the hard work and dedication of conservation-minded organizations and individuals, it does not warrant a full chapter.

This book is not meant to be an expert's catalog of every pool, riffle, and access point on every fly-fishable trout stream in the state. Nor is it intended to be a detailed analysis of Michigan's aquatic insects complete with fly-tying instructions. It is, we hope, a workable reference tool that will get you started with usable knowledge on some of the state's best trout waters. We have tried to be consistent in indicating which fish you will find, which tackle you will need, and what condition you can expect at various entry points, but we purposely did not list every fly-fishable trout stream of merit, or every access point along the streams.

Some people might argue with our selection of rivers and suggestions for access (either because we cover them, or because we do not), or with our recommendations on tackle and patterns, but disagreement based on experience and personal opinion is part of what makes fly-fishing for trout so intriguing. There is always something new to consider, something of value to learn.

The "Holy Water" of the Au Sable River System, near Stephan Bridge

Maps

The maps in this book are a compilation of information from many sources including maps available from DeLorme's *Michigan Atlas and Gazetteer* or the Department of Natural Resources' *Mapbook of Michigan Counties,* as well as state forest and national forest access maps and various regional recreation maps published by local organizations. In finding our way around the state we have found the most consistent source of useful information to be the DeLorme product, but no single source is perfect and we often cross-reference with the MDNR county maps and whatever other maps are available. You can purchase the DeLorme map book at most sporting goods stores, or you can order by writing to DeLorme Mapping Co., P.O. Box 298, Freeport, ME 04032; 207-865-4171. The *Mapbook of Michigan Counties* is also widely available, and it can be ordered through the Department of Natural Resources, Box 30034, Lansing, MI 48909. State forest maps are available through the MDNR in Lansing or at the district field offices listed elsewhere in this book. National forest maps are available as follows: Ottawa National Forest, Ironwood, MI 906-932-1330; Hiawatha National Forest, Escanaba, MI 906-786-4062; and the Huron-Manistee National Forest, Cadillac, MI 616-775-2421. Specific trail maps, such as the Shingle Mill Pathway near the Pigeon River and the Jordan River Pathway, can be obtained by writing or calling the MDNR or by stopping in at one of the field offices listed elsewhere.

The maps in this book have selected access points keyed by a symbol representing the top view of a Delta-Wing Caddis. These selected access points are *our* choices as representative of some of the better water in that general area.

Safety

Safety is, or should be, a matter of concern in any outdoor activity, and especially so when the activity takes place in largely rural and sometimes very remote areas.

WEATHER

Michigan is notorious for fickle weather. Carry a lightweight poncho in your vest, not just for rain but for added warmth as a windbreaker. Keep a spare blanket in your vehicle for added insurance. Sunstroke is not unheard of on glaring, hot days, especially around water. Wear a light hat or cap to reflect the rays. Keep a watch on the sky for tornadic or thunderstorm conditions with an eye to locating cover *away* from big timber.

DRIVING

Use your seat belt; it is, of course, prudent and it is the law in Michigan. A dashboard compass and road maps are valuable, and a CB or a cell phone could come in handy in emergencies, especially in the Upper Peninsula where passing vehicles on back roads can be rare. Gas up whenever you can. Sometimes stations are few and far between. Extra keys wired under a bumper can save a trip, and an all-around road kit is advised. Carry a shovel for sand, snow, and mud-stuck times, a saw to clear fallen trees, and maybe even a small winch or come-along if you are exploring off-road. They don't take up that much room and can save miles of hiking. Watch for deer. They are everywhere in Michigan, and deer/car collisions are a common occurrence. Remember, when one dashes across the road in front of you, there are often others to come.

Leave identity and destination notes on your vehicle. Tell someone (who cares) where you are likely to be. Keep a pad and pencil handy to record mileage driven and turns taken when you travel those two-track mazes that crisscross the state. It isn't always easy to find the same way out when you leave, especially after dark. A lot of drivers assume they are the only ones on the narrow trail; be alert for "incoming" cars even on the most remote track.

WADING

Michigan streams are often deceptive in their strength. They rarely look scary and can lull you into a troublesome situation. Wear polarized sunglasses to reduce glare, and carry (or cut) a wading staff for those faster rocky spots. Don't wade yourself into a corner; getting back is often more difficult than getting to a promising position. You won't always need felt soles, but it is smarter to wear them for the frequent times when you will. And watch out for slippery clay "shelves." Felts are great on gravel but not much help on the marl or clay bottoms. Carry waterproof matches. If you do the subsurface shuffle in cold weather, and the extra clothes (have them) are way back in camp, a fire can dry you and get you back on the stream, or prevent a life-threatening hypothermia situation. We have swum in our waders (for practice and by choice) and feel fairly confident of our abilities. If you haven't done this, it isn't a bad idea to experiment in a controlled situation. Know your capabilities and don't exceed them.

CRITTERS

Many of the same insects that provide protein for trout fatten up on the angler first. Mosquitoes, blackflies, no-see-ums, and deerflies are a thriving, unmanaged resource in Michigan. Carry your favorite bug dope. Often you won't even need to apply it, but a sudden "hatch" of bad-guy bugs can send you groping in your vest, and repellent can keep you from being driven from the stream. Wood ticks and deer ticks (carrying Lyme disease) are not a real problem except in the extreme western Upper Peninsula, especially in the counties bordering Wisconsin. Take appropriate precautions.

There are no poisonous snakes native to Michigan except for the shy massasauga rattlesnake. A bite is not usually life-threatening to an adult, but prompt treatment will ease painful effects. Open beverages, fresh meat, and sweets will often draw yellow jackets. They are no picnic. If anyone in your party has bee, wasp, or hornet allergies, carry appropriate medications, or a simple first-aid kit.

CAMPING

Don't neglect the obvious. Police a potential site for glass, nails, rain runoff, poison ivy, dead limbs overhead—all the things you learned in scouting, but sometimes need to relearn the hard way. Food, fish, and garbage improperly stored will attract pesky critters. Raccoons are remarkably bold, and a black

Kelly Neuman cooking client lunches on the Au Sable

bear, while generally harmless, is out of place in your camp. Bears can tear up gear, even coolers, in short order. An extra tarp or plastic sheet as an awning (and tent protector in *heavy* rain) is always worth the time it takes to stretch a rope or two as supports. When away from even a wilderness camp, lock valuables in your vehicle trunk. Unfortunately theft, though rare, is always a possibility. Get a (free) camping permit from any MDNR office or ranger station when staying on public land. Check regulations; much of the land along the Little Manistee, for example, forbids camping within 200 feet of the river. Clean up your camp. Leave the site in better shape than when you arrived.

Check out the general environs of your camp. It is disquieting, to say the least, to be awakened by the approaching rumble and whistle of an early morning freight a couple of yards from your tent, which you pitched hastily in the dark when you couldn't drive any more. But the ultimate camp-location faux pas came years ago after a midnight tent pitch near Marquette en route to the Yellow Dog River. Picture this: You are in the pristine far reaches of the Upper Peninsula sleeping at the end of a heavily wooded two-track. The sounds that first awaken you are not bird chirps or rustling leaves, but cymbals clashes, drumrolls, tuba oom-pahs, and the dis-harmonies of a high school marching band behind whose unseen football field we were cozily ensconced, until, that is, some Upper Peninsula admirer of Sousa decided on early morning brass-band practice.

"Okay, that's no train this time."

"Maybe it's a circus train."

Riparian Rights

First the good news. Michigan is blessed with countless miles of "navigable" public streams bordered by state and federal land. Where private holdings adjoin these waters, one need only stay in the river, where the state maintains rights to "such submerged land."

In questionable situations where private postings appear to refer to the stream as well as adjoining property, politely ask permission. Don't be shy. For the most part, people are friendly and have little gripe against property-respecting, catch-and-release, ever-considerate fly-fishermen. Case in point: We recently asked a landowner about a small parcel of federal property our maps showed to be landlocked beyond his posted land. He not only *led* us to it through a maze of trails, he spent two more hours driving us to other good stretches of fly water in obscure places along the Pere Marquette.

However, there is a slight downside to a Michigan angler's riparian rights; this involves the determination of the aforementioned "navigable" public water. Let us briefly plumb these murky depths beginning with a passage from the MDNR's *A Guide to Public Rights on Michigan Waters:* "The public or private status of a stream to date has been determined only by judicial action. Streams where such determinations have been made represent only an infinitesimal number of the state's total streams. No state agency can, under present conditions, satisfactorily respond to public inquiries as to their rights on streams, except in the few cases (45 streams) where litigation has resulted in Supreme Court decisions declaring the stream public or private."

Of course we scurried out and obtained the list of the "few cases" from the MDNR's legal division in Lansing. It bears this introductory caveat: "Care should be taken in reviewing the list of waters. In most cases that entire stream was not decided upon. This does not necessarily mean that stretches not mentioned may not be navigable." Hmm. The muddy waters, they be rising. Not a great help here, since we and most trout chasers of similar itinerant natures probably do not want to undergo the time and financial constraints of being test cases in a court system that has, the MDNR points out, "rendered sundry and often diverse rulings defining navigability."

The Michigan Supreme Court appears sympathetic, citing "the need for a comprehensive legislative solution," but its 1982 *Botts* case decision still left us with the somewhat vague "commercial use/log flotation test as the controlling legal test of navigability."

The MDNR would love to see a change in this, pointing out that "the old, but current, test . . . is fast becoming unprovable. . . . There should now be written into the law a means for determining . . . without need for judicial determination every time a dispute . . . arises." Our latest inquiries with the MDNR Law Enforcement Division reveal, however, no initiative to seek legislative clarification on navigability. Oh well. Perhaps, we hope, some clear legal finding will be made in the near future. (And perhaps we will land a 10-pound brown on 8X.) In the meantime, be cognizant of boundaries, ask permission or clarification when in doubt, respect the rivers and adjoining property, and your Michigan trout-fishing experiences are bound to be positive, enjoyable, and trouble-free.

Blue-Ribbon Trout Streams

In July of 1988 the Fisheries Division of the Michigan MDNR updated its list of the state's blue-ribbon trout streams with an eight-page publication detailing the rivers and the goals of the program. Streams qualifying for this designation must have a minimum average width of 15 feet, be largely fly-fishable, and have a good stock of wild trout. In addition, the streams should be clear for most of the spring and summer and have no important fishery for other species.

The streams are listed by peninsula and county, upstream and downstream limit, and the number of stream miles classified as blue ribbon. Most of the 51 rivers or streams are covered in this book, but a copy of the departmental listing is worth having and can be obtained free of charge by calling the Fisheries Division, Michigan Department of Natural Resources, at 517-373-1280. Additionally, the MDNR has published a document titled "Director's Order no. DFI-101.91." This document lists the designated trout streams for the State of Michigan. Its 41 pages define over 1,500 *designated* trout streams, by county, and it is worth noting that there are trout in streams that are not on this list.

Notes

You will notice that at the conclusion of each of our stream write-ups there is a brief listing of "notes." These are intended to complement the angling with nonfishing activities, either as a change of pace or as an explicit consideration for family members and/or friends who are not overly enthused at the prospect of a day on the stream. We have tried to list interesting diversions like scenic wonders (such as waterfalls), activities (such as golf or soaring), shopping, and dining that will supplement or be a happy footnote to your fishing trip.

Fly Shops, Outfitters, and Guides

There are many excellent fly shops that service the needs of Michigan's fly-anglers. Appendix B lists a *few* of the shops that represent a high standard of professionalism. They have a wide range of offerings, in-depth knowledge, and friendly, courteous assistance. There are other fine trout shops and we apologize for not listing all of the establishments in the state, but we could not personally visit each one, and that was an inviolate criterion for selection.

Appendix B also lists a few of the state's most highly regarded outfitters and guides. Again, this compilation is not complete, but the individuals listed are representative of the profession's finest. Consider using a guide anytime and weigh the advantages with the cost and available time. When first fishing big water such as the Manistee or the Au Sable, or when selecting an area rather than a river—such as a week in Sleeping Bear near Petoskey as opposed to a day on the Jordan River—a guide can be truly invaluable.

Conservation Behavior

It is worth noting that Michigan has many streams set aside for experimental, special regulations. These are always subject to change based on research data, but as a general rule the special regulations have proven effective in promoting quality trout angling. Barbless hooks and catch-and-release can only improve the future of trout fishing for all of us. Barbless hooks actually hook better and hold as well as the barbed versions, and a trout is much more easily released from a barbless fly. Even trophy-sized fish should be carefully released, because they are the most effective spawners. A clear, color photograph or slide will serve as the "trophy" and still allow the fish to reproduce as well as be caught again.

We had some interesting experiences in the process of exploration and research that produced this book. We heard coyotes sing and moose grunt, we were entertained by a strolling bluegrass minstrel, we spilled a perfectly good Suburban over the side of a sandy precipice into the unyielding trunk of a stout, punishing white pine, and we talked to many helpful, friendly people along nearly 38,000 miles of back road travel. Thanks to all.

I | THE CROWN JEWELS

The Muskegon River

Newaygo County

Our coverage of the Muskegon is new to this revised edition of *Trout Streams of Michigan*. Since the first edition was published in 1993 this river has developed as a phenomenal tailwater–spring creek fishery to the extent that it not only bears coverage, but must be fairly counted as one of the state's Crown Jewels. Correspondingly, it has grown in popularity among fly-anglers for trout, steelhead, and salmon and today ranks as one of the most angler-utilized bodies of water in the state.

The Muskegon system begins at Houghton Lake near the center of the state. Its flow is over 220 miles to the mouth at Lake Michigan. From Houghton Lake to Croton Dam near Newaygo there is a mix of fly-angling opportunities with both cold- and warm-water species dominant in certain stretches. The upper section has cold-water tributaries such as the Clam and Hersey that support wild trout. In Big Rapids the fly-angler will find some cool flows and quality riffles and pools that support stocked rainbows and browns with some overwinter survival.

Between Rogers Dam and Hardy Dam, Hardy Reservoir supports walleye, perch, bass, and northern pike. It is worth noting that each year several very large brown trout are caught here. Fish up to 8 pounds leave the cold-water tributaries such as Mack, Rosey Run, and Bennet Creeks and migrate down to the reservoir where they feed heavily on the Hex and *Ephoron* (White Fly) spinner falls, usually in July.

Between Hardy and Croton Dam the fly-angler will find a few trout, but this is largely a warm-water fishery. The brown trout that do show up here most likely migrated downstream from the Little Muskegon. The Little Muskegon and Tamarack Creek are stocked with both browns and rainbows and are a lot of fun to fish. We fished the Little Muskegon together and debated giving it separate coverage in "Veiled Treasures."

The superb trout fishing on the Muskegon begins below Croton Dam at

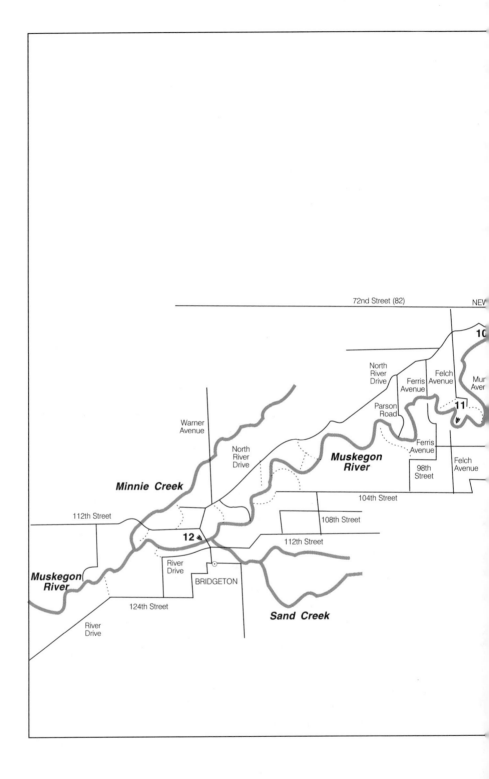

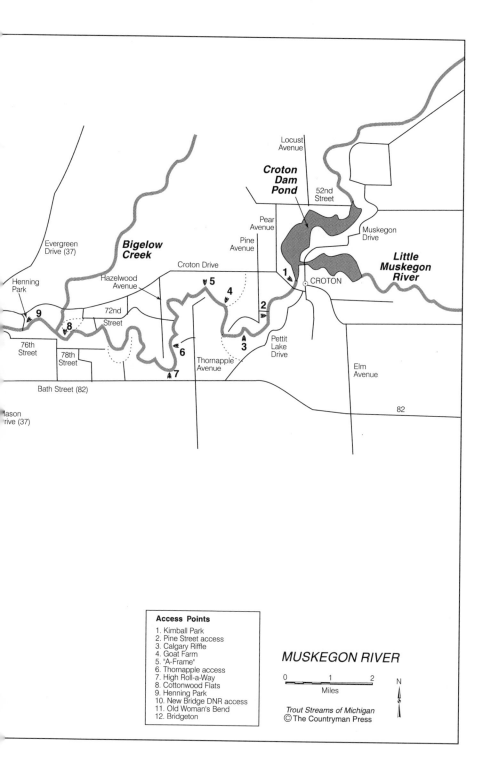

Locust
Avenue

**Croton
Dam
Pond**

52nd
Street

Muskegon
Drive

Pear
Avenue

Pine
Avenue

**Little
Muskegon
River**

Croton Drive

**Bigelow
Creek**

Evergreen
Drive (37)

Hazelwood
Avenue

Henning
Park

72nd
Street

5

4

1

CROTON

2

9

8

3

76th
Street

78th
Street

6

Pettit
Lake
Drive

Thornapple
Avenue

7

Elm
Avenue

Bath Street (82)

Mason
Drive (37)

82

Access Points

1. Kimball Park
2. Pine Street access
3. Calgary Riffle
4. Goat Farm
5. "A-Frame"
6. Thornapple access
7. High Roll-a-Way
8. Cottonwood Flats
9. Henning Park
10. New Bridge DNR access
11. Old Woman's Bend
12. Bridgeton

MUSKEGON RIVER

0   1   2   N
Miles

Trout Streams of Michigan
© The Countryman Press

Newaygo and runs to near Lake Michigan. This is "combination" tailwater-spring creek configuration with all the fine system characteristics attributed to famous western rivers. When the Federal Energy Relicensing Commission (FERC) settled negotiations with Michigan hydroelectric power producers, one of the key victories for cold-water fisheries was the establishment of stable flows (no "peaking" for energy production). These stable flows from the Croton hydro dam have benefited the food chain—mayflies, stoneflies, caddis, midges, baitfish—as well as some natural reproduction of stream trout, wild steelhead, and salmon stocks. Matt Supinski, a highly regarded guide on the river and owner of the Gray Drake Lodge, reports that 90 percent of the chinook salmon run and 60 percent of the steelhead are now wild (born in the river) fish. Correspondingly, natural reproduction in the stream-trout population is producing more vibrant additions to that population. The current (2000) stocking rate is 250,000 brown and rainbow trout (non-migratory strains), 50,000 Little Manistee strain steelhead, 190,000 chinook salmon, and 30,000 Seaforellen strain, migratory brown trout. With this large stocking program enhanced by increasing natural recruitment and a rich food base, it is no wonder that the Muskegon River is so popular with fly-anglers.

We have fished with Supinski on the Muskegon. Even on the coldest day imaginable in late February, we found willing takers of nymphs—brown trout to 18 inches and steelhead to 16 pounds. Wonderful! The air temperature was in the low 20s and the water ranged to a high of 36 degrees F. Still, the fish were actively feeding, robust and healthy. Our biggest problem was ice in the guides.

Most of the blue-ribbon fly angling for trout takes place from Croton Dam downstream to Old Women's Bend below the town of Newaygo. Some fine angling continues downstream to Bridgeton and there are additional releases of brown trout in this lower stretch.

One of the most popular reaches on the river is the "San Juan Flats" between Croton Dam and Pine Street. This area has excellent dry-fly and nymph fishing with heavy hatches of a multitude of caddis and a very good Gray Drake hatch and spinner fall. Access for wading anglers is available at Kimball Park at the dam and at the Michigan Department of Natural Resources (MDNR) site at Pine Street.

Between Pine Street and the MDNR access at Thornapple there are about 6 miles of excellent fly water. Local anglers and visitors with guides will concentrate on Calgary riffle, the Sheep Ranch, Rainbow Riffle, Carmichael Flats, and at the A-frame High Banks. From the A-frame High Banks to Thornapple the banks are private property and the river is only accessible by boat, but most of the water from Pine Street to the A-frame flows through land owned by the MDNR and is accessible from 72nd Street. This stretch has excellent fly angling throughout, all year long. It has diverse insect populations with hatches of caddis, mayflies, and stoneflies, as well as a healthy population of forage fish and crayfish. In between emergence periods and spinner falls a fly-angler is well advised to switch to a sinking line and "jerk-strip" streamers such as the Zoo Cougar and Woolly Sculpin or swing soft-hackle emergers for the willing browns and rainbows.

Continuing downstream, the run between Thornapple and Henning Park presents the greatest density and diversity of mayflies on the entire river. This reach produces superb angling to Sulphur, Gray Drake, *Isonychia,* and Brown Drake hatches and spinner falls. It is a paradise for the dry-fly addict with browns and rainbows of significant size eagerly feeding on the surface. At times, it rivals the very best angling on the most famous dry-fly western rivers in our country. Throughout this stretch underground springs add cold water to optimize conditions for trout even in the heat of high summer. Check out the new public access at High Rollaway Park. It has steps descending to the river and fine angling in the immediate vicinity. Access for wading anglers is also good at Henning Park and at Newaygo Park all the way to the MDNR access at New Bridge.

At Old Women's Bend there is an MDNR access at Feltch Road and there

MATT SUPINSKI

Average size for the Muskegon

Laurie Supinski fishing near the home pool of Gray Drake Lodge

is good pool and run fishing both above and below the access. Good hatches of Gray Drakes and *Hexagenia* take place near Bridgeton. Below Bridgeton and Maple Island, Cedar Creek is an excellent spring-fed wild trout stream. Other fine tributaries exist throughout the system, Bigelow and Penoyer Creeks being two examples.

From the first hatches of early spring through the deep cold of winter, trout in the Muskegon seem to like feeding on the surface—the coldest day will likely have fish sipping black midges near the Pine Street access. If not, it's a good bet they are burrowing for scuds.

The insect food base is so prolific and diverse on the Muskegon—more so than any other trout stream in Michigan—that it is appropriate to present some specific detail to aid you in your planning. What follows is an overview with appropriate dates. These dates may vary based on the severity and length of winter.

We suggest you check with a local guide or a fly shop for exact timing throughout the season. The information presented below is current through 2000 and we thank Matt Supinski for taking the time to compile and verify the hatch dates as well as for his generous assistance on all aspects of the Muskegon.

MIDGES

Black Midges—size 24—early November through early May

White Midges—size 28—mid-July through September

MAYFLIES

Sulphurs—invaria size 16; dorothea—size 18—mid-May through June

Tiny Blue-Winged Olives—size 24—late May through June, mid-August
   through September, and throughout November

March Brown—size 10—throughout May

Gray Drake—size 10—mid-May through early June

Isonychia bicolor—size 8—mid-May through late June

Brown Drake—size 8—throughout June

Yellow Drake—size 8—first of June through early July

White Fly—size 12—mid-July through August 14, 2000

Hexagenia limbata—size 6 and 8—on Hardy Reservoir and the lower river
   from mid-July through mid-August

Light Cahill—size 14—late May through August

Tricos—size 24—mid-July through mid-August

CADDIS

Cinnamon Caddis—size 16—mid-May through mid-October

Little Green Caddis—size 20—mid-May through September

Tiny Black Caddis—size 22—mid-May through June

Isonychia—an important hatch on the Muskegon

Zebra Caddis—size 12—mid-June through July
White Miller Caddis—size 14—early August through mid-September
Giant Brown Autumn Sedge—size 8—throughout October
Dot-Wing Sedge—size 16—mid-September through mid-October

STONEFLIES
Early Black Stone—size 14—early March through late April
Giant Michigan Stonefly—size 2—late May through July

TERRESTRIALS, OTHERS
Flying Amber Ant—size 22—early July through mid-August
Tiny White Aphid—size 26—late July through August
Scuds—size 18—throughout the year
Sowbugs—size 16—throughout the year
Dragonfly—mid-June through August

On those rare days when the Muskegon's trout are not looking upward, a healthy-sized streamer usually produces. Madonnas, Woolly Sculpins, Zoo Cougars, crayfish patterns, Rattlesnakes, and, of course, Woolly Buggers, will work for you. The strike may be a severe jolt; steelhead and migratory browns of magnum proportion show up throughout the year.

The Muskegon's fly-fishing opportunities are exceptional by any standard. It is a year-round fishery with stream trout, steelhead, salmon, and lake-run brown trout. Beginning in 2000, there is a 15-inch size limit from Thornapple downstream to Lake Michigan, and this will help protect the fish population. Still, more needs to be done to safeguard this shining jewel with its classic, westernlike riffle, pool, run, tail-out patterns. We need to encourage rigorous law enforcement and press hard for stretches of river to be designated as fly-fishing, catch-and-release only. And, because angling pressure can be high, it is important to diligently apply the highest level of stream ethics and courtesy.

There are eagles, osprey, kingfishers, herons, swans, ducks, geese, mink, muskrat, and beaver along the river. Sturgeon up to 90 pounds are making a strong comeback. Demanding, technical dry-fly-fishing with long, fine leaders and tiny flies to large, sophisticated trout; jerk-stripping big streamers on a sinking line through the heavy water; or nymph-fishing to chrome steelhead—you pick it and the Muskegon will deliver.

Notes:

- The Gray Drake Lodge (www.graydrake.com) is set high on a bluff overlooking the Muskegon. Its home pool has very good fishing and the lodge offers fine dining, first-class accommodations, and friendly service. The owner's phone number is 231-652-2868.

- There are several good fishing lakes in the area. For a change of pace, try Hess, Brooks, Bill's, and Pickerel. They have public launch facilities.
- The second largest city in Michigan, Grand Rapids, is just 1 hour south. It is a clean, friendly town with very good restaurants, excellent golf courses, shopping, and a major, full-service, international airport.
- Just north of Grand Rapids, the Rogue River (see page 221) flows through the village of Rockford. East of US 131 on Ten Mile Road, the Great Lakes Fly-fishing Company has everything you will need for either the Muskegon or the Rogue.

2 | The Pine River

Osceola County, Lake County, Wexford County, Manistee County

There are several Pine Rivers in Michigan, but the one that ripples and brawls its 40-odd-mile way through Osceola, Lake, Wexford, and Manistee Counties before emptying into Tippy Dam Pond and the Big Manistee is probably the best known. Environed by the Manistee National Forest and the Pere Marquette State Forest, the attendant public access makes it an intriguing river for fly-anglers to explore.

A lot of my time has been happily spent along its course over the past 40 years, first trout fishing the middle reaches, lately spending more hours higher up where grouse numbers and whitetail proliferation along its banks provided other (autumn) recreation.

Recent reacquaintance with spring and summer fly-fishing potential found me more toward the headwaters than ever previously, despite advice from experienced trout anglers that it was too tight for enjoyable fly-fishing up around Bristol. This proved to be mostly true, though dapping a fly through screens of brush can be fun; what was not fun was the tight posting encountered and the number of landowners who categorically refused access.

"Must be losing those old silver-tongued skills," I muttered on my way down to the Edgett's Bridge area on Raymond Road, where access on public land is no problem. "Oh well, didn't like those interlaced alders hiding the river anyway."

There is a great place to sample the upper Pine here by turning west off Raymond Road just north of the river where a faded access-site sign marks a trail that could easily be taken for the driveway of an adjoining farmhouse. After a couple of hundred yards the trail forks and the left turn leads to a little area that serves as campsite, canoe launch, and parking spot. It is unlikely many canoeists ever put in above this point, so an upstream foray eliminates the aluminum hatch concerns as well as giving anglers enchanting water to cover.

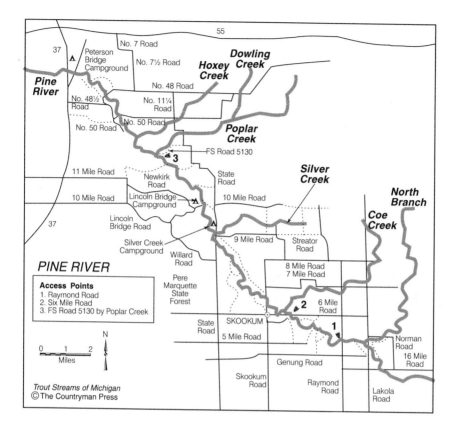

Trout Streams of Michigan
© The Countryman Press

It is a fun fish to Raymond Road (and beyond), pretty typical of the sort of water the Pine provides higher up—varied. The width ranges from 15 to 25 feet so casting isn't troublesome. Depth also varies. You can be working line from ankle-deep gravel bars one moment, then doing that "Oh-oh-oh" tippy-toe, arms-high crossing the next. My waders snug-up to armpit level but the limits can be easily tested hereabouts.

The wading angler will encounter every size rock imaginable in the upper Pine, most coated with greenish slime, the "moose snot" Canadians colorfully dub their Sault-Ste.-Marie-and-points-north algae. Whatever its nomenclature, felt soles are advised to keep ankle-twisting slippage minimal.

The upside to the rocky stretches is of course the broken water created when enough rocks cluster in the right gradient. To be on the river at the peak of the rock-rut when clusters are everywhere . . . Caddis (seriously now) flit about these pretty riffles, and tail-out runs and pools provide places to drift appropriate nymphs (stonefly and caddis variations) when surface activity isn't obvious—which seems my lot 95 percent of stream time.

Another good move here is to take the two-track on past the afore-

STEVE NEVALA

Typical riffle water on the Pine River

mentioned canoe-launch area straight west. It T's after 0.3 mile, the left turn quickly petering out as the river is approached. There is good fishing right at this juncture or one can take the right arm of the T north and parallel the river for quite a distance. Due to the "seasonal" nature (Michigan euphemism for muffler-eating mudhole) of this two-track, four-wheel drive is strongly advised. If vehicularly impaired, it is not a bad bet to park just off the T, walk downstream as far as time allows, and fish back to your ride.

This is a good point at which to share another hard-learned bit of river lore. Your vehicle, parked on higher ground, will often not be visible from the stream, so go to the nearest point of water and clearly mark an exit spot before walking off to a distant starting point. Oh, the stories that could be told of earnest, simple-minded anglers who got out too soon/late and slogged around in oxbow quagmires or took the wrong high-ground ridge off into the boonies while companions chafed, worried, and drank the last of the cold beverages as they waited. The entire length of the Pine with its countless twists and turns abounds with possibilities for this not-good scenario. Carry a compass, too.

Another good spot for a quick, easy access exists where Six Mile Road crosses the Pine. There is a small parking area on the north side of the road adjacent to the river, and a vague footpath allows one to walk downstream and then fish some frothy riffle water back up. The water above the bridge is similar, with perhaps more of those deeper bend pools filled with sunken logs, a preview of the characteristics of the bigger water awaiting your presentations farther downstream.

Just to the northwest Skookem Road spans the flow, and the North Skookem access about 200 yards north of the bridge is another of dozens of convenient spots from which to sample the Pine. There are still a few primitive campsites here, and a nice mix of sand, silt, sweepers, and undercut banks will keep your fish senses cooking.

The whole river system is beautiful, and some of the most attractive water can be accessed in the middle reaches just above and below the mouth of Poplar Creek. Get on 11½ Mile Road below Hoxeyville on the north side of the river and you can find Forest Service trails leaving the road just above and below this little feeder, which will lead you to within ½ mile of the Pine. My favorite is FS 5130, which is 0.2 mile southeast of the Poplar Creek bridge on 11½ Mile Road. This trail is generally in good enough condition to take any vehicle the 0.9 mile to the gate and the parking area.

It is an easy 3- to 4-minute walk to the river from the gate, and the holes, runs, bend pools—every type of trout cover you could name—are awesome both up and down. So too is the descent to the Pine. There are lofty heights to negotiate here in the federally protected corridor, which runs roughly 26 miles from Lincoln Bridge on down. Extreme care must be taken here to avoid a tumble or to cause bank degradation, the latter, it is said, very dimly viewed by the vigilant Forest Service. (So if you must tumble, don't degrade anything on the way down . . .) Give considerable thought in picking a passage down and back up, especially if late evening hatches might keep you in the gorge after dark—a productive, canoe-avoiding time to fish the Pine.

Longtime fishing companion and good friend Jim Scott and I recently worked our careful way down to the river here off FS 5130 and had a phenomenal 3 hours of action on a hot July midmorning. Bright sun, blue sky, and 14–16-inch browns willing to hit light-hued streamers seemed an odd mix, but we gloried in it, bringing several fish to hand, mostly Jim's hand.

Then the vanguard of a flotilla of canoes and kayaks approached, and their ingenuous "There's about an hour's worth of us still to come" decided the issue. Not that trout won't hit after canoeists go by—they have to be used to the traffic—we were in need of lunch and wanted to sample spots downstream. Grateful for a large block of undisturbed time on this popular river, we headed out (up), grateful too that we had marked a reasonable spot to ascend. Jim is in his 70s but held up remarkably well, hardly complaining at all about having to wait for me to catch a breath every 50 feet or so.

A relatively easy walk-in spot is at Elm Flats, marked by the bridge on No. 50 Road east of MI 37 in southwestern Wexford County. The fly-fishing is good both up- and downstream from this point. Last, what some say is the best reach to try is (of course) the most problematic. Take Sandy B's Road south from MI 55 (just west off MI 37) to a connecting two-track headed west. This trail parallels the river through its most scenic and productive run. Again, remember where you park your vehicle, carry a compass, and note and mark easiest up and down routes to the river.

If you are driving around someday (and you will be since trout driving is one of the earliest acquired, never lost "skills") considering where or whether to fish the Pine River, pull off by, say, the Hoxeyville High Bridge east of MI 37 and gaze down at the river below. Think about climbing back out again after a day of breasting current and clambering out of unwadable stretches. Think about an alternative my coauthor favors, certainly not because of advancing age, but because of "acquired wisdom"—that being a float trip.

With this approach there are two options. If you use your own watercraft, be it float tube, baloney boat, driftboat, or canoe, you must obtain a special permit from the U.S. Forest Service. Frankly, a hard-side driftboat is a bad choice. Even the new "shorty" models are too big to effectively maneuver some of the Pine's narrower widths and twisting turns and allow effective presentation of the fly. Launching and retrieval can be extremely

Jim Scott holding a typical brown caught in the Pine.

difficult. Winches are a big factor affecting watercraft and only licensed out-fitters have the necessary keys to operate the in-place winches on the Pine.

The second option is to hire a guide with the proper permits and expe-rience. The cost is reasonable, your workload negligible, and to be "coached" through some wild, untamed-country fishing for naturally reproduced brown, rainbow, and brook trout can be as good as it gets in the lower 48.

Schmidt Outfitters, owned by Ray and Angie Schmidt out of Wellston, Michigan, holds a permit for float trips on the Pine and offers a variety of floats on different stretches. They use low-impact, inflatable rafts and guide fly-anglers on no-kill floats down this fabulous river.

Ray is one of Michigan's premier guides and conservationists and he and his staff have a protective attitude when it comes to the Pine. Ray is quick to speak of the novel characteristics of the ecosystem, the fragile banks and low wetlands, the birds, plants, predators, and, of course, the trout. "People need to experience this special river to appreciate it. It is truly unique," he said. "But it's a delicate balance in terms of traffic. It's small and wild and, by definition, this puts it in some danger. The river needs friends to ensure its continued vigorous protection, but too many people might love it to death." Agreed. It is good that the lower Pine has restricted boat access and is difficult to reach and fish on foot in many of its reaches.

During a float or walk-in on the Pine you will be fishing for wild browns, rainbows, and brookies in (roughly) a 70 percent brown, 20 percent rainbow, and 10 percent brook trout ratio. They all present the extraordinary vivid hues of fish born in gravel. They grow hard and sharp with abundant food in the form of mayflies, stoneflies, caddis, crayfish, sculpins, darters, and more.

Seasonal hatches are strong and the Pine's trout are quick to rise to emergers, duns, and spinners fished drag-free. Hatches of note include Hen-dricksons, Sulphurs, March Browns, Brown Drakes, various Olives through-out the season, abundant caddis species, and stoneflies. Good searching patterns are large *dorsata* stoneflies, Adams, Madam X, the Tarantula and, in season, terrestrials such as hoppers, ants, and crickets.

Streamer fans should carry Madonnas in cream and olive, Rattlesnakes in yellow, white, and black, Zoo Cougars, and Woolly Sculpins. A fly that produces very well on the Pine, particularly in the riffles, is one like the Warbird that can be drifted as a nymph, then twitched and stripped as you would a streamer. This pattern closely resembles a Woolly Bugger with the addition of rubber legs and (critically) antennae.

A basic nymph/wet-fly selection is easy enough. Take along some Gold Ribbed Hare's Ears, Pheasant Tails, caddis larvae, small stoneflies, Prince nymphs, Zug Bugs, and an assortment of soft-hackle emergers. Beadhead versions of these nymphs are productive.

Although the Pine runs clear most of the time, it colors quickly with rain, and a quick switch in tactics might be required while on the water. A versatile rod capable of both dry-fly and streamer work is recommended; a good choice would be a 9-foot 5-weight. Bring both floating and sink-tip lines. There is no real need to carry two rods, one rigged for dries, one for streamers, as we often do on bigger water. Avoid lighter rods that may not have the stuff to beat some of the big browns and rainbows of the Pine quickly enough for a healthy release.

The Pine is a special river, popular and heavily used, yet wild and delicate, productive and beautiful. It is highly deserving of vigorous protection and the respect of all who use it.

Notes:

- In the town of Manistee there are a variety of attractions—museums, lighthouses, golf, boardwalks, and beaches on Lake Michigan.
- Close by is the Big Manistee River. Consider a two-day outing with one on the Pine and one on the big river.
- Birdwatchers can enjoy the Lake Bluff Audubon Center near Bear Lake (231-889-4761).
- Pine Lake in Manistee County has excellent angling for panfish, pike, and trout.

3 | The Au Sable River System

*Crawford County, Roscommon County,
Oscoda County, Alcona County*

Few trout rivers on earth are as well known as the Au Sable. It is one of the most written and dreamed about of this world's classic trout streams. Its heavy and reliable hatches and relatively easy wading and access, combined with a healthy population of wild fish (some very large), have produced a deserved international reputation.

And the angling is only getting better as we breach the 21st century. More and more large fish—over 16 inches—are being caught in the revered "Holy Water" stretch and true giants—trout exceeding 20 inches—have become relatively common in the designated Trophy Water between Mio and McKinley. Additionally, the run from McKinley to Forest Service Road 4001 produces trophy browns and rainbows, and the long reach from Alcona Dam to Loud Dam has a pleasant mix of giant browns, acrobatic rainbows, and exuberant smallmouth bass.

This is a river possessed of a great history, one of exploitation and extinction as well as resurgence and stewardship. This "river of sand," as it was called by early explorers, was home to the beautiful grayling. Its banks were lined with a fabulous wealth in the form of immense stands of virgin white pines, and the river itself provided the necessary, low-cost transport to convert the logs into cash.

The Au Sable also enjoyed a reputation as the center of a sportsman's paradise, and train and coach alike carried the nation's wealthy to its banks. As we entered the 20th century the pine and the grayling were gone. There remains a pitifully small stand of protected virgin white pine, the Hartwick Pines, near the town of Grayling, but the namesake fish is extinct. First brook, then brown and rainbow trout were introduced and they adapted very well, growing quickly and, because the river was slowly cleansing itself of silt and acid, reproducing effectively.

The river's reputation was reborn, and the sportsman returned, but this

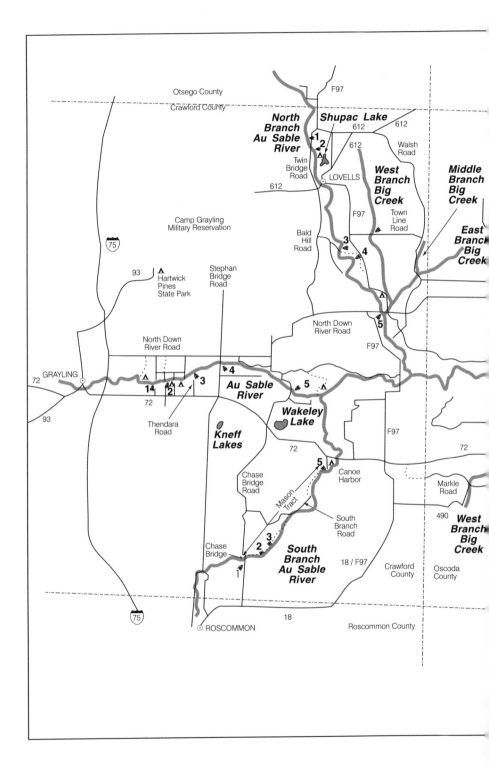

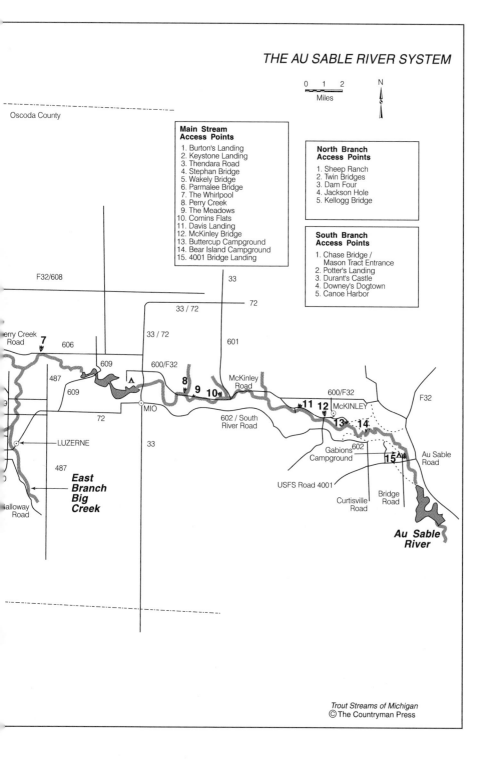

THE AU SABLE RIVER SYSTEM

0   1   2
Miles

N

Oscoda County

Main Stream
Access Points

1. Burton's Landing
2. Keystone Landing
3. Thendara Road
4. Stephan Bridge
5. Wakely Bridge
6. Parmalee Bridge
7. The Whirlpool
8. Perry Creek
9. The Meadows
10. Comins Flats
11. Davis Landing
12. McKinley Bridge
13. Buttercup Campground
14. Bear Island Campground
15. 4001 Bridge Landing

North Branch
Access Points

1. Sheep Ranch
2. Twin Bridges
3. Dam Four
4. Jackson Hole
5. Kellogg Bridge

South Branch
Access Points

1. Chase Bridge /
   Mason Tract Entrance
2. Potter's Landing
3. Durant's Castle
4. Downey's Dogtown
5. Canoe Harbor

F32/608

33

72

33 / 72

33 / 72

601

erry Creek
Road   **7**

606

600/F32

McKinley
Road

600/F32

F32

8

9 10

11 12 McKINLEY

609

487

609

13   14

MIO

72

602 / South
River Road

LUZERNE

33

Gabions
Campground

602

15

Au Sable
Road

487

**East
Branch
Big
Creek**

USFS Road 4001

Curtisville
Road

Bridge
Road

**Au Sable
River**

alloway
Road

Trout Streams of Michigan
© The Countryman Press

time with more of a sense of appreciation and responsibility. The Au Sable is the birthplace of Trout Unlimited and served as the institution's "nursery" in the early years. Today, there are many miles of water under special regulations that are designed to enhance, protect, and preserve the quality of the fishing experience. The Michigan Department of Natural Resources is quite conservative in applying its "blue ribbon" designation to rivers, or stretches of river, but still lists over 150 miles of the Au Sable in this classification. The Au Sable is arguably our finest and most varied trout stream east of the Rocky Mountains, and it ranks in the country's top 10 by any standard of measurement.

The Main Stream

THE HOLY WATER

The main stream is born in quiet and pristine anonymity. Deep in the cedars near the town of Frederic, Kolke and Bradford creeks join to form the headwaters of the Au Sable. There are no fly shops here, no requirement to match the hatch. Brown, brook, and rainbow trout are purely opportunistic here and pounce on Royal Trude, Mickey Finn, and nightcrawler with equal enthusiasm.

The little river flows almost directly south crossing CR 612, Batterson Road, and parallels Au Sable Trail on its way to Grayling and stardom. Within the city limits of Grayling it takes a turn to the east, swirls past the Fly Factory on MI 72, joins with the southward-flowing East Branch, and makes its way to Burton's Landing and the start of 8 miles of flies-only, no-kill—the Holy Water.

Devotees of the Holy Water have recently enjoyed an upward spike in the numbers of large trout caught. Beginning in 1998, bigger browns and rainbows than had been reasonably anticipated over the previous 10 years began to show up. The trend has continued. No-kill, flies-only regulations and intense habitat improvement work spearheaded by the Anglers of the Au Sable and supported by other Federation of Fly-fishers clubs and Trout Unlimited chapters throughout Michigan are showing positive results. The blue-chip dividends are trophy browns and rainbows that slam well-fished streamers, inhale nymphs, and suck down dun and spinner patterns during the major hatches.

The stream at Burton's Landing is easy to fish and wade. The bottom is a mixture of gravel, sand, and marl edges with easily identified holding water, feeding lanes, and deeper-water cover. There is a campground here and this is a very popular spot for the start of a scenic canoe trip, so it's wise to plan your fishing time around the hustle and bustle of an aluminum launch.

Fishing downstream to the next public access at Louie's Landing (about

⅔ mile by river) will take a morning or afternoon to work carefully. This is a pleasant, easy-to-wade stretch with firm bottom, mostly fine gravel, all the way. The selective trout will be found in the obvious places and will respond to accurate casts, fine tippets, and well-tied imitations of the naturals. This is very definitely match-the-hatch water. A dry fly needs to be the correct size and very close to natural color and proportion. In those periods before or after an emergence, a nymphal representation, sometimes drowned deep with a split shot and fished quartering downstream, is effective. At the very beginning of an emergence, when the first few duns are noticed, the soft-hackled wet-fly imitations popularized by Sylvester Nemes's books are very productive, particularly when fished with a crosscurrent, or slightly up-stream, twitch-and-drop retrieve. The soft-hackled wets do not seem to be fished a great deal by the Au Sable regulars, and this fact may contribute a bit to their effectiveness. These educated fish have not been stung quite as often when attacking food in this form or at this stage.

The next downstream access point is at Keystone Landing, a very popular spot with both fisherman and canoeist. It is extremely easy wading over firm gravel and sand and the prime cover and lies are readily identifiable.

Kelly Neuman holds a 24-inch Au Sable brown that ate a #18 pheasant tail nymph.

The late George Alexander guiding anglers near Stephan Bridge.

The early hatches—Blue-Winged Olive, Hendrickson, and Little Black Caddis—are strong and predictable in this stretch, and there is a noticeable increase in fishing pressure as the daily hatch time approaches. Still, there is usually plenty of room with a good population of fish between 12 and 15 inches, and an accomplished angler making accurate casts and delicate presentations can expect success.

Thendara Road is the next, eastward, approach from MI 72 and it is a favorite angling access spot, seemingly growing in popularity over the past several years. This stretch has excellent habitat, heavy and predictable hatches, and is easily navigable by the wading angler. The parking area will host license plates from Montana, California, New York, Virginia, Ohio, and just about every other state over the season's course. One early May afternoon mine was the only Michigan plate. Alaska, Idaho, Florida, and Ohio were represented. Little Black Caddis *(Chimarra)* were present and I took two fish of about 11 inches on a size-16 pattern with a bright green egg sac. Hendrickson duns began about 1:00 PM and came in 10-minute waves. The duns would emerge and the fish would feed for this interval and then the hatch would subside and the fish would go on hold. Then the emergence would start again and so would the fish. This went on for 2 hours or so. The other anglers I spoke with had experienced the same pattern so it wasn't peculiar to my little territory (about 200 yards downstream), and all had met with some success.

Between Thendara and Stephan Bridge the Au Sable is truly a raving beauty, a near–perfect 10. All of this water is actively fished by wading anglers as well as guides and their clients in the graceful Au Sable river-boats. But still there is room and, as an angler proceeds downstream, more and more room and sometimes even solitude. The wild-fish population, mostly brown trout, is very high here, and plenty of them go into and past the middle teens.

Gates Au Sable Lodge sits right on the southeast bank of the river at Stephan Bridge. In addition to the streamside motel there is a restaurant and a full-service Orvis Shop on the grounds. Rusty Gates and his knowledgeable staff can give you very precise information on hatches and other conditions. You can watch the insect activity and trout response yourself while having a cup of coffee in the restaurant or by stepping out of the shop and walk-ing 20 yards to the river. Just a few yards south of Rusty's shop there is a road that leads to a public parking area. This is an excellent starting point and beautiful fishing water with many fish and generally easy wading. Hatches are dependable and prolific with early Hendricksons, while in late May Sulphurs receive the most attention.

Continuing downstream from Stephan Bridge, toward Wakeley Bridge and the end of the flies-only no-kill water, the Au Sable remains premier water in every sense of the term. There are access points from both sides of the river, and in most places the wading, if not easy and carefree, is man-ageable with common sense. Two entry points from North Down River Road that are recommended are the Trout Unlimited access at Guide's Rest and the Pine Road River entry about 1 mile east of Stephan Bridge. Additionally, the TU Research Station south of the intersection of Conners Flat Road and Wakeley Bridge Road puts the angler on easily fished water with a high trout population density.

Wakeley Bridge is the downstream limit to the flies-only, no-kill stretch of the Au Sable. The launch area is often occupied by fly-tiers in the midst of preparations for the next emergence. There is excellent fishing here and, although the wading is a bit tricky, it is manageable with a measure of cau-tion. Deep holds and runs harbor some very respectable fish but can soak the unwise, and the cool waters of the Au Sable will make such a mistake an unforgettable experience.

WAKELEY BRIDGE TO MIO POND

From Wakeley Bridge downstream all the way to Mio Pond the Au Sable is prime habitat for its most famous insect. The *Hexagenia limbata* hatch in June and early July brings big fish to the surface and the season's heaviest concentration of anglers to the area. The Hex, or Michigan caddis, is a silt and marl dweller in the nymphal form. Burrowers, they reach their highest density and heaviest emergence and spinner activity in the stretch of river from Conners Flat to the Whirlpool access area on Cherry Creek Road just west of Mio.

Beginning in late May and up to the beginning of the evening appearance of emerging duns in mid-June, a slowly twitched nymphal imitation, especially the Wiggle-Hex pattern, is effective in the late afternoon and early morning hours. The emergence of duns, and the appearance of the more heavily fed-upon spinners, is a late evening and dark-of-night affair, and the addicted wading angler needs to thoroughly scout the selected nocturnal fishing spot by day, carefully noting logs, snags, drop-offs, and current strengths. Once the feeding begins there can be an almost irresistible temptation to move up, down, or out, just a bit, to reach that heavy fish. If you know your area well you will know the safety limit. Do not, under any condition, stray. Neighboring anglers (and they will be there) seem nettled by fishing time lost to rescue the reckless and foolish. They may be so intrigued by the fishing (or irritated) as to allow the chilled, floundering, and

BOB LINSENMAN

A brown drake—one of the "super hatches" on the Au Sable

sputtering adventurer to gurgle his or her way downstream to Mio Pond. If you insist on bravado and an "I can go anywhere" attitude, be sure to paint the felt soles of your waders a fluorescent, light-reflective color so that your remains can later be retrieved and identified.

This river section has taken on big-water status and attitude and although wadable in certain locations, it is best fished from a boat. Hire a guide. You will learn the river faster, catch more fish, and your guide will point out the best wadable stretches with public access for future reference.

In addition to the hypnotizing Hex hatch there is fabulous Brown Drake activity here. This emergence and spinner fall is also an evening affair, commencing, by calendar and clock, a bit earlier than the *limbata* festival. The Brown Drakes are eagerly awaited by the fish and literally pounced upon when they first appear. Two excellent spots for the cautious, strong wader to capitalize on both hatches are the downstream south bank (fish from the north side) at Parmalee Bridge and the downstream south bank below the tail-out of the Whirlpool at Cherry Creek Road.

This is a prime area for big fish, and although it is "open water" (general trout regulations apply) the pressure is only moderate. The fish population is high, with brown and rainbow trout, and occasionally brookies, actively feeding in the evening hours.

The South Branch of the Au Sable enters and greatly increases the flow between Wakeley and McMaster's bridges. The North Branch of the Au Sable similarly affects the river just downstream from McMaster's, and at Luzerne, Big Creek joins the rush to Lake Huron. This is very big, serious water, and all due caution and respect must be accorded.

The South Branch

The South Branch of the Au Sable originates at the outlet of Lake St. Helen in Roscommon County. It flows from that point northward and a bit west to the town of Roscommon through mixed forest and marsh. Although accessible by county and forest service roads, the fishing pressure is generally light. Wild brook and brown trout with an occasional rainbow are present and seem to respond all season long to a well-placed Adams in size 14. Woolly Buggers and Mickey Finns, Gold-Ribbed Hare's Ears, and Caddis Creepers are productive subsurface flies, and complementing the Adams with a Royal Wulff and Elk-Hair Caddis will generally complete the requirements for an enjoyable day of bridge-hopping from one county or forest service road access to another.

From Roscommon past the access at Deerheart Valley Road to the Chase Bridge boundary of the Mason Tract and downstream to its junction with the Main Stream, the South Branch is deservedly famous and receives a fair degree of pressure by both wading and floating anglers. Brown and brook trout are the dominant species with only a few rainbows in evidence until one reaches the Smith Bridge access very near MI 72 west of Luzerne.

From Chase Bridge to Canoe Harbor, the South Branch is enclosed by the protecting shield of the Mason Tract, a generous gift to the state by George Mason. Mason's will bequeathed, in perpetuity, the property on both banks of the river, once a private angling retreat, to be held in public trust. This magnificent gift to the people has returned to its natural state. Deer, ruffed grouse, and woodcock, along with the attendant predators, are abundant. From Chase Bridge to Canoe Harbor there are 21 parking and river-entry points easily accessible by dirt road. This stretch of river is a special place for the fly-rodder. Four miles, from Chase Bridge to the lower high-banks access, are reserved for flies-only and no-kill fishing. From the lower high banks to the river's mouth (11 miles) the fishing is restricted to flies only.

The South Branch hatches are prolific. Little Black Caddis and Hendricksons are dependable early season flies and reliably bring the brick-solid, wild trout to the surface. Sulphurs begin to appear in early to mid-May, depending on weather, and the fish seem particularly fond of both floating nymphs and soft-hackled emerging patterns when this hatch is in progress. March Browns start to show about mid-May and continue through early June. The Mahogany Dun is also a favorite menu item in May but by mid-June most of the attention goes to the Brown Drake and Hex activity. Mayflies the size of small hummingbirds create quite a stir (literally—the sound of a swarm of mating *limbata* spinners is distinct and unforgettable) in the late evening hours. The biggest fish in the river feed on top during June and early July and, due to the special regulations and excellent habitat, fish over 20 inches are caught and released every day.

The experienced South Branch angler fishes a hatch predictably. The first few duns, or spinners, are taken in splashy rises by immature brown trout and eager brookies. They are left alone by the wading fisherman. Once the more stoic, substantial but conservative rise forms begin to show in the heavier, deeper water the angler may make a first approach but likely waits a few more minutes, until an actual rhythm is discernable, before casting to the more substantial fish. Quite often, multiple, drag-free casts are required to perfectly intercept a larger fish's feeding rhythm. Such fish are often holding tight beneath a stump or under the protective covering of a sweeper. The bigger fish are never easy to reach and are difficult to fool, but a patient approach to the opportunity will generally bring a heart-thumping reward.

At Chase Bridge there are entrances to the Mason Tract and its fabulous fishing on both the west and east sides of the river, but there are many more access points on the west side, and most local and visiting anglers

Ron Brillinger fishes the "White Fly" near Perry Creek.

favor this approach. Although not always marked as such, the two-track fire trails heading eastward lead to parking areas and paths that will take you streamside.

Some of the more historical (and famous) locations in the Mason Tract are Potters Landing, Durant's Castle, High Banks (two sites here—the lower high banks marks the end of the no-kill water), Baldwin's, Fisherman's Chapel (a spot for reflection and thanks), Downey's Dogtown (probably the most popular parking spot on the South Branch), and Canoe Harbor. Downstream from Canoe Harbor there is a stretch of water that is surrounded by private property. The landowners are friendly, reasonable folks, and their property should be accorded respect. Just before reaching the MI 72 bridge the Mason Tract resumes for the very short flow to Smith Bridge, a popular spot for canoe conclaves.

One recent May afternoon I fished the South Branch at Canoe Harbor and at Smith Bridge. On the next day I fished farther upstream in the vicinity of the Fisherman's Chapel. Both days were warm and clear, and there was little insect activity and no visibly rising fish until late afternoon. At about 5:30 PM on both days, waves of egg-laying Popcorn Caddis *(nectopsyche)* began to appear and the first slash rises of the eager, smaller fish showed in the shallows. By 6 PM the first struggling Sulphur Duns were in evidence, and 10 minutes later, respectable rise forms were beginning to pattern.

I started with a soft-hackle emerger pattern that sports a trailing shuck of antron. This produced moderate action, a mix of solid takes and missed slashes, until 7 PM By now the emerging Sulphurs formed a steady parade and there were rhythmic rises everywhere. A high-riding thorax tie produced until about 8, when although the Sulphurs were still coming they seemed to ride the feeding lanes in complete safety. Fish were still rising but not taking the obvious. I retreated to the bank, removed the Sulphur pattern and, flyless, watched the river. When I looked up for some forgotten reason, I noticed the mating swarm and luckily, swirling at my feet, found a Hendrickson spinner. The feeding continued until full dark, and it was my good fortune to land and release four solid browns between 12 and 15 inches and two handsome brook trout, one approaching 12 inches.

Downstream from Smith Bridge to the mouth the river flows through privately held property. Many of the cottages have docks and landings for canoes and riverboats and these are surprisingly good spots for larger fish. This section is best fished from a boat (or with a landowner's invitation in hand) and it is a full day's float, so be prepared for several hours on the water. Rainbow trout are more common in this stretch, coinciding, it seems, with a general fade in the brook trout population.

Throughout its course, from Chase Bridge to the mouth, the South Branch is wadable and a joy to fish. The deep holes, snags, and heavy-water runs are easily identified and avoided with a little prudent forethought. Plan on a fishing width averaging 40 to 50 feet. A 9-foot, 4- or 5-weight rod is ideal. The hatches are reliable, sometimes very heavy, and the fish are willing respondents to a studied approach and careful casting. Gates Fly Shop at Stephan Bridge has reliable information on the hatches throughout the Mason Tract and from Smith Bridge to the mouth. Roscommon is a real trout town. You'll likely see wader-clad folks just about everywhere.

The North Branch

The North Branch of the Au Sable is born in the Mackinaw State Forest at Otsego Lake in Otsego County. It flows southeasterly and crosses into Crawford County near F 97 a few miles west of the town of Lewiston. Flowing southward and generally parallel to F 97 (Twin Bridges Road) it approaches the hamlet of Lovells, with all the characteristics of a large spring creek.

From the Sheep Ranch access north of Lovells to its junction with the Main Stream, the North Branch is under the protection of flies-only angling. This 21-mile span has, at this writing, an extended season making it the ideal center for a "cast-and-blast" outing combining the best of upland bird hunting and colorful, crisp angling.

The start of the flies-only water at the Sheep Ranch access is, with the exception of a narrow chute downstream from the sign at the special-regulation boundary, mostly wide, flat, and shallow water with brook trout and smaller browns spread throughout the 50- to 60-foot width of the streambed. Watercress beds and grasses provide cover late in the season, and small scud patterns drifted in the channels and in the deeper water around snags will produce wild and scrappy, if somewhat small, naturally reproduced trout. The Sheep Ranch is only 2 miles north of town on Twin Bridges Road and 0.5 mile north of Twin Bridges. It is reached via an easy to see, two-track dirt road leading off to the left. Do not proceed down the hill to the left. Park at the top and walk to the river as the soft, black, low ground will mire even a stout four-wheel drive.

The property on both sides of the river at Twin Bridges is private, and care should be taken to stay in the river, but this is very easy wading and should present no problem. There is more trout cover from here downstream to and through Lovells proper, and the wild fish average larger than upstream. This area supports good hatches of all major mayflies and caddis with the Hendrickson, Mahogany Dun, Sulphur, and March Browns producing excellent fishing.

Downstream, south of Lovells on F 97/Lovells Road, there is an easy access with excellent fishing for both brook and brown trout at Dam Four. Drive south from Lovells about 4.5 miles to the first graded road heading west. There is a sign at this turn that reads DAM FOUR. Follow this road about 1 mile to its dead end at the river. Private property surrounds the North Branch here and the no-trespassing laws are enthusiastically enforced, so be sure to stay in the river.

The river here is wide and easily fished. The bottom is mostly gravel and sand and quite firm. Holes, runs, and obvious riffles, as well as bankside edges, hold abundant brook and brown trout. The best cover and larger fish, in my opinion, are downstream from the access point, and this area is best fished with long, slack-line casts, quartering down and across. Hendricksons, Sulphurs, Caddis, and Gray Drakes stimulate heavy feeding in this section. The fish are quite demanding relative to both presentation and exactness of imitation, and particularly so during the Sulphur hatch when I found that only a parachute tie would reliably produce. There is a good ratio of larger brook trout both up- and downstream from Dam Four access, some approaching 13 inches, and they should all be carefully released. They are incredibly beautiful, richly colored fish, and a photo or two shouldn't hurt them.

The Jackson Hole (yes, you are still reading about Michigan) Campground access is downstream from Dam Four about 1 mile on the Lovells Road. Turn west and take the right fork around a sharp curve and down the hill to the campground. This is a very popular place for campers interested in tubing and canoeing as well as fishing, so it's wise to make a quick tour of the grounds and scout the prevailing water sports before selecting a spot to fish.

Some time ago, I ran into Matt Wilhelm at Jackson Hole, and our compared notes showed a consistent preference by the fish for the Sulphur dun over the Hendrickson dun or spinner. At the same time emerging caddis were heavy but the fish did not respond at all to them. The parachute-hackle Sulphur dun and, earlier, the soft-hackle emerger were the keys to success.

The fishing is generally very good in this area. At Jackson Hole the river varies greatly in width and depth and a little more care is called for while wading. The stream here has excellent cover, good hatches, and a healthy trout population with many large trout being taken throughout the season. For hatchless periods, a small Clouser Minnow or yellow Marabou Muddler

BOB LINSENMAN

Steve holds a nice Au Sable brown that ate a Hendrickson spinner.

is effective. Caddis Creeper nymphs, Gold-Ribbed Hare's Ears, and Pheasant Tails produce all season long. Crickets, ants, grasshoppers, and beetles work during mid- and late summer. Otherwise, the Adams and Elk-Hair Caddis are good search patterns. The Trico hatch in late summer is top entertainment, and an early-rising angler should carry the little spinner patterns in sizes 22–26.

At Kellogg Bridge on North Down River Road, the North Branch is about 70 feet wide and carries a heavy current with deep runs and good cover for large trout. You may see rising fish immediately up- and downstream from the bridge, but these are most likely small brookies. The best fishing from this access is upstream for several hundred yards throughout several river bends with deep holes, swift runs, and bright, sunlit riffles. The banks are private property and the courteous angler will stay in the river.

This is one of the more heavily fished sections of the North Branch, and exact imitations of the prevailing hatch are worth the extra effort. Sculpin and small olive or tan crayfish patterns are effective at dawn and dusk, and a moonlit drift with a size-4 Deer-Hair Mouse is an adventure. Big Creek enters the North Branch downstream from Kellogg Bridge and increases depth and flow considerably. The access at the dead end of Morley Road is reflective of this increased flow and is generally representative of the North Branch downstream to its junction with the Main Stream. More care is required to safely wade the remainder of the river. A good case in point is the stretch just downstream from the Morley access. The river flows into a gentle curve against a high bank area, and this curve and its deep water is a superb fishing spot, with or without a hatch. The shallow east side is very manageable, but because the banks are private, a long, upstream, and very tiring wade is required to reach the access point. Normally this will present no problem, but high water or an overtired pair of legs can make the return trip a dicey proposition.

I have fished the North Branch extensively and find it a lovely, peaceful, and pleasant river to explore. The trout rise to any reasonable volume of insects and, during hatchless periods, respond well to attractor patterns. It is generally a safe place to wade, a good place to learn, and, overall, a varied and rewarding experience.

Trophy Waters

A vigorous stocking program has supercharged fly-fishing for trout below Mio. From the boat access just east of the highway bridge in Mio through the Trophy Water stretch, which ends at the bridge in McKinley to the backwaters of Alcona Pond below FS 4001, the annual stocking program releases large numbers of rainbow and brown trout that quickly grow to respectable size. And there is good survival through the warm water of summer and bitter cold of winter. Rainbows and browns in excess of 20 inches are commonplace. True "giants," those fish over 24 inches, appear during the Brown Drake and Hex hatches, but most often eat large streamer patterns representing sculpins or crayfish.

There is now more angling pressure than when we wrote the first edition, but this is a good thing. The increase in ethical anglers, many of whom carry cell phones to report violators, has the effect of discouraging and reducing, if not eliminating, the activities of poachers. The MDNR law enforcement officers from the Mio office are vigorous and dedicated. Support them.

From the Department of Transportation roadside park in Mio to the bridge at McKinley the big river is under special regulations intended by the MDNR managers and biologists to produce trophy-sized trout. Artificials-only fishing and a minimum size limit of 15 inches for brown trout and a creel limit of two fish per day has, over the years, allowed the growth of very large fish and the development of a premier trophy opportunity.

The river below the Mio Dam, visible from MI 33, is big even by Rocky Mountain standards. It can be easy to fish with careful wading in a few places near the many public access points, but more often it is too much river for the first-time visitor without a guide. There are many holes deep enough to sink a Suburban without a trace. Its runs, both near the banks and midstream, seem manageable due to the firm bottom, but the current is heavy and relentless and many anglers have been toppled after staying out too long, deceived by the appearance of casual flow and becoming too tired to wade safely back to calmer water or the bank.

In addition to the safety factor, a guide provides access to otherwise unreachable feeding zones via the driftboat and, of course, knows with intimacy the best riffles and pools and locations for peak hatches and large fish. Another benefit is that knowledgeable river guides, like Kelly Neuman and Mike Bachelder, have developed a schedule to beat the "canoe hatch," putting an angler ahead of the aluminum flotilla and into good fishing.

With a little luck and some planning, an angler can reasonably expect trophy-size trout rising to the dry fly throughout this stretch of river. There are fewer fish overall between Mio and McKinley, but there are many more real bruisers, big fish over 20 inches that look topside during a hatch. Key emergences here are pretty much the same as in the upper river with a few notable deviations. There is only very limited Hex activity between Mio and McKinley, but Little Black Caddis *(Chimarra)*, Hendrickson *(subvaria, invaria,* and *rotunda)*, Sulphur *(dorothea)*, various Olives, March Browns *(vicarium)*, Brown Drakes *(simulans)*, the White Fly *(Ephoron leukon)*, and selected terrestrials, especially flying black ants, are reliable big-fish producers.

One afternoon a few years ago, I floated the Mio-to-Comins-Flats stretch with Ron Brillinger. After shuttling automobiles and launching at the Mio access at 2:00 P.M. we drifted lazily for several hundred yards casting Hendrickson nymphs to deeper runs and looking hard for the first sign of emerging duns. The air was a cool 58 degrees F and the water temperature was 52 degrees. The wind came hard, gusting from the southwest, and the rolling buff-colored clouds gradually gave way to a gathering roil of thunderheads.

By the time we had passed the power line that marks the start of the trophy, special-regulations water (this is just about ½ mile downstream from the Department of Transportation roadside park on MI 33) we had seen two wading fisherman and only a dozen or so duns. Ron (who was still guiding fly anglers at that time but no longer does) explained that on the previous day he guided on this same stretch and that the hatch had not started to reach interesting volume until about 4:15 PM; the fish had started feeding actively by 4:30 and from that time until dark the action had been constant. His client had taken several good fish on a cul-de-canard Hendrickson emerger, one a 20-inch male brown and the other a female of 21 inches.

As we passed the first public access point off McKinley Road to the north, a few more duns formed miniature regattas and drifted harmlessly through what appeared to be excellent holding water. My nymph and emerger pattern had not produced anything beyond a suspicious flash in midstream, and I asked Ron if I should change over to a streamer, at least until the hatch picked up in intensity. "No, but put on a size-14 dun and be ready to cast to any suspected rise or swirl," he answered as he lowered the boat's stern-mounted chain to slow our progress. After two rods had been loaded with 4X-tipped, high-riding dun imitations of *subvaria,* we slipped down to the edge of a long, dark run on the south bank. As we approached we noticed a parade of Hendricksons drifting through a serpentine back eddy, out into the main current and down the far edge of the run. At the precise edge of the slack and moving water there was a smooth, deliberate rise. First the head up and out about an inch, then the heavy shoulders and dorsal, and, finally, the tail slicing downward smoothly in a rainbow arc.

"That was a big fish, cast right away," Ron directed as he anchored and stopped the boat. Two dozen seemingly perfect casts later had produced no indication of interest. I tried several more casts, changed to an emerger and then to a nymph without reward. "The duns have stopped," Ron explained. "They're coming in spurts of about 10 minutes' duration. That's when the fish have been rising. Let's move on down. There are several fish working the edge of that sweeper on the left-hand bank."

We floated a full 60 yards before I could pick up the rise forms downstream about 45 yards. "Try these," he instructed. "Give your fly at least a 6-foot drift to the fish." Out went the bad cast, in came the bad cast. Out went the good cast, and a trout slashed and missed. "Let it drift." The fly floated another 10 feet and was taken with confidence by the next fish. The small rainbow was quickly released and the fly was back in the air toward the most distant feeder. This one, another small rainbow of about 10 inches, sucked in the fly without any hesitation. After its return to the water, Ron suggested that since the hatch was becoming heavier and the fish had begun to take the duns, we should move down to the area near the mouth of Perry Creek, a prime spot for big fish on the dry fly.

The float to Perry Creek encountered one heavy squall that had us scurrying into rain gear. It also stayed the emergence until we had anchored and started our stakeout at one of Ron's favorite "heart-jumper" spots.

I put on a fresh fly and fidgeted for a full 10 minutes until we both saw two simultaneous rises near the bank. The upstream fish was closer to us, perhaps 10 feet out from the sweep of an old cedar stump. My excited and clumsy cast produced a wind knot, a scared fish, and a thoroughly drowned dry fly. The lower, bankside fish rose again with a satisfied "schlup," and Ron and I exchanged rods as a quick solution to my problem. My first cast was about 16 inches short and after it had drifted past the hot zone I picked up and tried again. The little fly perked nicely, drifted 2 feet, and disappeared into the vortex of a rise form. I raised the rod tip and felt heavy resistance. "Good fish, maybe 15 or 16 inches," I said to Ron. Just then the trout turned nuclear, a display of pure Nautilus power, and ran all the line and 30 or so yards of backing straight out into the river with real purpose to the far bank. "I'd say that fish is a bit over 16 inches," Ron noted dryly, and the real excitement commenced. After 10 minutes the big female was in the net, quickly photographed, taped, and released. She was 23 inches long with a beautiful deep golden sheen, large vibrant spots, deep girth, and small head. We guessed her at near enough to 5 pounds. Whew!

The rest of the float to Comins Flats produced more large fish, rising to both duns and, near dark, to spinners, but nothing in the 23-inch class. When we loaded the boat on the trailer the clouds had gone and bright stars flooded the sky.

The early season until about June 1 provides very good streamer fishing during hatchless periods. After early June streamer productivity drops, although large fish are still taken on crayfish and sculpin imitations. The river has many areas of heavy aquatic vegetation that are home to a thriving scud population, and a number-12 or -14 tannish Olive or gray scud pattern fished dead-drift through the grass channels upstream from Comins Flats can bring some surprisingly large fish to your attention. After mid-June the warmer air temperatures push the main hatching activity to early morning and late evening, which is just fine, because the midday hours are peak canoe time.

BOB LINSENMAN

Bruce and Carl Chin with an Au Sable bruiser. Carl caught the big male on a streamer in August 2000.

Access throughout this stretch of river is very easy. Bordered largely by public lands (mostly national forest), there are many forest service roads off McKinley Road that lead directly to riverside parking. The fishing experience itself is one of near-wilderness impressions. The cedar lowlands and pine and hardwood high banks are haven to grouse, deer, turkey, assorted predators including bobcat, coyote, mink, and otter, and the majestic eagle. There are few cabins in evidence except in the immediate areas of Comins Flats and McKinley, and the "ride" is pure joy even without the big fish.

Some access points to consider for relatively easy wading and reliable fishing are reached via McKinley Road. Both up- and downstream from the parking area at Davis Landing (3.0 miles upstream from McKinley) there is good fishing for browns and rainbows in the near-bank riffle. The "Meadows," upper and lower, can be reached via forest service access 0.5 mile east of Perry Creek, and there are reliable hatches with easy casting from the bank. This is a good area for terrestrials, especially flying ants and grasshoppers, later in the season. Just upstream from the boat ramp at McKinley Bridge there is a very nice long run on the south side of the river. It extends from below the ramp, where it drops into a handsome riffle, upstream for about 100 yards to an old, clearly visible protruding snag. This is excellent morning and evening dry-fly water and wadable for anyone with an I.Q. above the freezing mark.

Downstream from McKinley the river leaves the special-regulations section and generally runs a bit warmer through high summer, but good numbers of trout (some very large) are still available. There is reasonable public access for the wading angler throughout the run to FS 4001, but the best way to fish this stretch is from a driftboat.

Major hatches are Hendricksons, Mahoganies, Brown Drakes, *Isonychia,* various stoneflies, Hex and the White Fly *(Ephoron leukon).* Streamers like the Zoo Cougar, Woolly Sculpin, Madonna, and Kiwi Muddler, which represent sculpin, and the Trick or Treat, which mimics a crayfish, are consistent producers of heavy brown trout.

Kelly Neuman, a top Au Sable guide, and I often fish this stretch together on "days off." We always keep two rods at the ready. One is a 6- or 7-weight rigged with a short, stout leader, a full-sinking line, and a large streamer. The other is a 4- or 5-weight with a floating line set up with the dry fly of the moment. We fish streamers with a vigorous, jerk-strip retrieve until we spot rising fish. Then, a quick switch is made. This rotation continues through the 11-mile float.

May through mid-June and late August through season's close are the best periods in this section. The entire course is through the Huron National Forest. There are no cabins here (no buildings of any kind), only wild Michigan as it might have been long ago. Kingfishers, eagles, osprey, mink, otters, deer, the occasional bear, bubbling springs, singing riffles, and placid pools delight the senses. And just when your mind wanders—when you relax too much—a long, deep trout will charge your Zoo Cougar and bring you back to full alert.

The Au Sable is a rich and varied trout stream. Over its lengthy course to Lake Huron it harbors diminutive headwater brookies, sophisticated, critical rainbows, trophy browns, and in the last reach below Foote Dam, spawning steelhead and salmon. It hosts plumbers and sheiks, movie stars and cops, executives and children seeking release, joy, excitement. It is gentle and downright scary; sometimes crowded and often deserted. It is one of the most fabulous trout streams on earth.

Notes:

- Be sure to visit Hartwick State Park just north of Grayling. The centuries-old virgin pines are inspiring.
- The "rolling thunder" you hear on clear, dry days is artillery fire from the military base. Those low-flying, hair-raising jet fighters get your attention, don't they?

- There are general festivals and jamborees in this area throughout the summer months. If you're interested, check a community calendar or information boards at any of the local businesses for a schedule.
- Lovells, Grayling, Luzerne, Roscommon, and Mio have good restaurants, motels, and most everything you might need.
- The Au Sable River system is north of the "tension line." Relax and enjoy your stay.
- Lumberman's Monument west of Tawas City at the junction of Monument and River roads features the Stairway of Discovery, a 260-step descent of over 160 feet to the Au Sable River.
- Several champion-class golf courses are located in the area.
- Big Creek Preserve just south of Mio on CR 489 offers private trout ponds and upland bird hunting.

4 | The Manistee River

Antrim County, Otsego County, Crawford County, Kalkaska County, Wexford County, Missaukee County, Manistee County

Since publication of the first edition of this book in 1993, the angling in the Manistee has actually improved. From the upper headwater reach northwest of Frederic to the mouth at Manistee, the river is presenting more and bigger fish to fly-anglers. Stocking programs have certainly had impact, but as important is the effect of stewardship by conservation organizations and alliances. Habitat improvement and a sense of responsibility and restraint that comes from education are key elements. Trout Unlimited, Federation of Fly-fishers (specifically Anglers of the Au Sable), the Upper Manistee River Restoration Committee (UMRRC), the MDNR, homeowners associations, and other groups are making an impact that is calculable in the numbers of wild brook trout, healthy browns, and rainbows throughout the river's flow. The "flies-only" water has been enlarged, the number of true trophy-status browns and rainbows has increased in the middle section of the river, the Hodenpyle stretch gets better each year, and the flow below Tippy dam, long considered premier steelhead, salmon, and lake-run brown trout water, is now providing excellent fly angling for resident trout throughout the year.

The Manistee River's headwaters are just a very few miles west of the Au Sable River's birthplace and it takes but a few minutes to drive from one to the other. After a few short miles of southward flow, both rivers turn. The famous Au Sable heads east to Lake Huron and the Manistee turns westward to Lake Michigan.

Long famous as a premium steelhead and salmon river (below Tippy Dam near Wellston), the Big Manistee is also an excellent blue-ribbon fishery for stream trout, from the narrow confines above Mancelona Road downstream to the wide reaches and deep pools near Sharon and on downstream past Smithville, through Hodenpyle Run, and below Tippy Dam.

Perhaps it is due to less exposure in print, but it is interesting to note that, although the Manistee has excellent fly-fishing for brook, brown, and rainbow trout, has easy access and special regulations to protect the resource, and is close to major tourist areas, it has much lower pressure from visiting anglers than the nearby Au Sable. Knowledgeable local anglers and guides often prefer the Manistee for their personal fishing due to its relative solitude and highly productive flow.

In its upper reaches the Manistee is home to wildly aggressive, vividly hued brook trout. Some sources of information state flatly that the river is not suited to fly-fishing above the Mancelona Road (C 38) culvert just east of the Antrim-Otsego county line, but we have fished this area extensively using fairly long rods (8½ feet) and had little difficulty with back casts. In a few spots roll casts were necessary to present the fly without mishap, but as a rule there was little problem even with the longer fly rods. There is, however, evidence of beaver activity in the area. A well-placed dam could change the situation overnight.

Upstream from the culvert the Manistee is reminiscent of a smallish Montana spring creek with a smooth sand bottom, fine gravel ribbons, and black mud edges. It is about 20 feet wide and ranges from about 6 inches to 3 feet deep. The cover is largely natural with old cedar and birch logs, undercut banks, and a few deep, midstream pockets. In addition, there are the remnants of man-made CCC-type diversion wings and other such structures that provide shelter for the eager brook trout. During a recent visit, 10 brook trout were caught and released in 40 minutes within 200 yards of Mancelona Road. These fish took an egg-sac Irresistible without hesitation on a bright Saturday afternoon during the peak of the tourist season. No canoes, no other anglers, no paths, nothing to be found here but clean water and wild fish.

Downstream from the culvert the little river ranges from 20 to 25 feet wide and its sand and fine gravel bottom supports various aquatic grasses. The water is clear to the point of being deceptive. While most of this stretch is 1 to 2 feet deep there are many pockets that, in fact, are much deeper. An angler can easily be distracted by the beauty and serenity and ship some ice water into a pair of hip boots.

About 50 yards downstream from the culvert, and entering from the east, there is a 4-foot-wide feeder spring with 6-inch-deep water and 3 feet of soft muck. Be very careful crossing this feeder; a mistake will take a few minutes of effort to correct. The banks are very difficult to walk in this section. The ground is spongy at best and the many muck holes and the thick foliage dictate navigation from the stream.

There is ample room to fly-fish, although short roll casts are often a necessity. As is the case above Mancelona Road, downed trees and undercut banks are where you will find the trout. Several healthy brook trout jumped on a small Woolly Bugger, and a small brown inhaled a Hare's Ear during a short, recent foray. This upper section of the Manistee is wild and pristine.

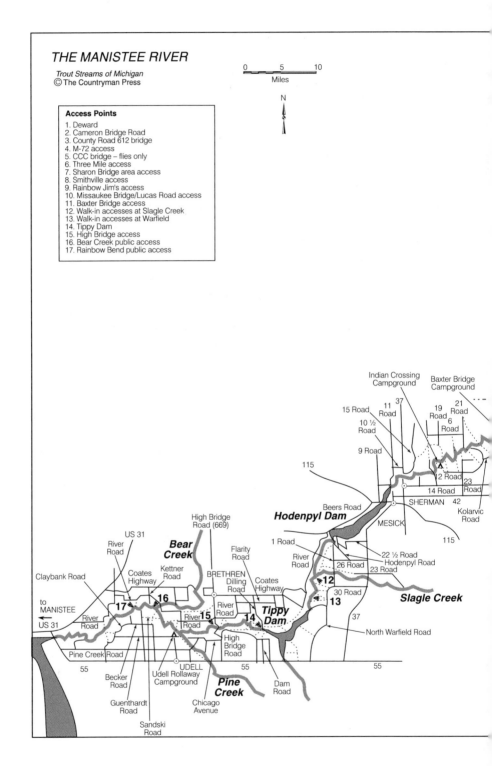

THE MANISTEE RIVER

Trout Streams of Michigan
© The Countryman Press

0   5   10
Miles

N

Access Points

1. Deward
2. Cameron Bridge Road
3. County Road 612 bridge
4. M-72 access
5. CCC bridge – flies only
6. Three Mile access
7. Sharon Bridge area access
8. Smithville access
9. Rainbow Jim's access
10. Missaukee Bridge/Lucas Road access
11. Baxter Bridge access
12. Walk-in accesses at Slagle Creek
13. Walk-in accesses at Warfield
14. Tippy Dam
15. High Bridge access
16. Bear Creek public access
17. Rainbow Bend public access

Indian Crossing
Campground

Baxter Bridge
Campground

15 Road

11
Road

37

19
Road

21
Road

10 ½
Road

6
Road

9 Road

115

2 Road

23
Road

14 Road

SHERMAN   42

Beers Road

Hodenpyl Dam

MESICK

Kolarvic
Road

High Bridge
Road (669)

US 31

River
Road

**Bear
Creek**

Flarity
Road

1 Road

River
Road

22 ½ Road

115

Claybank Road

Coates
Highway

Kettner
Road

BRETHREN

Dilling
Road

Coates
Highway

River
Road

26 Road

23 Road

Hodenpyl Road

12

30 Road

13

Slagle Creek

to
MANISTEE

US 31

River
Road

17

16

River
Road

15

River
Road

14

**Tippy
Dam**

37

North Warfield Road

Pine Creek Road

55

Becker
Road

High
Bridge
Road

55

**Pine
Creek**

Dam
Road

55

UDELL
Udell Rollaway
Campground

Guenthardt
Road

Chicago
Avenue

Sandski
Road

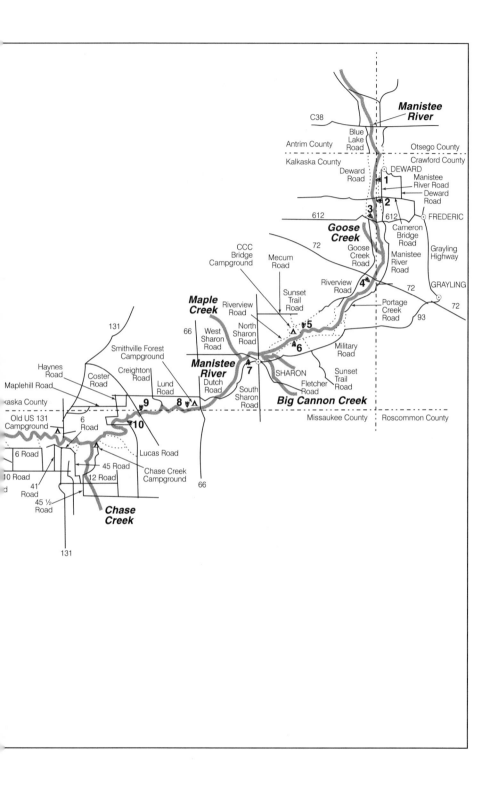

The trout are eager, there is no pressure, and the wildflowers are spectacular.

Downstream from Mancelona Road the next major access point is at the ghost lumber town of Deward. The Deward access, in extreme northwestern Crawford County, is easily reached via Fayette Road south of Mancelona Road and north of Cameron Bridge Road. The Deward parking area is approximately 4 miles south of Mancelona Road on Fayette Road. Note that when Fayette Road crosses into Crawford County from Otsego County (heading south) the name changes to Manistee River Road. If you are driving north toward Deward from CR 612 you will be on Manistee River Road for about 2.7 miles before the westward turnoff to the Deward parking area.

The river here has been enlarged by springs and Frenchman's Creek and averages about 35 feet wide. It has a firm sand and gravel bottom and excellent trout cover in both natural and man-made forms. The oxygen-rich water, gravel, muck edges, and rotting vegetation produce optimum conditions for aquatic insects, and mayfly, caddis, and stonefly species are present. Generally speaking the fly-casting and wading is easy and, although this area receives more pressure than others, the fishing is quite good for brook trout with an occasional outsize brown thrown into the mix.

Downstream from Deward, and upstream from Cameron Bridge Road, the water is a fly-fisher's paradise. Running from 35 to 45 feet wide with long runs, deep holes, alternating pools and riffles, and deep undercut banks, the Manistee offers low angling pressure, only moderate canoe traffic (the upstream limit for most canoe journeys is Deward), and a very healthy population of sizable browns and handsome brook trout.

For the adventuresome angler, one not afraid to walk several hundred yards, a westward compass heading through the public land in the Deward region will take you to good fishing. Probably the best way to reach this water is by taking Manistee River Road north from Cameron Bridge Road for 0.6 mile to a sand two-track heading west. Take this road to a pair of private property signs and park off the road to the south (be sure to stay on public lands). From here you can walk approximately 250 yards southwest to a pipeline trail. Follow this trail 250 yards to the river.

Although they are few, canoes are present due to the Deward access upstream. Fish the back eddies, undercut banks, foam lines near the shore, anywhere that can float a trout and not a canoe. If fish are actively rising and a canoe appears, be patient, wait a few seconds, and the fish will resume their feeding.

You can fish any length rod in this section of the Manistee as the stream is generally wide enough to keep your back cast clear of the brush. An 8½- or 9-foot for a 4- or 5-weight line is just about ideal in that it will present a small fly on a fine tippet with delicate accuracy (required in this crystalline water) as well as punch out a 50-foot cast with a weighted nymph.

Woolly Buggers, Zoo Cougars, Woolly Sculpins, and Muddler Minnows are effective streamers and should be tried here. Terrestrials, especially grasshoppers from late June to season's close, produce well, and a general assortment of nymphs and dry flies would include the Gold-Ribbed Hare's Ear, Caddis Creeper, Pheasant Tail, and Brown Stone for subsurface work, and Adams, Light Cahill, Henryville Caddis, and Rusty's Spinner for top-water action. If there is a hatch in progress, you must match it fairly closely, so be sure to carry faithful imitations of the bug du jour.

Cameron Bridge is an extremely popular starting point for general canoe hoopla and is best fished in the early morning and late evening hours. The river near Cameron Bridge is much the same in character as the Deward section with the notation that there are numerous homes bankside and, because the property is private, the angler must stay in the river. Just east of Cameron Bridge (0.3 mile) there is a dirt road to the north that leads to a public access built by Trout Unlimited. Additionally, there is a private southward sand two-track 100 yards east of Cameron Bridge. An angler wishing to fish in the immediate area can, with permission, walk down this two-track and fish back up to the bridge, or reverse the process and fish downstream for a few hundred yards and then walk the two-track back to Cameron Bridge Road.

The river here is 50 to 75 feet wide and 1 to 4 feet deep. The bottom is sand and gravel with deep bankside cuts. There are many logs and tree stumps that provide excellent trout cover and some tricky wading. Be careful. Despite its popularity with canoeists the fishing is quite good here, and even at midday fish will resume feeding moments after a flotilla has passed.

The bridge on CR 612 is another popular canoe rendezvous, but this should not be a deterrent to fishing. This area has some excellent cover for large fish and produces some very large brown trout on a regular basis. Here the river is wide and flat with logs and partially exposed stumps providing cover for both brook and brown trout. The river at the bridge on CR 612 is about 60 feet wide and therefore casting is not a concern. The water remains very clear and cold with depths up to 5 feet or more in some of the holes. Hip boots are out of the question.

Both brook and brown trout, and an occasional rainbow, respond very well to a small Royal Wulff or egg-sac Irresistible when fished on a fine tippet. The usual nymphs work as expected, and a Mickey Finn in size 10 is a popular addition to the more somber-hued streamers mentioned earlier. Downstream from the bridge there are areas with silt banks that are home to the Hex and Brown Drake nymphs, and the late June and early July emergences of these insects produce superb late evening dry-fly angling.

There is a large campground downstream from CR 612 just off Goose Creek Road. For the most part this section of the river is just too busy with boat, kid, and pet traffic to recommend for fishing. Still, it does have a

Lunch break on the "flies-only" section of the Manistee River

healthy population of trout and it is a beautiful spot to try in the early morning or late evening hours.

Also downstream from CR 612 (but east of the bridge and accessed from Manistee River Road) is Long's Canoe Livery. On your way south from CR 612 toward Long's on Manistee River Road, you will notice a two-track lane 0.25 mile south of CR 612. Take this two-track 0.25 mile west to the river. This sure beats parking at the bridge if you want to fish close to CR 612.

Continue south on Manistee River Road to Long's Canoe Livery. Anglers are very welcome here, and car parking is allowed for a small fee. The river here is split into many channels and provides surprisingly good fishing in the morning and evening. From this point, and continuing downstream to the end of the trout water, the wading becomes more problematic and the inexperienced or weaker angler will be wise to fish from the safety of a boat with a guide in attendance.

The "flies-only" stretch of the Manistee has recently been lengthened and now begins (upstream boundary) at the bridge at MI 72. The positive impact of this has been immediate. The fishing has improved both in number and average size throughout the flow from MI 72 to the CCC Bridge and and below. All of the major hatches—Hendricksons, mahoganies, sculpins, Brown Drakes, *Hexagenia,* and *Isonychia*—are producing superb dry-fly angling. Cloudy days are best for streamers. Carry crayfish patterns like the

Trick or Treat and sculpin imitations in yellow, olive, brown, and black.

During the peak of the Hex hatch favorite floats for guided trips will likely include "access" points that have excellent fishing but generally difficult wading. These floats will start, end, or take you past the MI 72 bridge, and the Riverview and Yellowtrees areas. This stretch has excellent dry-fly fishing for big fish and is a favorite with the guides. Up-to-date information on hatch activity can be obtained at the Fly Factory in Grayling or at Gates's Lodge at Stephan Bridge just east of Grayling.

The next convenient access point to the Manistee is at the CCC Bridge on Sunset Trail Road in Kalkaska County. Sunset Trail Road is best reached by driving west from the bridge on MI 72 about 6 miles. Drive south on Sunset Trail approximately 8 miles to the bridge and the adjacent campground. This is the downstream limit of the area reserved for flies-only angling and is an excellent starting point for an upstream excursion. The river in this immediate area ranges from 80 to 130 feet in width. The bottom is composed mostly of firm sand and gravel, and the cover, as usual, is provided by logs and sweepers, deep pools and riffles, and the very deep hole in the bends.

From the CCC Bridge upstream to Yellowtree and downstream to Sharon there is excellent habitat for aquatic insects, and the hatches are prolific and heavy. This larger water is an obvious favorite for the angler and the guide.

Over a two-day period in late June the following insects were evident either in dun or spinner stages: *Hexagenia limbata, Stenonema canadense* (Light Cahill), *Ephemera simulans* (Brown Drake), *Ephemerella lata* (Slate-Winged Olive), and *Siphlonurus rapidus* (Gray Drake). Additionally, several different caddis species appeared along with a random sample of terrestrials and midges. Fish were honed in on the Hex duns during the cloudy afternoons and evenings, and the anticipated spinner falls produced trout in the wee morning hours. It's a special thrill, an eerie excitement, to crawl out of a tent at 3 in the morning and hear rises that sound like bowling balls being dropped in the river.

Using the CCC Bridge as a base point, there are several easy access points to this section of the Manistee in both up- and downstream headings. To stay in the flies-only restricted area, follow the dirt road south of the bridge in a northeasterly direction. There are several good access points along this road with room to park one or more vehicles. The river winds through a series of slow bends with deep holes and excellent habitat for aquatic insects. Soft-muck banks in some areas require a studied approach, but they make up for the inconvenience with dense populations of the "super bugs." Not all the access points—and there are several between CCC Bridge and Portage Creek—are shown on the county maps, so drive slowly and explore, and take notes on your route. The roads in this area are confusing.

From CCC Bridge downstream to Sharon the Manistee is again under general trout regulations, and bait- and spin-fishers are intermingled with the fly-rod addicts. Float-tubing is becoming more and more popular as a means of reaching the best water, and it is particularly convenient due to the number and close proximity of the access points. The best route to reach the Sharon area from CCC Bridge is via the gravel road about 200 yards south of the bridge on Sunset Trail. If you turn right you will be following the river downstream past three good access spots with ample parking. The first parking area is about 1 mile south of Sunset Trail. The next access point downstream is another 1.5 miles farther on this gravel road. It is marked Three Mile Road, and has a circular parking area and wooden stairs leading to the river. The initial view of the river from the parking area at Three Mile is deceiving in that the first impression is of a much smaller river than observed just upstream. The river at this point is split into two flows by an island, and thus the deception. Up- and downstream from the island the river is over 100 feet wide and varies from 1 to 6 feet in depth with a moderate flow.

Upstream from the parking area there is an excellent area for fly-fishing with a combination of deep runs, large holes, pools, riffles, snags, and sweepers providing ideal trout cover and a multitude of opportunities for both dry-fly and wet-fly techniques. There is a small island just upstream from the access point, and at the head of the island where the river splits, two very good holding areas have formed. Farther upstream mud banks and marl strips edge the river with perfect Hex and Brown Drake habitat. If you're there at the right time, you can actually hear the big Hex duns "pop" their nymphal shucks.

Very robust brown trout and lively rainbows with the thick bodies and small heads indicative of rapid growth and fine health look to the surface during any reasonable hatch, and they seem overly eager for the opportunity to take a large dun or spinner on cloudy, overcast days. If no hatch is in progress the fish usually stay deep, so general prospecting is best conducted with subsurface nymphs and weighted streamers. The Fox Squirrel nymph and the Clark Lynn or Spring's Wiggler are good, general-purpose patterns for this part of the Manistee. As is nearly always the case on nearly every stream, the Gold-Ribbed Hare's Ear and Pheasant Tail are very effective. Streamers are best fished deep and slow. The Light Spruce Fly, Olive Woolly Bugger, and Zonker are good choices, and a bright fly like the Mickey Finn is worth trying during slow periods.

The Sharon Bridge accesses are the next downstream entry points and are the last that will be covered in this chapter. There is a veritable tangle of roads, a rural spaghetti junction, at Sharon, and a close scrutiny of county roads is a requirement. West, South, and North Sharon roads converge with Riverview Road, Sharon Refuge Truck Trail, King's Road, and Dutch

John Road (no, you are still in Michigan, you have not been transported to Utah) within spitting distance of the Upper and Lower Sharon accesses.

At the Upper Sharon access on North Sharon Road there is ample parking on both sides of the bridge, and the decision to fish up or down is academic—the angling is very good in either direction. Upstream from the bridge the river ranges from 100 to 130 feet wide with clear water flowing over sand and gravel. There are deep midriver runs, dark bankside holes, and glistening pools tailing out into tempting riffles. The fish-holding water is generally obvious, but it is worth noting that there are many hard-to-see pockets of slightly deeper water. These pockets hold fish and it is worth the effort to wade carefully and be on the lookout for them.

As you face upstream you will notice a high sand bank on the right. At the base of this hill's sweep is a deep run that holds a number of large brown and a few brook trout. Farther upstream, on the right bank, a small feeder stream enters the Manistee, and at this junction a deep, dark, and very strong run is formed. This run holds some large rainbows in addition to browns and is worth fishing carefully with a heavily weighted nymph or streamer.

The lower Manistee, like the lower Au Sable, is a big, powerful river that requires thoughtful wading.

Wading this section of the run is best left to the cautious and strong. In several places it is necessary to get out of the river to avoid deep water or obstacles. This is prime big-fish water with a pleasing vista in all directions.

Downstream from the bridge the river splits around a sizable island. Fish a nymph or streamer down the right fork and still a bit beyond where the river rejoins. Then, if so moved, fish a dry fly on the way back upstream to the bridge. The river here is very clear and deceptively deep in spots. Be wary! The bottom is a mix of sand and gravel with stretches of grasses and cress beds. The flat, open stretches seem barren, but on close examination will reveal semihidden pockets that almost always hold a trout.

Good hatches bring the fish up and once up they seem willing to take any reasonable representation of the prevailing insect. One fish in particular was aggressively feeding on struggling Hex duns but took a Brown Drake imitation on the first drift without hesitation. This was a 14-inch brown, not a reckless 8-inch brookie.

From Sharon to Smithville at MI 66 and downstream to the access at Lucas Road near the county lines of extreme northwestern Missaukee County and extreme southwestern Kalkaska County, the river gains width, depth, and strength. When you explore these "middle grounds" do so with a measure of caution. Although this reach has lots of wonderful riffles and pools that are easy to wade, its power is formidable. Make your first visits during daylight hours. There are several dirt roads and two-tracks that come close to the water on both the east and west sides. Shirley Road (on the west side) runs north and south. At the south end, it branches into several trails that take you very near the river. On the east side, Military Road parallels the stream for several miles.

From Smithville to the Missaukee Bridge access (at Lucas Road), the river is again accessible via two-track trails on both sides. One of the most convenient (with boat launch) is "Rainbow Jim's" access off Coster Road in southwestern Kalkaska County.

The "middle grounds" section produces large fish throughout. It has very good populations of mayflies, caddis, and stoneflies as well as significant forage fish numbers, crayfish, and lampreys. Streamer fishing can be excellent. The number one guide service for this stretch of river is run by The Troutsman in Traverse City. Kelly Galloup, the owner of The Troutsman, recommends Zoo Cougars, Blondes, Woolly Sculpins, Madonnas, and Rattlesnakes in a variety of colors for this stretch and downstream past US 131, Baxter Bridge, and beyond.

Perhaps the most scenic stretch of river in Michigan, certainly in the lower peninsula, is the Hodenpyle dam at the Wexford-Manistee county line to Red Bridge in Manistee County. This is a 13-mile reach through a non-motorized, semiprivate protected area. It is big water with beautiful and productive riffles and pools. It has log jams, gravel, silt, sand, boulders, under-cut banks, and very large brown trout. Early and late season hatches are strong and bring good fish to the surface, but streamer fishing is probably the best method for the real bruisers, the trophies over 20 inches.

There is walk-in access from the east side via two-track trails at Slagle Creek at Warfield Road. My suggestion is to float this stretch with a knowl-edgeable, experienced guide. Schmidt Outfitters in Wellston is my first choice. Ray Schmidt and his cadre of guides provide first-class service on this stretch. Regardless of what time of year you fish or which hatch you may be targeting, be sure to bring a selection of *large* streamers.

Last, the fly angling below Tippy Dam has improved dramatically in the last few years. It is no longer reserved for migratory steelhead, salmon, and brown trout. The hatches are reliable and the streamer fishing can be superb. Not only will you find healthy, robust, radiant browns and rainbows, but it is entirely possible (even likely in certain months) to hook up with a 10-pound-plus summer-run steelhead and a monster brown on the ascent from Lake Michigan.

The Manistee offers a fly-fisher just about anything and everything. Depending on your inclination, you can select a day on small water with light tackle for wild brook trout; choose to fish bigger water with prolific hatches and critical, sophisticated browns and rainbows; elect to join the burrowing muck dwellers and skulk along a silt bank near CCC Bridge at midnight waiting for the Hex spinners; or journey on a productive float with an experienced guide from Wellston, Traverse City, or Grayling. Whatever your initial selection might be, it is a sure bet that you will be back for more of the same and to sample the rest.

Notes:

- Kalkaska, home of the Trout Festival, and Grayling are the major com-mercial centers near the Manistee. Both towns have golf, good restau-rants, accommodations, resorts, and a full range of services.
- The little hamlet of Frederic has a nifty old-time saloon, the Swamp II, with a full menu and evening entertainment. It is only a 5-minute drive from the upper Manistee to the upper Au Sable in Frederic on CR 612.
- Canoe liveries are everywhere and it's worth noting that the canoeists on the Manistee, for some reason, seem to be more thoughtful and courte-ous than on other rivers. Many will actually go to great effort to disrupt your fishing as little as possible. One canoeist recently handed Steve a cold beer on the way by, along with an admonishment not to litter.
- For a change of pace, try fly-rodding for panfish or bass on one of the many fine lakes in the area. Lakes Mitchell and Cadillac are two possibilities.

5 | The Little Manistee

Lake County, Mason County, Manistee County

I suspect that many, if not most, of the fly-rod anglers who make the Little Manistee a "must-fish" stream during the regular trout season were first beguiled with the little river's charms during a spring or late fall steelhead foray. For years it has deservedly maintained its reputation as one of Michigan's very finest steelhead rivers, and it is still one of the prime sources of fertilized eggs used to stock other waters.

But once the steelheaders thin out in early May, miles and miles of beautiful, productive water are available for some of the finest resident trout fishing in the state, and the pressure is surprisingly light. Those same gravel riffles and fast slicks that hold the magnificent steelhead in late fall through early spring become fertile feeding haunts for browns and rainbows, many of them in trophy sizes.

The rainbows in particular come readily to the dry fly and have given us some unforgettable 30-plus-fish days. These rainbows, unlike the browns, are generally eager and unsophisticated. They attack and slash rather than sip or gulp. White-winged patterns such as the Trude flies or the Royal Wulff are easy to spot in a dancing, sunlit riffle and will bring the rainbows rushing to the surface.

The brown trout in the Little Manistee are more secretive and reserved, and many of the largest specimens show a decided, wise preference for nocturnal feeding. Look for the browns in the deeper holes and pools, under bankside cuts, and deep in the heart of the most tangled logjams. A slow, deep drift with a large nymph, or a teasing retrieve with a marabou streamer or crayfish pattern is usually the productive method for making contact with the large specimens.

There are some brook trout to be found in the headwaters of the Little Manistee around the Luther area in Lake County east of MI 37, but the river is pretty small here, running from 12 to 18 feet in width, and fly-fishing is further restricted by a prolific growth of tag alder and other brush, which can bridge the stream in places.

Access is somewhat limited by private land, but if you choose to sample this 20-odd miles of smallish water, try taking Dillon Road west from Luther 2.0 miles to King's Highway. A quick turn to the north will put you on the river, and the downstream flow goes through public land for a considerable distance. It's tight fishing in many places and your roll-casting skills will get a thorough workout, but there are some very good trout in this section and you will often have it pretty much to yourself.

You will find easier fishing (and more pressure, of course) immediately below MI 37. Access is no problem. Park at the west end loop of Old Grade Campground, immediately to the northwest of the MI 37 bridge. If you are willing to hike downstream a decent piece across the public land, you will find very pretty water that doesn't get fished to death. The stream is shallow and clear, about 25 feet wide, with a bottom mix of gravel and sand. There are good pools here and there, and small dancing attractor patterns will often coax up surprisingly big fish. There are good hatches of caddis, various Olives, Sulphurs, Brown Drakes, and *Hexagenia* in this stretch. Besides the standard attractor patterns, carry an assortment of Rusty's Spinners, Robert's Yellow Drakes, and Elk-Hair Caddis to match an emergence or spinner fall. Olive patterns should be tied in either thorax or parachute style, in sizes 16 through 22.

Rod selection is not critical on the Little Manistee, but you will want something that can cushion a light tippet as well as control a streamer or weighted nymph. An 8½-foot rod for a 5-weight line is a good all-around choice and will give you at least a glimmer of hope should you hook into an off-season, full-figured visitor from Lake Michigan.

Spencer Bridge, the first bridge below MI 37, can be reached by taking Four Mile Road west to where it meets Peacock Road. Turn north on Peacock for about 1 mile and you will hit the bridge. There are cottages and private lands upstream, requiring you to stay in the river for the most part, not a problem under normal water conditions. There is a MDNR access site just a hair southwest of the bridge with plenty of room to park. Enter the water downstream from the bridge to fish some appealing twists and turns of the Little Manistee. For several years the angling in the vicinity of Spencer's Bridge has been restricted to "flies only," but you are advised to check the regulations as things do change.

Speaking of change, I recently pulled in to Indian Bridge on the Irons Road to fish an area I had not hit in several years. The state maintains a small campground here to the northeast of the bridge. Used to be you could pull in here and then hike way back into Indian Club property, private land generously left open to the public. But when I came to their property line at

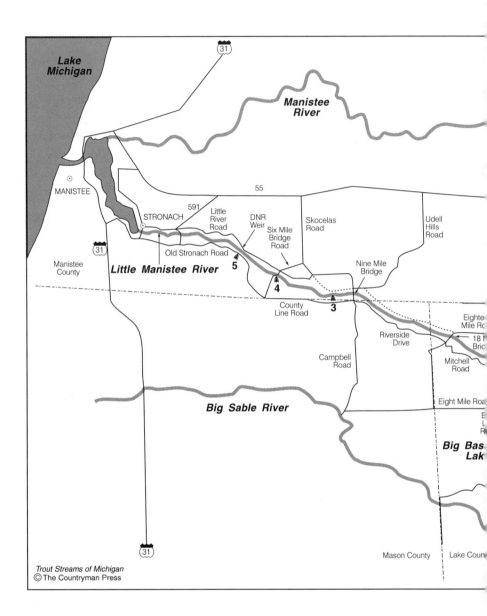

Trout Streams of Michigan
© The Countryman Press

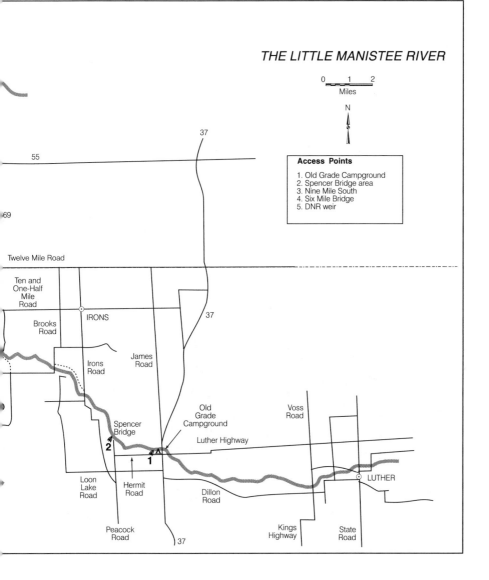

THE LITTLE MANISTEE RIVER

0   1   2
Miles

N

Access Points

1. Old Grade Campground
2. Spencer Bridge area
3. Nine Mile South
4. Six Mile Bridge
5. DNR weir

the east end of the public access site, a real disappointment met me: BECAUSE OF PAST ABUSE . . . THIS LAND CLOSED TO PUBLIC . . . FOR ALL PURPOSES glared the sign over what used to be the footpath back into the famous "numbered pools." What an unfortunate testimony for our ever-increasing need to be cognizant of the expectations, rights, and goodwill of property owners.

Now one has to get in the river on state land and *stay* in the river, greatly limiting the amount of easily fished water. I gave it a good effort anyway, and as I remembered, it sure is a pretty stretch. Productive too. I was pleasantly surprised with half a dozen 10- to 12-inch fish on a small yellow hopper—especially since the stream had to have been recently fished by other anglers, judging from the half-dozen cars parked nearby.

When fishing this general area, we often headquarter near the town of Irons 5.0 miles west of MI 37 on Ten Mile Road. Overnight, or weekly, rental accommodations are easily found, and just about any road you take south, east, and west will put you within a short walk to a productive stretch of the Little Manistee. The Irons business community publishes a recreation map that provides a very good overview of the whole river system from its headwaters near Luther to its outlet into Manistee Lake. These maps are available at restaurants, grocery stores, and sporting-goods stores throughout the community.

The numerous bridge access points south and west of Irons let you easily skip from spot to spot and sample the varied currents, riffles, hides, and

Caddis are important and prolific on most Michigan trout streams.

holds of this intriguing stream. Go south out of Irons on Brooks Road to Johnson Bridge—it's gorgeous water there. Between this bridge and DeWitt Bridge, the next crossing to the west, we've taken many good browns, and moved some that, as Mark Twain would say, would clean "give you the fantods."

When I was younger and more spry, I used to make a long trek up from DeWitt Bridge a couple of times a year just to try for one old soaker under a cedar sweep. I would see him about every other time when he would ghost out to look with disdain at my updated Spuddler or Spruce or whatever I fancied as the right streamer that year. I couldn't imagine a trout that big bothering with a lesser mouthful. Never hooked him/her, but that fish will always be in my memory bank.

We will often go west out of Irons on 10½ Mile Road until it meets Bass Lake Road, then head south to Fox Bridge. There is a good parking area here and the pretty water continues. Or just as likely, we will cut west off Big Bass Lake Road just a mile south of the intersection (watch for Driftwood Valley Campground signs just past the Elbow Lake Access on your right) on the 10½ Mile Road (FS 5357) continuation. You will note as you cross Pole Bridge that the river bottom is looking a lot sandier. This will predominate, with some infrequent gravel areas, pretty much to Nine Mile Bridge. Access is quite easy off FS 5357 (signs soon deem it River Road) at Driftwood Valley, a popular, scenic, and well-maintained public campground, or from the similar Bear Track Campground, another 2.5 miles to the west. Except for peak times, these campgrounds are not usually full, but if you want to really dodge campers, go another 1.5 miles west past the Bear Track entrance and you'll come to a two-track leading to a scenic overlook on state land.

The river is wider and quite open here, as at Bear Track and Driftwood, but there are enough logjams, cress, and sweeper cover to hold good fish, and there is enough silt and muck for the desired burrowing nymphs. The scarcity of gravel keeps down the steelheaders, so incidental catches of large browns are not as heavy as in some other areas, leaving more for the summer angler. If you are in this area during the Hex hatch, the bugs do come off pretty well hereabouts.

A size-6 Robert's Yellow Drake is a very good imitator of the Hex dun and also works during a heavy spinner fall. Try a "wiggle" Hex nymph any time during the season in this stretch, especially during early June. Soft-hackle wets seem to be effective in the evening hours, and a Tups soft hackle, with that pink, eggy-looking thorax, should be allowed to dead-drift through the deepest pockets and runs, and then be retrieved with a painfully slow twitch and drop-back motion. Any holdover steelhead will likely gobble a Tups fished in this manner; resident browns, ever watchful for dislodged steelhead and salmon eggs, will take it as eagerly.

This is a good stretch to fish terrestrials. Both black and cinnamon ants join beetles, crickets, and grasshoppers as favored menu items. A high-visibility dot on your ant and beetle patterns makes them much easier to see and does not seem to bother the fish. A Griffith's Gnat and a few midge pupae in sizes 20 and 22 will cover any tiny fly and calm-water requirements you are likely to encounter. The ultimate terrestrial, in my opinion, is the mouse. A chamois- or marabou-tailed Deer-Hair Mouse tied chubby on a size-6 hook can be an excitement overload during the late evening or very early morning hours. Perhaps the words of Super Dave would apply: "Kids, don't try this at home." Equally rewarding can be the deep and short erratic dart of an olive-tan crayfish imitation. Try fishing one of these from an upstream position into a deep hold or logjam with a repeated short pull and drop-back presentation.

As you move west toward Nine Mile Bridge on River Road, there are a couple more unmarked public two-tracks and attendant rustic overlooks that put you on similar water. The river is close to the road and canoeists and tubers will occasionally launch at these spots, but you will frequently have them to yourself.

There is a parking area and an access site at Nine Mile Bridge, and the water upstream has some variation before you get in the aforementioned sand flats. We prefer to fish down from this bridge into even better water and will beat the "bridge traffic" by going south from Nine Mile Bridge on Skocelas Road back to River Road, turning right (west) 0.1 mile to the second turnoff, a horseshoe loop of public land (called Nine-Mile South on some forest service maps). This is a nice place for a rustic camp (no facilities) within easy range of some tight bends and deep holes with every conceivable kind of cover. We hit this area several times during the season, usually with good success. Since it is easy to find, it is one of my first choices of where to send a friend who wants a good place to go trout fishing, and I don't ever recall hearing a disparaging remark. More often it's "Wow, what a nice spot; we even caught fish." This access point gets a lot of activity during steelhead runs, but competition is minimal at other times.

The state has started posting maps to other Little Manistee access spots at places like this, but they are often "borrowed," leaving a puzzling blank signboard. If you find one intact or get one from a district office, it can be very helpful, but it is still sometimes tricky to hit the desired area as there is a mix of private as well as public drives along here.

One such public trail well worth trying lies 2.0 miles west of the Skocelas River Road intersection. If the forest service trail sign is there, look for road marker 8479; if this sign is missing (people take the strangest things), use the 2-mile measure referred to above and look for double entrances about 50 yards apart. A single, greenish cabin sits on the opposite

BOB LINSENMAN

Steve releases a smallish steelhead that took a stonefly nymph immediately after a brief, late April snowfall.

(south) side of River Road for a further reference point. If you are coming from the east, odometer 1.5 miles from where Six Mile Bridge hits River Road to this same spot. This trail takes you a couple of hundred yards in before the road is blocked, necessitating a walk of another 200 yards or so to the river. Access both up- and downstream is now easy for long stretches in both directions.

When the steelhead first made their big comeback in the early 1960s, this was where Jim Scott, the late Glenn Snook, and the late Bob Willacker, all of Whitehall, Michigan, and all fishermen of no small repute, instilled in me a long and abiding fascination with the Little Manistee. The still-fresh memory of an 18-pound buck steelhead may also have something to do with this. He took the egg fly softly, but that was the only thing soft in our encounter. He did everything a monster, fresh-from-the-lake steelhead could do, and when he landed and released me, I was forever imprinted with the Little Manistee. There is everything and then some throughout this section of the river. The hydraulic gradient increases dramatically, and for a small river, you can slip into some roaring chutes that will test your leg strength and the gripping properties of your felt soles. These chutes tail out into well-oxygenated holes and slicks. Then maybe you will find a wide stretch of gravel flats where the water will frisk along at a brisk pace before hitting an abrupt bend with a whirling pool framed by old, leaning cedars and half-sunken logs. Be sure to hit those off-current slack spots where white foam collects. A lively feeding station on any river, the "foam pockets" on the Little Manistee have been especially productive for me over the years. If fishing a dry pattern, take the time to change flies and dunk a weighted marabou streamer whenever such a scenario appears.

This area has the ideal combination of holding and feeding water to shelter larger-than-average resident fish and to attract extended "layovers" by the migrant spawners. There are wide, slow stretches with deep, silt-edge holes that produce significant Brown Drake and Hex hatches. Olives, Hendricksons, Gray Drakes, Sulphurs, Tricos, and a caddis bonanza complement terrestrials, midge, crayfish, minnow, and trout/salmon eggs. A deadly combination, during periods when there is no visible surface feeding, is a size-10 Dark Brown Stonefly nymph, with a pale cream abdomen and thorax, as the point fly, and a Micro-Egg (size 12) tied on as a dropper. Fish this duo with a dead-drift through the deepest runs next to the banks, through the pools, and next to the logjams.

The abundance of gravel and shallow riffle water between Nine and Six Mile bridges can generate phenomenal action for small rainbows both on dries and nymphs. The darker, slower water hides browns in the 20-inch range. It is just a beautiful all-around experience. The river here presents several different faces and its charms are many and varied. I've had a bald eagle glide just overhead with a ghostly flap just as an early-run August salmon leviathaned by. Deer are very often in evidence, wading and browsing, and mink can be seen scrambling along the banks. The Little Manistee here ranges from 40 to 70 feet wide and from inches to many feet deep. The relatively fast current, tight bends, narrow chutes, log hazards, and occasionally very shallow, gravel flats (especially after a dry period) keep canoeists to a minimum. Those you might encounter will often have that wild-eyed "get-me-out-of-here" look, and an imploring "How far to Six Mile?" is likely to be their initial greeting. I once overheard a calloused angler respond with "Just 2 miles past Dead Man's Falls." This earned an instant and pitiful repeat of the wild-eyed look. They're an entertaining breed at times, as the canoeists career about in water unsuited to their sport. Take a lesson from their problems: If you wade when the water is "up" be extremely careful. This fast current combined with rolling gravel underfoot can put you under in a heartbeat. Felt soles are a definite plus.

The gradient eases and the current slows as you near Six Mile Road, and there is a mix of both productive and sterile water around Six Mile Bridge with forest service parking areas on either side; you can also access the Little Manistee downstream at Old Stronach Bridge nearer the lake and via numerous two-tracks. The Department of Natural Resources weir, besides being a point of viewing interest, is an excellent access point for general trout fishing. Several signs make it easy to find from Old Stronach Bridge (about midway between Six Mile Bridge Road and Old Stronach Bridge), and there are toilet facilities, camping, and parking spaces for a large number of vehicles. It's a real circus here during steelhead season or during the fall salmon rodeo, but it's relatively uncrowded and peaceful at other times.

There are a couple of interesting trails going toward the river off Old Stronach Road above the weir, but one has to do considerable brush-busting and mud-slogging to reach the main flow. It's far better to go down to the weir proper and enter the river just above it if you wish to fish toward Six Mile Bridge. Since much of this is open, uninspiring sand bottom for a long way, a better choice—a *good* choice—is to walk the high bank on the south side, which is public land downstream from the weir, and fish back upstream. There is a pretty fair path/deer trail for a half-mile or so, and you can glimpse the river periodically on your right. There is some absolutely gorgeous-looking water down here—big, slow at times, dark, and wrought with promise as it slides around bends, runs between chained log structures, and chews at immersed stumps and half-submerged sweepers. It makes you drool to contemplate what might rise to evening hatches of *simulans* and *limbata,* munch a crayfish imitation, or intercept your streamer.

Width and depth vary considerably in the lower river. It can flatten out in a mixed gravel and sand "spread" and approach 100 feet in width, or it can narrow to 50 feet and channel all that flow into a deceiving, powerful force that will pile up against a careless wader in a hurry. You can find yourself spinning your wheels in the sand and shipping icy water if not careful.

I wax enthusiastic about this stretch, perhaps because I've never taken that many fish here, certainly not as many as appearances suggest I should. Yet this disquieting water has grudgingly given me my biggest brown trout ever: a 27-inch, 7-pound male on a *Hexagenia* nymph. It's as if a taunting yet beckoning voice says "You won't get many of us, but when you do . . ." And I do go back and go back.

The Little Manistee, from its headwaters near Luther to the mouth at Manistee Lake, is one of the very finest trout streams in Michigan. Its gifts to the fly-rod angler are a measured blend of sparkling riffles with eager brookies and rose-tinged rainbows slashing at a colorful Trude; deep and inky-black logjammed holes with the unseen, but sensed, critical inspection of a weighted nymph by a wise old brown; and the electric rush of a holdover steelhead through a heavy run. Fish it once and you will go back and go back.

Notes:

- The Oak Grove Tavern in Irons has good food, excellent service, fair prices, daily specials, and satellite television.
- The Little Manistee River weir on Old Stronach Road is a major egg-taking facility with peak salmon activity from mid-September to mid-October and steelhead in April. There is no charge to watch the operations. Call the MDNR office in Cadillac, 231-775-9727, for details.
- Manistee to the west and Cadillac to the east are the largest towns in the vicinity. They both have luxury accommodations, fine resorts and restaurants, shopping, and excellent golfing facilities.
- The surrounding area has dense populations of deer and wild turkey. An evening drive should present several photographic opportunities.

6 | The Pere Marquette
Lake County, Mason County

A nglers in pursuit of stream trout in the Pere Marquette represent a small percentage of the river's wader-clad visitors. Most wielders of glass, graphite, and cane are engaged in the passionate hunt for fly-hooked steelhead and salmon. They congregate at a few selected fly shops in Baldwin and at two or three of the most widely known parking and public access points along the flies-only stretch. Their hands are rough and chapped, their eyes are glazed, and their feet are cold because their waders have just begun to seep.

It is excitement in overdrive when a fresh 9-pound steelhead takes your Black Stonefly nymph, makes a blistering 25-yard run, and snaps your tippet at the end of a 4-foot somersault, but there are less-dramatic ways to have fun on the Pere Marquette. If you are willing to cancel the crowd and the high drama (often comic tragedy) then you should give strong consideration to fishing the Pere Marquette during normal business hours of the regular trout season for its everyday citizens, beautiful and healthy brown trout.

The Pere Marquette is a large system and, like the Manistee and Au Sable, presents a wide range of experiences and water types. From the diminutive, sparkling headwaters to the slow, powerful flow of a big river, the Pere Marquette can challenge and bedevil as well as soothe and reward.

For our purposes, the river is divided into three sections with emphasis on one, the flies-only water. The upstream, or top, section is that water above the bridge on MI 37 in Lake County; the flies-only water runs from this same bridge to Gleason's Landing, some 8-plus miles downstream; the lower river is the truly big water from Gleason's Landing through the Walhalla-Scottville reach, all the way to Lake Michigan.

The top section of the Pere Marquette has very good fly-fishing for brown trout and, compared to the flies-only stretch, enjoys only light to moderate angling pressure even during one of its most productive periods, the midsummer grasshopper dance.

The Rosa Road area is about the upstream limit for comfortable fly-fishing. It is easy to find; simply drive east on US 10 approximately 7 miles from Baldwin to the burg of Nirvana, and Cedar Street. Take Cedar Street south for 1.0 mile to 56th Street and drive west to Rosa Road. A southward turn on Rosa Road will deliver you to the bridge after 1.0 mile and a hard right turn.

This is the Middle Branch of the Pere Marquette. It averages 20 feet in width and has depths that, depending on conditions, range from 6 inches to 3-plus feet. The bottom is sand and fine-to-medium gravel with silt edging. The banks are well sheltered and the deeper holes in the bends and the undercuts hold some very respectable brown trout.

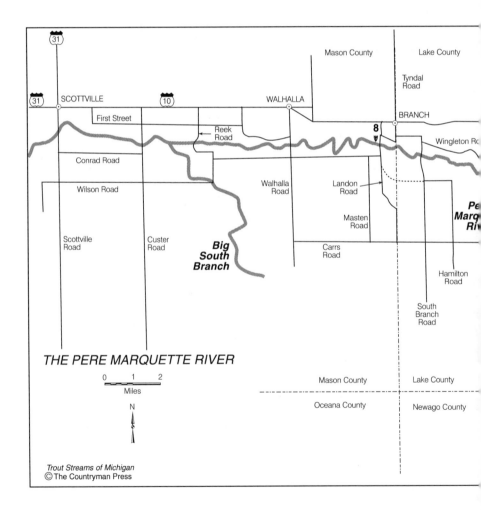

THE PERE MARQUETTE RIVER

Trout Streams of Michigan
© The Countryman Press

There are dependable hatches of both mayfly and caddis in this stretch of the river. Hendricksons are reasonably heavy beginning in early May. This is the first mayfly hatch that brings sizable fish into an active, calculable top-water feeding pattern. The Little Black Caddis, also in May, and the Sulphur, Popcorn Caddis, and Gray Drake in June will bring most of the fish in the river to a very active condition. These hatches precede the Brown Drake and some limited *Hexagenia limbata* appearances (most of the really good Hex fishing is downstream quite a distance), and throughout the season, Blue-Winged Olives and terrestrials are in evidence and eagerly taken by the trout.

The grasshopper fishing has for many years been extremely good on the upper sections of the Pere Marquette and particularly so between Rosa Road and Switzer Bridge. Checking a fishing diary from several years ago, an entry for early June brought a pleasant memory. I had been fishing a good-

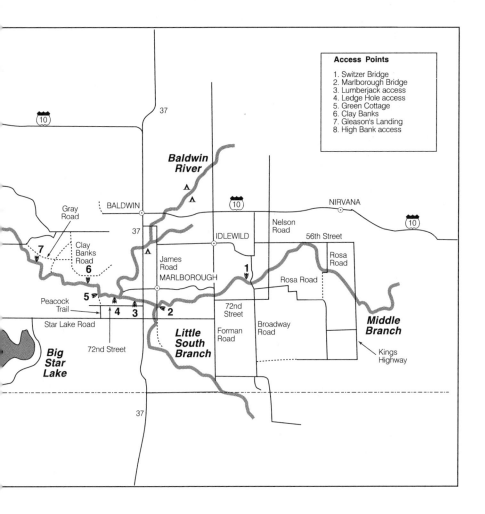

Access Points

1. Switzer Bridge
2. Marlborough Bridge
3. Lumberjack access
4. Ledge Hole access
5. Green Cottage
6. Clay Banks
7. Gleason's Landing
8. High Bank access

sized pool edged by a healthy tangle of logs and an undercut bank. There was a nice 2-foot-deep riffle at the head of the pool and, at the tail-out, a wide, smooth, slick tapered slowly to a shallow spread. Fish were rising, but these were not the deliberate takes one would expect during the Gray Drake bonanza. These were boiling, high-speed, dash-and-slash rises, and I thought "caddis," but could not see any. In fact, despite a hands-and-knees inspection, I could not find anything at all on the water.

I tried a parachute Olive, a Gray Drake, a Goddard Caddis, a stonefly nymph, assorted spinner patterns, a floating nymph in size 20, and a Royal Wulff with no reaction from the trout but total indifference. The frenzy continued and I sat on the bank (probably to cry) and watched. The breeze puffed just a bit and with the puff came a burst of rises. The wind picked up again, and again the rises concentrated. Then the trout gods smiled and I noticed a tiny grasshopper with a bright green abdomen sail into the flow. It was immediately charged and eaten by a 12-inch brown and I became an instant genius.

A size-14 green-bodied Elk-Hair Caddis was as close as I could come to what was being eaten, but it was close enough. The first cast brought a chunky 11-inch trout to hand and the second left my fly on a tree branch. Two more green-bodied lovelies were in the caddis box and before they were chewed beyond recognition, I had experienced a blue-ribbon day. I've not been able to find a repeat of these conditions since that time, but I now carry an even-dozen diminutive Deer-Hair Hoppers in size 14—just in case.

Downstream from Rosa Road there is good access to the Middle Branch at the foot of Nelson Road, at the camping area on the river at Rolles Bridge, and at Switzer Bridge. These three entry points are within a short westward drive of the Rosa Road bridge, and for the most part display very similar stream conditions to those found at Rosa Road.

Nelson Road intersects both US 10 to the north and Rosa Road to the south of the river, and it's an easy matter to find the bridge. There is a sign for public access off Rosa Road 2.5 miles west of Rosa Road Bridge, and this sign directs you north for a very short distance to the access. If you come to Broadway Road you have passed this area by about 0.5 mile. Switzer Bridge is at the foot of Broadway, 0.5 mile downstream from Rolla and 3.0 miles downstream from Rosa Road Bridge.

Good fishing can be experienced at all three of these sites. There is abundant cover, and a healthy population of resident browns. The casting lanes are reasonable although roll casts are often necessary. An 8-foot rod for a 3- or 4-weight line is about perfect, and a 9-foot leader tapered to 5X is as long and fine as you will need.

Hatches need to be matched on this water. The fish are not foolhardy and will shy away from poor presentation or improper fly selection. Parachute and Compara Dun patterns work extremely well, and if you do not tie your own flies, complete selections at reasonable prices are available at Pere Marquette River Lodge and Baldwin Tackle, and at other sporting-goods retailers in Baldwin.

Between hatches a simple selection of general attractor patterns will suffice. The Royal Wulff, Adams, Rusty's Spinner, Secret Rubber Bug, ants and grasshoppers, and Lime Trude will rustle up some surface action. Black and Brown Stonefly nymphs in sizes 8, 10, and 12 are very productive along with Hare's Ears, Pheasant Tails, and caddis larvae. The Light Spruce and Muddler Minnow have been my favorite streamers for this water over the years.

Downstream from Switzer Bridge the quality fishing continues, and there are access points at Watermill Bridge on Forman Road, at Marlborough Bridge on James Road, and at MI 37. After the Little South Branch joins the flow near James Road, the river's volume and width is significantly increased and reflects the stream conditions typical of the flies-only water between MI 37 and the junction with the Baldwin River. This is bigger, but still very manageable, water. Widths run to 50 feet and depths to enough to dampen your hat, but the wading is generally easy and the casting is open.

The bridge on MI 37 marks the upstream boundary of the special-regulations, flies-only section of the Pere Marquette. This run of approximately 8 miles (to Gleason's Landing) has a wide diversity of water types and fishing opportunities. This stretch, and the town of Baldwin, has as many expert guides as the Madison near Ennis, Montana, or the Henry's Fork near Last Chance, Idaho. If the naked truth be known, your chances of taking a real thumper (say, a trout of 5 pounds or better) on a fly are much, much higher on the Pere Marquette.

The new millennium should see only increased success in this quality water section of the Pere Marquette since it was recently designated totally no-kill. "I attribute this change to the best fishing I've had in 20 years," said Joe Heywood (best-selling Michigan author whose recently released fly-fishing yarn *The Snowfly* is a recommended read). He regaled us with accounts of 18- to 22-inch browns on dries amid very light competition—all near the easy public access areas.

The traditional access and meeting spot on the flies-only water is the Green Cottage. This is far and away the most popular section of the river. The MDNR has recently acquired property and constructed a large parking area to better handle the vehicular requirements of the peak steelhead and salmon months.

This will be our focal point for the flies-only stretch. The Green Cottage sits on the south bank of the river at the foot of Peacock Road. Peacock Road is reached by driving west on 72nd Street (this is the first west turn south of the bridge on MI 37) 1.5 miles from MI 37. Turn right at Peacock

BOB LINSENMAN

Winter angling near the bridge on MI 37

Road and you will reach the river and the parking area after 0.25 mile.

The Pere Marquette in this reach ranges from 50 to 80 feet in width. The depth ranges from 1 to 6 feet over a sand, gravel, and mud-banked bottom. There are well-worn paths along the river banks in both directions, sometimes traversing private property. Stick to the marked paths or, if in doubt, the river to avoid trespassing.

Excepting periods of abnormally high water, this part of the river is easily wadable. The holes and deep, powerful runs are obvious and easily avoided, but are for the most part approachable to within comfortable casting range. The habitat is ideal for a wide array of caddis and mayfly species and, in addition, the trout dine on minnows, crayfish, terrestrials, and an abundant supply of steelhead and salmon eggs.

This is entertaining water. It is lively, clear, and cold. It dances and swirls and glides and tumbles. There are trout next to the banks, under the logs, in midstream riffles, at the tail-outs of dark and secretive holes, and in the heavy runs and in the fast-water pockets. Robust, healthy browns and immature steelhead are found exactly where they should be, and ever present is the well-founded hope that a real giant will intercept your streamer or nymph.

The fishing is very good in both directions from the Green Cottage, but my feet seem most often to turn to the right, in the upstream direction.

Favorite spots include the Island Hole, where my good friend Walt Bishop of Park City, Utah, landed his first-ever salmon; Basswood Run with its wide reaches, shining gravel, and deep bankside cuts; and the Whirlpool, where Steve Pensinger of Boston floated his hat—twice in one day. This area is a very productive stream-trout fishery, and the successful and continuing efforts of the Pere Marquette Watershed Council to improve the habitat and control erosion are readily apparent.

Dark Brown and Black Stonefly nymphs in sizes 8 through 12 are effective all year on the Pere Marquette. Latex Caddis, the Zug Bug, Gold-Ribbed Hare's Ear, Pheasant Tail, and, in the deep holes, olive-brown dragonfly nymphs will earn fish on a regular basis. Muddler Minnows, Woolly Buggers, and various shades of the Spruce Fly will suffice for the streamer category. The Adams, Elk-Hair Caddis, Borcher's Drake, and Lime Trude should be in your box along with some ants, beetles, and Griffith's Gnats. During emergence periods or spinner falls it is necessary to match the naturals as closely as possible. Accurate information on the hatches is cheerfully supplied by the experts at Pere Marquette Lodge on MI 37. Not so coincidentally, they also have a wide selection of proven fly patterns in all the right sizes and will sell you some if you ask.

About halfway between Peacock Road and the railroad tracks on 72nd Street there is an access path on the north side of the road. A break, or "gate," in the wooden fence and a small sign indicate the anglers' footpath that winds through the woods for about 200 yards before reaching the river. Approximately 100 yards upstream from this spot you will find the junction pool where the Pere Marquette is met by the smaller Baldwin River. The large hole at this point of merger is very productive. It has been, and continues to be, an outstanding producer of big fish. Just upstream is a short, straight stretch before the river bends sharply to the left. At the outside edge of this bend there is an extremely productive hole of moderate depth. Two large cabins sit on the high bank overlooking this hole and assist in its precise location. At the tail-out of this hold you will notice the darker, deeper water flowing tight to, and sometimes partially under, the southeast bank. This long, continuing run is crowded by brush and complicated a bit by several log tangles, but it is one of the better areas, day to day, month to month, for brown trout and, at appropriate times, steelhead.

Favorite patterns for this stretch, both above and below the Baldwin River, are the Light Spruce Fly, Silver Hilton, Egg-Sucking Leech, and Marabou Muddler. A particularly effective arrangement is the use of a weighted Black Stonefly nymph with a Micro-Egg fly as a dropper. Dead-drift this combination into the deepest water you can reach and you should be rewarded with a hook-up.

Continuing back toward MI 37 on 72nd Street, you will come to what is known as the Lumberjack access about 200 yards before crossing the railroad tracks. This is a very short trail that turns north off the street next to a cabin on the Flint Rainbow Club property. Park your vehicle on the shoulder on 72nd Street and walk down the hill on the anglers' path. The bankside property in both directions is guardedly private, and it is strongly suggested that you stay in the river during your exploration.

A short distance upstream from the Lumberjack footpath you will notice a stout footbridge that crosses the river. Directly beneath this bridge lies a deep hole that should be fished thoroughly. Continuing upstream you will find a series of loops and bends that push water into handsome runs, glides, and more deep, inviting caverns. This upper section of the flies-only stretch, all the way past the railroad trestle to the bridge on MI 37, is prime brown trout water, and you will no doubt notice the stretches of beautiful gravel that attract the big rainbows.

A short distance downstream from the Lumberjack trail, the Pere Marquette forms two tight, adjacent loops that, in effect, create two mini-peninsulas with deep holes at the outside of the loops. This entire run through the loops is worth fishing carefully with nymph or streamer if no hatch is in progress. As you approach the second loop, you will notice a very attractive cabin on your left. The run next to and in front of this cabin is narrow and deep, a bit tricky to wade, but usually productive. Try a Black Stonefly nymph, a Woolly Bugger, or large, dark Hare's Ear for the first pass. If unsuccessful, slog back upstream and try again, but this time use a Light Spruce or Marabou Muddler.

The water between the Green Cottage and Gleason's Landing is bigger, heavier, and more "western" in its overall appearance than the upstream section. The holes are—or seem to be—deeper, the flats are wider, and the runs are more intimidating. Much of this water is best fished with a guide's direction and a riverboat for transport. First-class guide trips can be booked through several local businesses, including Baldwin Tackle and Pere Marquette River Lodge. The guide fares on the Pere Marquette are not cheap, but they are reasonable and of real value. The guides' boats will deliver you to the best locations without hassle, and their expertise will be appreciated at famous spots like the Birch Hole, the Grayling Hole, the Snag Hole, and the Railroad Bridge Hole.

The driving and walking angler can reach into the lower stretch of the flies-only water at the Clay Banks near the dead-end parking area at the foot of Jigger Trail. To reach Jigger Trail take 56th Street west from Baldwin to the intersection with Astor Road and drive south to the first right turn. Take this road for about 0.25 mile to Jigger Trail (aka Clay Banks Road) and follow to the southwest about 1.5 miles to the dead end.

From the parking area a path leads through a very narrow corridor of public land to access points at the Clay Banks. This narrow path is surrounded by heavily posted private property, and it is easy to be misled into thinking you might be trespassing. The path will eventually lead you to a stretch of very appealing water with a series of tight loops and bends, deep holes, and impressive, deep-water runs. The bottom consists of sand, gravel, and, you guessed it, stretches of slippery clay. The depth ranges from 2 to 6-plus feet and the current is strong across the 70- to 80-foot width.

There are some very large brown trout in this area, and they typically lie deep in the darkest holes and runs. A sink-tip line has value here since your fly will need to sink quickly to reach the largest fish at the bottom of these inky lairs. Lead-eye leech patterns tied with marabou or philoplume feathers are quite effective. A mottled gray-olive-tan color scheme seems to work best. Marabou Muddlers in yellow and black persuasions are almost as effective. The browns also like the stonefly nymphs mentioned earlier, and it's a good idea to take the extra time to tie on a dropper with a small egg pattern.

Gleason's Landing is the downstream limit for the special-regulations water and serves as the take-out point for most guided float trips. Gleason's Landing is easily reached by driving west from Baldwin on Carr's Road to 62nd Street (about 2.5 miles). Turn left and follow 62nd Street for 0.5 mile to Shortcut Avenue. Take Shortcut Avenue to Gray Road and turn right. Follow Gray Road for 0.5 mile to the well-marked entrance road to Gleason's Landing.

This is big water that must be waded with care and respect. The river is more than 75 feet wide in most places and carries a considerable volume. Many holes are well over the head of a tall man, and the powerful bankside runs are often complicated by a confusion of logs and stumps.

With the necessary cautions duly delivered, it is appropriate to state that the fishing around Gleason's Landing can be superb. The heavy, deep flow is secure harbor for resident browns and migrating steelhead and salmon. Even the peak summer months carry strong potential for large steelhead now that the summer-run Skamania strain has found the Pere Marquette to its liking. June is probably the only month of the year that the river is relatively free of anadromous fish. And June is the prime time for the largest of the brown trout to feed on the surface. Brown Drakes and Hex begin to appear in mid-June and the evening dry-fly action can be incredible. The large Gray Drake is also on the water during June and it too triggers a heavy surface feed by the trout.

Gleason's Landing is a good choice for the trophy seeker. It has excellent habitat for a variety of aquatic insects and sufficient flow and depth to satisfy the safety instincts of the river's biggest fish. This same flow that is protective and assuring to the trout can be a serious problem for the angler, so extreme caution is again strongly advised.

Steve and I schedule a yearly, pre-snowmelt, spring steelhead visit to the waters around Gleason's Landing. The fish are always in this stretch and are often receptive to egg patterns, stonefly nymphs, and wiggler flies: Spring's Wiggler, June Wiggler, the Clark Lynn, and the Latex Wiggler. It is the end of winter and the water is as low and as clear as it can ever be. We fish upstream for a short distance and then move downstream. We will catch and release a fish or two and shortly arrive at a deep inviting hole with a strong entry run that is about 30 yards in length. At the tail of the hole the water curls into another powerful bankside run of approximately 45 yards in length. These runs are close to 4 feet deep and block a wading angler's route to the far bank, where you must be to fish this spot, but at the very head of the upstream run there is a narrow patch of high gravel that spans the river to the far bank.

Every year we stare at this spot for a few moments and then Steve will say, "We can make it this year. The water is really low. We can cross here." "No, we can't, don't try. It's too cold." Steven then shuffles his feet a bit before the decision. "That hold-and-run has to be stacked with fish. *I* can make it!" "Okay Steve, hand me your camera." Shortly, we will be back at the car. I will be taking pictures of Steve changing into dry clothes. The snowflakes and the blue legs show up nicely in the photo album.

Below Gleason's Landing, the Pere Marquette is largely a float-trip fishery. Certainly the best way to sample its treasures is to hire a guide, but for those who have some Jim Bridger in their soul, there are downriver access points reachable by car and foot travel that offer some limited safe wading in close proximity to prime, big-fish water. Some of the trout in this lower section of the river are truly immense and when they rise to a struggling *limbata* dun or spinner on a warm summer evening your heart will pound, guaranteed.

Branch is a small village 9.0 miles west of MI 37 on US 10. Landon Road runs south from US 10 in Branch and crosses a set of railroad tracks after 0.4 mile. Immediately south of the tracks a poor two-track runs west and parallel to the tracks. Follow this trail for 1 mile (watch for ruts) to a Y in the road and bear left to a small parking area on a high bank overlooking the river.

A direct descent down the steep and sandy slope is not advised, and I have a clumsy patch in the seat of an expensive pair of neoprene waders to remind me. To the left of the parking area the slope of the hill is more gradual and you will find a faint path that will lead you to the river at the inside of a long, rock-walled, sweeping curve. This hold, and most of the river in the area, has mud banks that are home to the large burrowing nymphs. Both the Hex and the Brown Drakes produce heavy nocturnal hatches in this section of the Pere Marquette, and the fishing can be superb.

Under low-water conditions, a wading angler can get around in this area if intelligence and caution are applied to the process. Heavy, tinted water or low-light conditions should ring the alarm bell. Do not even consider taking the risk.

Downstream from the big hole and directly under the hill where your car is parked, there is a long, straight stretch with deep water on the bank and a heavy, gravel-based run at midstream. This long run produces good brown trout fishing and is a favored holding area for steelhead. Almost any emergence or spinner fall will bring feeding fish to the surface of this run.

Farther downstream at the end of the long run, the river curves left and forms another deep hole. This hole and the waters below float some monstrous browns that look for a sizable meal. If hatches of the big bugs are not in season, you might try a large Deer-Hair Mouse or moth pattern for surface work. Try a nymph-and-egg combination or a large streamer on an overcast day and be prepared for a heavy strike. It could be a brown or it could be a steelhead. You probably will be too busy to care.

There are, of course, many more access points along the length of this great river than have been mentioned here. Bowman Bridge, Rainbow Rapids, and Indian Bridge are a few that come immediately to mind. All of these have their relative merits, but the sites described in this chapter are the authors' favorites.

The Pere Marquette has many loyal fans and dedicated friends, and their coalition, in the form of the Pere Marquette Watershed Council, has worked long and hard to restore the river to glory. The council is active in erosion control, fish population studies, the lamprey issue, and anything and everything that affects the watershed.

Notes:

- Baldwin has some good restaurants and a couple of nifty saloons. If it's raining hard you can shoot pool and play the jukebox, or hang out at one of the fly shops and tell lies.
- Ludington, at the mouth of the Pere Marquette on Lake Michigan, is a larger town with more shopping. There is a nice golf course on the north side of town near the Lake Michigan shore.
- There is a shrine to the near south of Baldwin that is open to the public. The very large cross and quiet grounds are worth the short time it takes to visit.

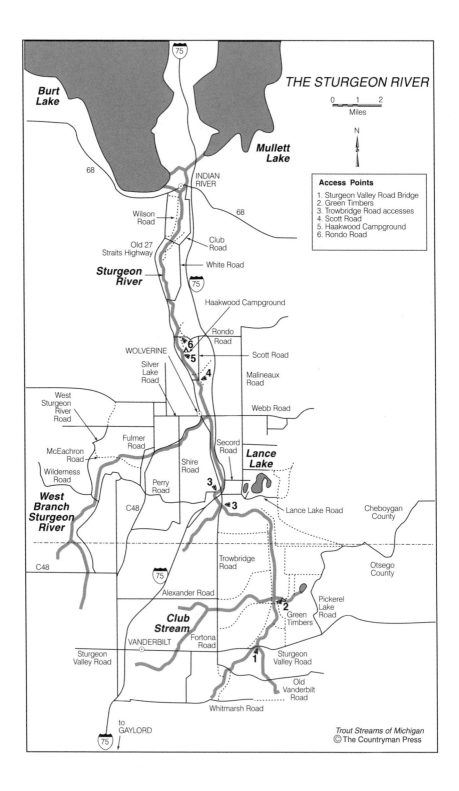

THE STURGEON RIVER

0   1   2
Miles

N

Access Points
1. Sturgeon Valley Road Bridge
2. Green Timbers
3. Trowbridge Road accesses
4. Scott Road
5. Haakwood Campground
6. Rondo Road

Burt Lake

Mullett Lake

75

68

INDIAN RIVER

68

Wilson Road

Club Road

Old 27 Straits Highway

White Road

Sturgeon River

75

Haakwood Campground

Rondo Road

WOLVERINE

Scott Road

Silver Lake Road

Malineaux Road

4

West Sturgeon River Road

Webb Road

Fulmer Road

Secord Road

McEachron Road

Shire Road

Lance Lake

Wilderness Road

Perry Road

3

West Branch Sturgeon River

C48

3

Lance Lake Road

Cheboygan County

Otsego County

C48

Trowbridge Road

75

Alexander Road

Pickerel Lake Road

Club Stream

VANDERBILT

Fortona Road

2

Green Timbers

Sturgeon Valley Road

1

Sturgeon Valley Road

Old Vanderbilt Road

Whitmarsh Road

to GAYLORD

75

Trout Streams of Michigan
© The Countryman Press

7 | The Sturgeon River

Otsego County, Cheboygan County

The Sturgeon River flows northward from just east of the city of Gaylord through the rugged Pigeon River State Forest and the heart of Michigan's elk country to the town of Indian River, where it empties into Burt Lake.

The upper reaches of the Sturgeon, from its headwaters near Gaylord to the bridge on Sturgeon Valley Road east of Vanderbilt, are problematic for the fly-fisher. In many areas the combination of jackstrawed logs and tight, overhanging foliage make wading and effective casting nearly impossible. In other spots large sand traps, installed by the Department of Natural Resources as a means to improve brook trout habitat, make wading dangerous. The signs marking the locations of the sand traps are occasionally vandalized or removed by cretin humorists, and this can cause a very serious problem for the visiting angler. Last, sections of the upper river have been the subject of litigation relative to navigability, riparian rights, and access by the general public. Combine all this with a relatively low fish population in the upper reaches and the obvious conclusion presents itself. Concentrate on the lower river from the bridge at Sturgeon Valley Road downstream to the Rondo Road bridge just south of Indian River. This is, for the most part, prime fly-fishing water with the ever-present potential of hooking an explosive trophy lake-run rainbow or brown trout.

At the bridge on Sturgeon Valley Road (east of Vanderbilt about 5 miles), the river averages 40 to 45 feet in width and 1 to 4 feet deep. On the upstream side of the bridge, the river is open and almost barren in appearance. It is approximately 40 feet wide and quite clear. It runs over a smooth, sand bottom with the major percentage of trout cover near the banks and the cooling shade of the vegetation.

The property on the upstream side of the bridge is private, but there is a decent path paralleling the river's east bank for quite a distance. This path starts at a two-track trail, blocked by a huge log, that is clearly visible from

Sturgeon Valley Road. An angler can follow this path upstream and fish back down to the bridge with emerger, nymph, or streamer patterns, or reverse the process and fish upstream and follow the path back to the bridge. There are two marked sand traps upstream from the bridge and extreme wading care is a necessity.

A more serene, or relaxing, approach to this section of the Sturgeon is to walk downstream (there is a faint and difficult path on the west bank) and fish back up to the bridge. The river is full of submerged timber and insists on a cautious step, but this same crisscrossed timber provides excellent shelter for the trout and is well worth a little extra time and effort to navigate.

An alternative to struggling with the bankside jungle is to fish downstream with a long line and fine tippet, rest the water for a few minutes, and fish back up to the bridge. Another approach worth consideration is to follow the marked hiking path north (this path begins 0.1 mile west of the bridge and is an old two-track that is now off-limits to motorized vehicles), paralleling the river's course for a selected distance. Then, compass in hand, the Kit Carsons among us will find the river after an eastward hike, and will be rewarded with excellent, near-wilderness fishing on a wild stream.

The trout population in this section consists mostly of browns and a few rainbows. Brook trout were once dominant and now, thanks to study and habitat work, appear to be making a measurable comeback. The University of Michigan Biological Station at Pellston has been engaged in habitat research, analysis, and improvement directed specifically at the brook trout population, and this work seems to be having the hoped-for effect.

Grasshoppers, crickets, ants, and beetle imitations are good mid- to late-summer dry-fly choices for this piece of water. The Elk-Hair Caddis, Adams, and Wulff patterns should be carried as well. Effective nymphs include the Woolly Worm, Gold-Ribbed Hare's Ear, Pheasant Tail, and Latex Caddis larvae. The Light Spruce Fly, Muddler Minnow, Woolly Bugger, and Clouser Minnow are recommended streamers. Your streamer selection should also include some larger weighted flies, sizes 4 and 6, such as the White Marabou, Egg-Sucking Leech, and Black Zonker. The larger offerings will more likely motivate the very large (up to 10 pounds) migrating browns and rainbows that ascend the river from Burt Lake.

There is an access point to this piece of the Sturgeon River between Sturgeon Valley Road and Trowbridge Road that needs to be mentioned. The Green Timbers access area was formerly a private club, but is now owned by the State of Michigan. It is reached by driving east from the bridge on Sturgeon Valley Road for 1.5 miles to a hard-packed gravel road on your left. Take this road north to the MDNR sign and turn left. You will circumnavigate several large sand and gravel mounds and end up at a designated parking area near a path to the river.

Follow this path downhill to the river and be sure to note the sign indicating the presence of a sand trap near the foot of the path. Downstream from the path, the river winds its way past the old Green Timbers lodge on its path to easier access and fishing at Trowbridge Road. The river in the vicinity of the lodge is extremely difficult to fly-fish due to the very tight tree cover and an incalculable number of intertwined logs and blowdowns throughout the length and breadth of the stream.

There are some very large resident and, at certain times of the year, anadromous fish present, but it is quite difficult to present a fly let alone land a trout of substance amidst this tangle. If you have hotshot fly-fishing associates who think they have done it all, take one of them to Green Timbers for an ego-leveling excursion. You can later refer to the expert's travail as the "Bungle in the Jungle."

Upstream from the footpath and the sand trap, the Sturgeon is a bit more open and limited fly-casting is possible. The river in this direction is about 35 feet wide and still presents the jackstrawed logs, drowned stumps, twisted roots, and deep muck edges to the explorer. Despite these obstacles it is possible to fish this piece of water. Sometimes dapping is the only way to present a fly. In most cases, roll casts are all that will be allowed by nature's circumstances.

Weighted wets, nymphs, and streamers seem always to snag on the logs, so dry flies are the obvious choice. A long leader with a fine tippet is not necessary; in fact it will only cause more problems with snags and break-offs. If you plan to visit this area on a hot day consider wading wet. This will eliminate the risk of tearing those new neoprenes and allow more agile maneuvering through the timber.

The next downstream access (really a series of access points) is at Trowbridge Road in the immediate vicinity of I-75. These points can be reached from the Vanderbilt area by taking the expressway north, or, if you are in the vicinity of the bridge on Sturgeon Valley Road, by driving north on Fontinalis Road to the Trowbridge area. From Wolverine, simply take Trowbridge Road south about 3.5 miles to the intersection. There is access at the bridge over the Sturgeon at Trowbridge Road and at several convenient, short two-tracks (park short of the railroad track!) between I-75 and the town of Wolverine.

The river, from the expressway to its junction with the West Branch of the Sturgeon in Wolverine, ranges from 25 to 35 feet wide with a fast, heavy current flowing over a gravel and sand bottom at a depth ranging from over 1 to 4-plus feet. The river is high in oxygen, and its clear, cold water is ideal habitat for aquatic insects, forage fish, crayfish, and, of course, trout. Various persuasions of Blue-Winged Olives are prolific here, and both mid-morning and afternoon hatches bring browns and rainbows into regular, topside feeding rhythms. In late July, emergences of Slate-Winged Olives peak around 5:30 PM. Trout generally rise freely, if not recklessly, in the softer side currents, at the tail-outs of pools, and in eddies and slack water near the banks. A size-18 dark Olive with a pale dun hackle tied parachute style over a slate post wing will bring strikes from most fish that are decently covered. This stretch can also present exciting dry-fly fishing with terrestrial patterns, especially when the wind pushes hoppers and crickets into the flow. Any high-floating deer-hair hopper will work, but the Dave's Hopper and the all-deer-hair pattern created by Bill Koernke of Lovells are exceptional seducers of larger-than-average trout.

Because of the abundant Olives, a Pheasant Tail nymph is very effective in this stretch of the Sturgeon. The Gold-Ribbed Hare's Ear in dark and olive shades, and various colors of Latex Caddis larvae and pupae consistently produce fish. Large, weighted streamers should be carried throughout the season. Marabou Muddlers, Grizzly and Light Spruce, Zonkers, and Woolly Buggers are all good selections, particularly on cloudy days.

This section of the Sturgeon can be difficult to wade safely, and extra care must be taken during periods of high water. Fishing this area at night for the large Burt Lake browns and rainbows is very tempting, but definitely not for the careless or infirm. Pre-scout your intended fishing area thoroughly, make a practice foray or two during daylight hours, and do not stray after darkness settles.

At the town park in Wolverine, the Sturgeon is joined by the West Branch and the flow is correspondingly increased. The West Branch is a very good small trout stream on its own merits and is definitely worth fishing at several easy access points along Old 27, which parallels the river for several miles between Wolverine and Vanderbilt. The West Branch supports brook, brown, and rainbow trout that respond eagerly to a well-presented fly, and there is a reasonable chance, from late July onward, of hooking an outsized migrant brown.

Meanwhile, back at the park, the main river downstream from the West Branch confluence averages 40 feet in width with a fairly heavy flow that insists on careful wading. The depth fluctuates from 1 to 4 feet and considerably more, while the numerous logs and ideal spawning gravel make this a prime spot to probe with large streamers and Micro-Egg patterns for lake-run fish. This is a convenient and relatively hospitable area to fish at night for trophy trout. The park has the expected amenities (such as a picnic table to hold a lantern for changing flies and so forth) and the open grounds to allow room for the lengthy back casts necessary to reach holding lies on the far side of the river. Night wading should be undertaken with great care and only in the presence of a colleague. Assistance may be required.

Downstream from the Wolverine town park and north toward Indian

River, there are several convenient parking areas along Old 27 that are within an easy walk of the river. The first access is at Scott Road, which is just 1.0 mile north of Wolverine. Turn right at Scott Road and, after crossing the single-lane bridge, turn right again and follow the road to the parking area at the canoe-launching site.

The river at the launch and take-out point is roughly 45 feet wide and relatively fast. It flows over a gravel, stone, and sand bottom with silt edges. It ranges from 1 to 4 feet deep and supports heavy mayfly and caddis populations. Fishing in both directions from the launch site can be very good when insect hatches activate the browns and rainbows in the morning and afternoon hours. During hatchless periods a smallish Muddler Minnow is an effective searching pattern. Fish it across downstream and retrieve with short jerks and a low, swinging rod tip. Make the fly dart erratically along the bottom, and you will shortly find yourself connected. There is a path from the parking area that leads upstream to a small meadow at the edge of a deep, quiet run. At the head of this slick run is a deep hole with a clustered tangle of roots and debris near midstream. Facing upstream, you can cast to solid fish holding in the deep run next to the left bank and in the deep hole close to the structure. Continuing upstream, you will find several readily identifiable covers that shelter healthy, sizable resident fish and, in season, migratory brown trout.

Downstream from the launch, and upstream from the one-lane bridge on Scott Road, you will notice a deep, bankside cut next to several dead, standing trees. This deep, dark water is often the resting-staging area for spawning browns of serious poundage that have made the late-summer ascent from Burt Lake. In late July there are often large, noticeable spawning redds just across and slightly downstream from this spot. Another location that consistently holds the super trout is the very large and very deep hole immediately downstream from the Scott Road bridge.

Large, dark, Matuka-style, fur-strip streamers will work on the lake-run fish on overcast days and during the evening and dawn hours. One would assume that large, western-style stonefly patterns such as the Girdle Bug and Yuk Bug would be effective if fished patiently. In addition to the patterns for spawners, your streamer book should include sculpin imitations and Woolly Buggers. Black and Brown Stonefly nymphs in sizes 8 through 12 should be in your arsenal along with the Clark Lynn or Spring's Wiggler nymph. Oftentimes a small Pheasant Tail tied on a dropper will produce fish when the heavier fly takes it deep. If a hatch is in progress, the naturals should be closely matched. Look for olives and caddis just about anytime. The Borcher's Drake and Rusty's Spinner in sizes 12 through 18 will adequately mimic many Sturgeon River emergences and spinner falls.

Continuing downstream, you will find incredibly beautiful fishing water in the vicinity of Haakwood State Campground. This campground is clearly marked by a large sign on Old 27 and is right on the river's banks. Campsite number three is at the end of a blocked two-track trail that winds from the campsite through an open field to a line of trees that mark the banks of the Sturgeon. At this tree line you will find foot trails that follow the river's course throughout the campground area and beyond. There are some fairly steep banks along the way, but generally speaking, the trail is easy enough to follow right to the water's edge.

This stretch of the river is just about as pretty as anyone could reasonably expect to find anywhere on this planet. The stream is 40 to 50 feet wide (wider in some spots) with a fast, strong flow that literally dances over rock ledges and a mixed sand and gravel bottom. The depth ranges from 1 to 4 feet with a few holes that are deep enough to rinse your hair. There are some spots that show extremely slick clay and they should be avoided. Because of the relatively steep gradient, the riffles are very lively until they dive into the deep swirls and holes at the river's bends. Long, gliding tail-outs are typically found downstream from these holes, and they usually provide excellent dry-fly fishing.

Excepting periods of high water or conditions of insanity, the river is wadable in the Haakwood stretch. Reasonable care and felt soles are not optional, and a wading staff would be helpful for those who are not strong in the legs. A dependable flashlight and a companion are necessary for any twilight or nocturnal excursions.

Haakwood Campground is another prime locale for the lake-run magnums. Every 50 yards or so sports a deep hold or smooth, dark pool with enough structure to make the torpedoes feel secure. The riffles and runs have abundant gravel, and this combination of holding water and spawning area is ideal for the trophy-seeker. A 9-foot fly rod with backbone, some weighted streamers, perhaps a crayfish pattern, and a warm late summer evening can package splendid memories.

The campground's meadows and banks are thick with grasshoppers, and a high-floating imitation with a pale yellow body is good throughout the summer. Lime Trudes, Goddard Caddis, Adams, Royal Wulff, White Wulff, and Griffith's Gnats are productive in the riffles as well as the glassy slicks at the tail-outs of the pools and deeper holds. Haakwood is a great place to spend the better part of a day.

The next convenient access is at Rondo Road, just about 1 mile north of Haakwood. This spot is clearly marked by the MDNR as a boat-launch area and features parking for several vehicles, an outdoor toilet, and a wooden stairway leading down a short embankment to the river.

The water at the base of the wooden steps is scary. Not even Crocodile Dundee would wade here. The water rushes into this inky dark, swirling hole with considerable gusto. It is forced into a chute by the adjacent railroad trestle and creates whirlpools with separate back eddies on both banks. Even a very heavily weighted fly rarely ticks the bottom, and quite often it is necessary to add a split shot or two to present the fly to the feeding trout. This deep cavern, with its twisting side currents and back flows, is an ideal rest stop for migrating browns and steelhead, but even when the big fish are present you will find resident browns and rainbows rising to the parade of insects near the foam line. This big hole tails out into a wide, smooth pool with a firm sand and gravel bottom. A soft-hackled emerger can work wonders in this pool and in the riffle immediately below. Farther downstream the river alternates between pool and riffle, or hole and deep run, for a considerable distance. This area has big fish and heavy water. It is navigable, with great care, by a strong wader with felt soles and a staff, but it should only be explored under optimum—low water, high visibility—conditions.

Downstream from Rondo Road the river is accessible at White Road, Fisher Road, and at Burt Lake State Park. The river in most of this lower stretch is fast, deep, and downright scary and, although it holds very large trout, it is not suited to fly-fishing.

Overall, the Sturgeon is a beautiful and productive wild river. It has dependable hatches, clean, cold, clear water, and naturally reproducing trout. With the added bonus of migrating giants and the nervous edge produced by a heavy current, any visit to the Sturgeon is ripe with the promise of high excitement. With the application of common sense and care in wading, that surge of adrenalin is confined to your contact with the fish amidst a beautiful countryside.

Notes:

- Indian River is a tourist mecca. Many fine restaurants and motels are close by.
- Gaylord is a major commercial center in northern Michigan. The city has a styled Bavarian alpine atmosphere, superb dining, excellent resorts, and some of the finest golf courses in the central United States.
- This area is the home of Michigan's elk herd. Some of the best areas for viewing these magnificent animals are east of Vanderbilt and Wolverine in the Pigeon River State Forest. Horseback trail rides can be arranged. Complete information is available in Gaylord.
- The Pickerel Lake Campground, east of Vanderbilt, has 39 lakeside campsites, hiking trails, nearby horseback trails, and immediate access to several elk-viewing areas.
- The Windjammer Marina on Crooked Lake, just west of Burt Lake, rents pontoon and runabout boats for scenic cruises through Burt Lake and Mullet Lake.

8 | The Escanaba River
Marquette County

This is one of the largest river systems in Michigan. The East Branch, Middle Branch, and Big West Branch drain the wilderness of the central Upper Peninsula from just south of the city of Marquette on the shore of Lake Superior to the river's mouth at the city of Escanaba on Lake Michigan. The town of Gwinn on MI 35, 28 miles south of Marquette, is the point of merger for the East and Middle Branches and is the birthplace of the main river and a reasonable base for trout-fishing the system.

The East Branch of the Escanaba hosts both brook and brown trout throughout its course from just south of the town of Palmer to its junction with the Middle Branch within the city limits of Gwinn. A major brook-trout study program has been in effect on the East Branch, and anglers are asked to report catches of tagged and otherwise specially marked fish. Department of Natural Resources signs are prominently displayed at several access points, and these bright yellow placards give directions for submitting data for analysis by the research team. Perhaps this is one of those rare cases when killing a fish (for study) is more valuable than releasing it.

County Road 553 runs due north from Gwinn to Marquette and is the main artery for access to the upper East Branch. MI 35 and CR 553 intersect just east of Gwinn and from this corner it is 6.3 miles north on CR 553 to a good gravel road headed west. Take this gravel road for 0.1 mile and turn left on another hard-packed gravel road. Follow this road for 2.2 miles to a bridge over the East Branch.

Here the river averages 28 feet wide with a strong, cool flow of water stained the color of weak tea. The bottom is a mixture of soft sand, granite, coarse gravel and slag, logs, and stumps. Some minimal aquatic vegetation and overhanging brush provide the habitat for trout. Moderate depths (plan on 4 feet, but be on the lookout for deeper pockets) and a fairly open field for casting provide a pleasant avenue and some easy casting approaches to the shy brook trout of the upper East Branch.

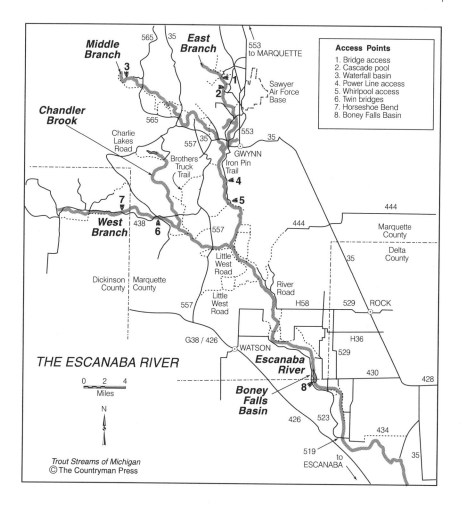

Access Points
1. Bridge access
2. Cascade pool
3. Waterfall basin
4. Power Line access
5. Whirlpool access
6. Twin bridges
7. Horseshoe Bend
8. Boney Falls Basin

THE ESCANABA RIVER

0   2   4
Miles

N

Trout Streams of Michigan
© The Countryman Press

Downstream from this bridge the fly-fishing has typically been more productive than the upstream section. Just below the bridge and for a considerable distance downstream, the water is faster and shallower and the lively current, with its inviting pockets, dancing riffles, and slower poollike glides, is easier to probe with nymph, streamer, or dry than are the deeper flat slicks farther upstream.

Brook and brown trout populate the upper East Branch and both species are generally eager to sample a reasonably presented fly. The Light Spruce, Mickey Finn, and Muddler are effective streamers when fished methodically with a slow, pulsing action through the deeper runs and close to the banks. Size 10 is about the right hook for these patterns, and a bit of weight in the fly, or a small split shot on the tippet, is helpful in swimming them at the proper depth. Effective nymphs include the Pheasant Tail in sizes 14 through 18, the Hare's Ear in 12 and 14, the Prince in 14, the Caddis Creeper in 12, and the black Woolly Worm in size 10. The Irresistible is a very effective dry fly for the Escanaba system, and the egg-sac version is particularly productive. Additionally, the Adams, Royal Trude, Renegade, and Elk-Hair Caddis should be in your box along with a supply of Blue-Winged Olives in sizes 16 through 20.

Proceeding downstream toward Gwinn, your next reasonable access to the East Branch is 3.7 miles north on CR 553 from the MI 35 junction, or 2.6 miles south on CR 553 from the previous turnoff. At this point a firm, sand-based two-track heads west for approximately 2.0 miles to the river. This road is passable for most of the year by ordinary automobiles, but it does have some very deep ruts, and the extremely close confines make tight turns a matter of keen interest. At the end of this trail you will find a circular parking area with a poor two-track continuing downstream and paralleling the river. If you have a four-wheel-drive vehicle you can take this trail another 0.1 mile to a dead end at streamside and begin fishing at the foot of the lively cascades just a few yards upstream from the parking spot. If you are driving a traditional vehicle, it is best to park at the upstream location and walk down to the cascade where the water shudders over large granite boulders into the deep calm of a tremendous pool of indeterminate depth. The bottom in this area is mostly granite slab, rubble, and sand. The lightly stained water averages 1 to 4 feet in depth, but some very deep holes and scattered patches of soft sand require careful, attentive wading.

Downstream from the cascade pool, the East Branch meanders through a thick growth of pine and cedar. The aromatic banks, beautiful surroundings, and the flat, calm, gliding surfaces belie a steady, pushing current and deeply undercut banks. The overhanging timber provides cooling shade and a heavy, continuing parade of land-based critters to the watchful trout. Beetles are effective at all times of the year and a black pattern, with a high-visibility dot, is a good first choice. Black and cinnamon ant patterns will take fish just about as well, and someday someone will take a real trophy on a dark Deer-Hair Mouse with a black marabou tail.

In the dark expanse of the cascade pool, both Light Spruce and Mickey Finn Clouser streamers have proven their individual merits. A deeply drifted Hare's Ear or Fox Squirrel nymph will usually bring strikes on the East Branch, and, excepting periods of active emergence or spinner fall, attractor dries such as the Royal Trude and Irresistible are good bets for surface work.

There is very good fishing in the relatively short stretch upstream from the cascade to the foot of a solid beaver dam. The current is moderately fast with firm footing and easy wading. The brook trout are found in midstream pockets, at the base of log structures, and under, or near, the overgrown banks. Bright attractors—nymph, streamer, or dry—will bring the fish to hand.

Upstream from this beaver dam the backwater effect makes Branch too deep to wade for quite a distance. Very heavy new grow alder and aspen make bankside navigation extremely difficult. N there are some very large fish behind the beaver dam, but safely ex one is a puzzle of consequence.

Continuing downstream into the city limits of Gwinn and to the confluence with the much larger Middle Branch, the East Branch continues to offer good fly-fishing. There is a robust brown trout population co-residing with the tagged brook trout in the waters that flow though the town park. It is sometimes possible to be entertained by an open-air concert while fly-casting to free-rising browns and brookies, and this is a most engaging way to spend a summer's evening.

The Middle Branch of the Escanaba officially forms near CR 581 just south and west of Ishpeming, the hideout of the late John Voelker (aka Robert Traver). The Middle Branch flows through some extremely rugged country without comfortable automobile access, and several waterfalls discourage (or should) amateur exploration by boat, canoe, or float tube. The joyous prose of *Trout Madness* describes the countryside, the insects, and expeditions to the Escanaba by "fish car" and canoe. Although *Trout Madness* includes no maps to the Escanaba's treasures, it gives full flavor and color to the stream's character.

There is a bridge over the Middle Branch on MI 35 within the city limits of Gwinn. From this bridge it is a 5.0-mile drive west, then north, on MI 35 to a left turn on CR 565. Drive west curving north on CR 565 for 5.7 miles to a bridge over the river at a beautiful stair-step waterfall and rapids. The banks in this gorgeous location are privately owned and wading would be dangerous, at best, close to the bridge, but it is possible to gain access and fish the enticing pocket water from the bank if permission to trespass is granted. Be sure to ask before squishing across someone's lawn.

If you continue to drive north past the bridge for another 0.9 mile, you will come to County Road MWD, a gravel trail that heads north by northwest. Take this trail for 1.4 miles to a dead end at a very dramatic and photogenic waterfall that plunges into a large (several acres) basin. The banks and bottom are granite ledge and the depth is beyond measuring with a sink-tip line and weighted nymph. Mixed hardwoods, with a heavy crimson maple influence in the fall colors, along with pines and cedars forest the surrounding hillsides. Mink and otter along with deer and bear are common in the region, and coyote serenades at dusk and dawn are a thrilling bonus. Most important, large brown trout and few outsized brookies cruise the deep water of the basin in search of a meal.

Deep sinking lines and weighted flies are necessary to reach the fish in this basin unless there is a hatch in progress. Clouser Minnows and lead-eye leech patterns are both fast sinkers and good choices for exploratory work, and marabou damselfly and dragonfly nymphs will take fish during hatch-less periods if fished deep with a slow, hand-twist retrieve.

Downstream from the basin the river is slow, calm, deep, and quite difficult to wade. County Road MWD parallels the Middle Branch for nearly all its length (MWD's length), but parking, turnaround spots, and streamside pathways throughout the jungle-thick shrubbery are scarce at best. A short, carefully scouted float in a belly boat might just be the best way to fish the Middle Branch of the Escanaba. This branch has many miles of water that receive minimal pressure and, as a result, harbor very large trout.

The Big West Branch of the Escanaba rises in northeastern Dickinson County and crosses into Marquette County near CR 438 approximately 12 miles southwest of Gwinn. CR 557 intersects CR 438 7 miles south of Gwinn and from that intersection it's 4.3 miles west on CR 438 to a set of two bridges over the Big West Branch.

The river in the vicinity of these two bridges (they are only 0.2 mile apart by road) averages 25 feet in width and from 1 to 3 feet deep. The largely sand bottom has intermittent stretches of fine gravel and dispersed areas of mud and silt. Undercut banks, heavy overhanging shrubs, and downed timber provide cover for the trout. There is space to park a vehicle near both bridges and, in addition, there is an old logging trail paralleling the river on the north side just 50 yards east of the first bridge. This is "tight" fishing that demands roll casting your fly into a narrow window opening between the shrubs on both banks. The good news is that the fish are rarely selective, and well-placed casts with attractor patterns such as the Adams, Gold-Ribbed Hare's Ear, or Mickey Finn will bring the desired result.

A bit farther west, 3.6 miles from the twin bridges, CR 438 crosses the Big West Branch in northwestern Dickinson County. This may be the upstream limit for fly-fishing in a conventional manner. The stream at this bridge, and in the immediate area, has depths ranging from 1 to 3 feet, a firm sandy bottom, and a light tea stain to the water. Undercut banks and overhanging shrubbery provide cooling shade and good trout cover but also reduce the casting channel to less than 12 feet in most cases. Roll casts are often required even though the streambed is close to 30 feet in width.

Downstream from the bridge there is a large horseshoe bend with deeply undercut banks, and this is a good location to test the receptivity of the trout on any given day. Cast a small baitfish or leech imitation to the edge of the bank and give it a twitch as it sinks. Allow the fly to drift under the bank and downstream a bit and give it a hard jerk or two. If the fish are on the prowl you will quickly be aware of the fact.

Further exploration can be conducted from CR 438, which parallels the stream for several more upstream miles, but a more productive expedition would be to probe Chandler Creek from the bridge on CR 438 (2.5 miles west of CR 557) downstream for about 1 mile to the junction with the West Branch, then fish back upstream to the bridge and your automobile. This is not any easy hike or fish, but wild fish are plentiful and you will have the stream to yourself.

The junction of the East and Middle branches forms the main channel of the Escanaba River within the city limits of Gwinn. Iron Pin Trail parallels the main river and provides the best access to this fishery for more than 5 miles. From MI 35, in downtown Gwinn, take Johnson Lake Road south for 0.7 mile to Iron Pin Trail and follow Iron Pin Trail (still angling south) for 3.1 miles to an ample parking area near a power line. A trail runs for only 20 yards to the river's edge.

The mainstream at the power-line crossing is 50 to 60 feet wide with a hard bottom. Granite boulders, rubble, and shale litter the banks and river bottom and produce current breaks and eddies throughout the flow. Generally speaking, the depth is negotiable to about 3-plus feet, but the iron-red

BOB LINSENMAN

Brook trout haven on the East Branch

tinge to the water makes visibility, particularly under low-light conditions, problematic and it is best to proceed very cautiously. As a safeguard, only wade when and where you can see bottom for several steps in the direction you wish to wade.

Upstream from the power-line parking area, a washed-out two-track parallels the river for several yards, but do not attempt to drive this trail. Rather, walk up the river and fish back or reverse the procedure. This upstream section is wider and has less depth than downstream from the power line. It has silted edges, many logs and stumps, and some fairly deep riffles and pools. It is easy to wade with plenty of room for long back casts when they are required.

Brook trout have been reintroduced to this brown trout stronghold, and they are the object of close scrutiny by the Michigan Department of Natural Resources. The brookies inhabit the faster riffle water while the browns seem to prefer the calmer flow of the pools and bankside eddies. Both are pushovers for a Griffith's Gnat fished on a long leader and light tippet. The brown trout rise deliberately in the slick tail-out of the pools or under the

A pool of several acres on the Middle Branch

sheltering boughs of the cedar overhangs, while the brook trout make slashing, enthusiastic strikes in the faster currents.

There are dense caddis populations in this upper section of the Escanaba's mainstream, and a complete selection of patterns will include Henryville, Goddard, and Elk-Hair Caddis from size 12 through 18. Nymphal impressions can be confined to the Caddis Creeper, latex larva, and antron sparkle emergers in sizes 10 through 16. In addition to the caddis patterns and Griffith's Gnats, carry some colorful attractors such as the Royal Wulff and Lime Trude; a selection of dun- and cream-colored, high-floating variants; and parachute Olives in sizes 16 and 18. Streamer patterns are very effective in the Escanaba's mainstream and should be fished methodically when no surface feeding is in evidence. The Spruce (light, dark, and grizzly-wing variations) and dark sculpin imitators will do a good job.

It is about 2 miles from the power-line access to the end of Iron Pin Trail. At the 1.9-mile mark you will come to a circular turnaround and parking area on your left and a very poor logging road proceeding downriver. Park at the end of Iron Pin Trail and use the logging trail only as a footpath.

The river in this area continually repeats a pool-and-riffle configuration and is wide enough and open enough for lengthy back casts. The bottom is firm with a mixture of sand, gravel, and rock. Overhanging pines and cedars shelter and shade the fish and act as conveyors of wind-blown terrestrials. Midriver runs and pockets and the deeper holes at the river's bends also hold trout and should be fished carefully. The very deep whirlpool at the base of the hill near the parking spot holds some large fish and should be given at least 10 more casts than would seem to make good sense. Use a deep-sinking dragonfly nymph or Clouser Minnow, a slow, twitch-and-dart retrieve, and patience.

Farther downstream there is access to the mainstream of the Escanaba from Little West Road and from various logging trails in south-central Marquette County. Near the Delta County line (extreme southern Marquette County), Boney Falls Basin absorbs the Escanaba's flow for a brief respite and then releases the river's energy at the power dam on CR 523 in western Delta County, about 18 miles northwest of Lake Michigan and the city of Escanaba.

The river at its escape from the dam and Boney Falls Basin is more than 100 feet wide with a fast current pounding over granite ledge. The resultant riffle is streamwide and heavy and harbors large and robust brown trout that are vigorously pursued by knowledgeable anglers. Below Boney Falls Basin the water retains its light-tea coloration, and this amber shading combined with the speed of the current produces a wading condition that necessitates felt soles and extreme caution. A wading staff is highly recommended and the buddy system should be employed if at all possible.

Streamers and large nymphs are the top-drawer choices of experienced fly-fishers on the lower Escanaba. Marabou Muddlers, lead-eye leeches, and large Clouser Minnows produce heavy strikes, long runs, and fish-chasing scrambles. Rubber-leg nymphs such as the June Wiggler, Girdle Bug, Yuk Bug, and Black Stone are used in the morning, evening, and throughout the day under overcast skies. Large attractor dries and Elk-Hair Stonefly patterns will bring the trout to the surface when the water is clear.

Downstream from the power-dam access, the Escanaba can be fished by the wading angler in the vicinity of the bridge on CR 519. High banks with steep, rocky gradients, both upstream and downstream from the bridge and on both sides of the river, require a careful approach to the fishing. Viewing the river and the angle of the hillsides, it is easy to visualize a misstep, an energetic scramble, and a quick, bumpy entry to the water.

The river's characteristics at CR 519 are very similar to those found just below the power dam at Boney Falls. Navigation is tricky at best and great care should be applied to each foot placement in the rapid current. This is big, spooky water with a healthy measure of solitude, particularly during midweek.

The Escanaba system is beautiful, productive, and largely remote. From the quiet, cold wilderness headwaters to the rushing brawl of the lower river, it offers a range of angling experiences that is hard to duplicate in the central United States. Moose, bear, and the rare timber wolf roam the upper reaches. Roads are few and maps are sketchy. One September day we were questioned by a MDNR researcher about our success with brook trout. When asked for directions to another specific bridge access, the researcher could not explain the route, even with a map, so he led us there. Shortly after we parked our vehicle near the bridge, a Michigan State Police officer stopped and asked us for directions to the highway!

The lower mainstream might remind you of a western river, perhaps the Madison below Quake Lake or the stretch between Varney Bridge and Ennis where safe wading is as prime a motivator as are the big fish.

If you bring current maps, a good compass, and some high-test mosquito repellent along with your felt-soled waders and other trout gear, you will thoroughly enjoy fishing the Escanaba.

Notes:

- There are numerous beautiful waterfalls in Escanaba territory. The drive from Marquette to L'Anse and Baraga will take you very near several of these dramatic cascades.

- The Lumberjack Tavern in Big Bay has very good food. Some of the filming for *Anatomy of a Murder* was conducted on site.
- The Red Horse Ranch near Gwinn offers fine food, lodging, and hayrides.
- Marquette on Lake Superior is a large town with all imaginable products and services. There are first-class golf courses in the immediate area.

9 | The Ontonagon River

Houghton County, Ontonagon County, Gogebic County

The East Branch of the Ontonagon River becomes fly-fishable as it leaves Lower Dam Pond in extreme southern Houghton County just 2 miles north of the Iron County boundary. The large, deep hole at the base of the twin culverts, which pour water from the pond, has a double whirlpool, one on each side of the stream, and the feeding fish can be oriented in all possible compass headings.

Flowing north and then west to the town of Kenton, the East Branch crosses CR 161, roughly parallels FS 138 for a brief run, and then turns due west toward Kenton. On the way to Kenton the East Branch cuts through some very wild country, picking up additional water volume from Smith and Stony creeks. County maps show several points of access from the south but most of these (surprise!) dead-end into posted, private property. Summer cottages and hunting camps are numerous in this area, and direct access to the river between Lower Dam and Kenton is problematic.

Between the outlet and the bridge on CR 161, the East Branch runs between 15 and 20 feet wide. It flows over rocks, small boulders, and gravel with some sand. Its banks are lined with spruce, cedar, tall ferns, and all types of branched back-cast bedevilers. Roll casting and an upstream approach are necessary for success, but because this section is lightly fly-fished, the rewards are plentiful for the adventuresome.

Brook trout predominate in this stretch of the river. Occasionally immature steelhead are taken, and early in the season it's a good idea to strengthen your tippet and be cognizant of the possibility of hooking a silver bullet. The fish are not at all selective, even during an emergence, but presentation is important.

Pattern selection is not a critical issue. Attractor dries work very well, and a selection of Adams and Trudes will more than suffice. The Hare's Ear or Fox Squirrel nymph and a Woolly Bugger and Mickey Finn or Light Spruce Fly will cover wet-fly needs.

As the stream approaches Kenton it has gathered volume and breadth and is more easily fly-fished. Averaging 30 feet in width, the East Branch bends through a series of slow curves with deep holes and undercut banks as it enters the town proper. Despite the proximity to "civilization," this is a good place to fish, and since it is now possible to present the fly in a downstream attitude, either an upstream or downstream decision is workable. There is a parking area next to an old railroad trestle just north of MI 28 on Forest Highway 16, and the fish in this area, both brook and rainbow, have a fondness for the Grizzly Spruce Fly and Silver Hilton in size 12. During the summer a grasshopper pattern will bring some respectable fish to the surface.

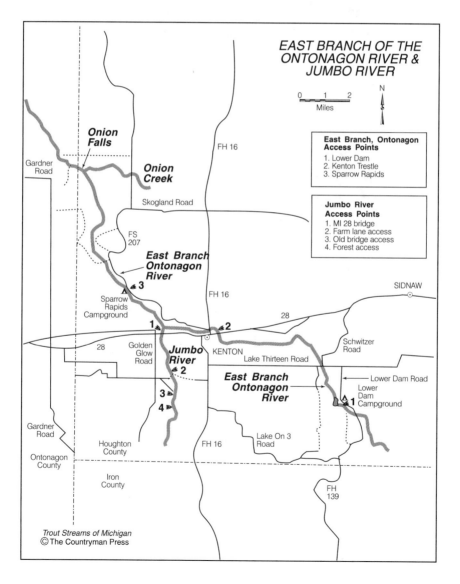

EAST BRANCH OF THE
ONTONAGON RIVER &
JUMBO RIVER

0   1   2
Miles
N

East Branch, Ontonagon Access Points
1. Lower Dam
2. Kenton Trestle
3. Sparrow Rapids

Jumbo River Access Points
1. MI 28 bridge
2. Farm lane access
3. Old bridge access
4. Forest access

Onion Falls
Onion Creek
FH 16
Gardner Road
Skogland Road
FS 207
East Branch Ontonagon River
3
SIDNAW
Sparrow Rapids Campground
FH 16
28
1
28
Golden Glow Road
Jumbo River
2
KENTON
Lake Thirteen Road
Schwitzer Road
Lower Dam Road
Lower Dam Campground
1
East Branch Ontonagon River
3
4
Gardner Road
Houghton County
FH 16
Lake On 3 Road
Ontonagon County
Iron County
FH 139

Trout Streams of Michigan
© The Countryman Press

Lower Dam Pond on the East Branch near Kenton

Downstream from Kenton the river parallels FS 207 as it approaches Sparrow Rapids. There is a clearly marked sign on FH 16 just north of town that indicates the road and mileage to Sparrow Rapids and the U.S. Forest Service campground at that spot. The river flows through a continuing series of S-curves throughout its course to the rapids. The small valley is largely public land and since the river is very close to the forest service road, it is possible to walk (south) to the river from the road in many locations. A compass is a requirement.

Averaging 35 feet in width to the point where the Jumbo River enters (see separate coverage of the Jumbo River) and 45 feet thereafter, this section of the East Branch will produce brown trout as well as brooks and rainbows. They are all suckers for a Woolly Bugger or Light Spruce Fly fished deep with a quick, erratic retrieve. A dead-drift with the Hare's Ear, Fox Squirrel, or small black Montana nymph is also productive. Dry patterns are the obvious. Match the hatch if in progress. Otherwise, an Adams, Irresistible, or Royal Trude will bring fish topside.

As the river enters the rapids area it sweeps into high banks and in the outside curves the deep holes and following tail-outs hold some very nice fish. Here the East Branch is nearly 50 feet wide (and considerably wider in some spots) and carries a significant volume, particularly in the spring or after a rain. Wading care and common sense will be necessary, but, for the most part, difficult water is easy to spot and avoid.

The rapids proper are easily reached from the USFS campground, which features a convenient wooden stairway to this photographic attraction. Do not be deterred by the term "rapids." The water here is very fishable and highly productive for the skilled and patient fly-rodder. Deep holes carved into the ledge rock by the pounding of the stair-step rapids harbor many trout, and it is not unusual to take brook, brown, and rainbow on successive casts. In addition to the holes and wide pools, fish hold in midstream pockets, and every likely looking sanctuary should be productive.

Olive Woolly Buggers with just the slightest touch of Flashabou or Krystal Flash in the tail are well received. The Hare's Ear, Fox Squirrel, Black Stonefly, caddis pupa, and Halfback nymphs are generally taken with surety, and the old standbys, the Adams and Elk-Hair Caddis, the grasshopper, Royal Wulff, and Lime Trude are good dry-fly choices.

Downstream from Sparrow Rapids the river takes on additional volume from springs and small feeder streams. It winds, in a series of tight curves, northward to Onion Falls right at the Ontonagon County line. FS 207 closely parallels the river for the first 2.0 miles below the rapids and then breaks away in a sharp right-hand curve while the East Branch continues northward. Below Onion Falls the East Branch is marginal trout water.

Access to the river after FS 207 breaks away is by hiking, and the fishing pressure is almost nonexistent. Be sure to carry a compass, fresh water, and a vigorous state of mind if you intend to embark on this wilderness outing. A four-section pack rod and lightweight stockingfoot waders will be appreciated during the jungle navigation. This section of the river has some very deep holes that require a careful approach, but the resident fish are ample reward.

Very respectable trout are common in this stretch of the river. Brook trout exceeding 12 inches and browns considerably larger can munch your streamer or crayfish pattern on almost any cast. In the spring and late fall (at this writing the East Branch has an extended season downstream from MI 28) be aware of the presence of Lake Superior steelhead. Fishing a Micro-Egg dropper in combination with a stonefly, Clark Lynn nymph, or Woolly Bugger can bring a big rainbow into contact.

Although the East Branch below Kenton seems to cloud quickly after a rainfall, it is exciting water to fish with the fly rod. It harbors steelhead, large browns, and colorful brooks in good numbers between Lower Dam and Onion

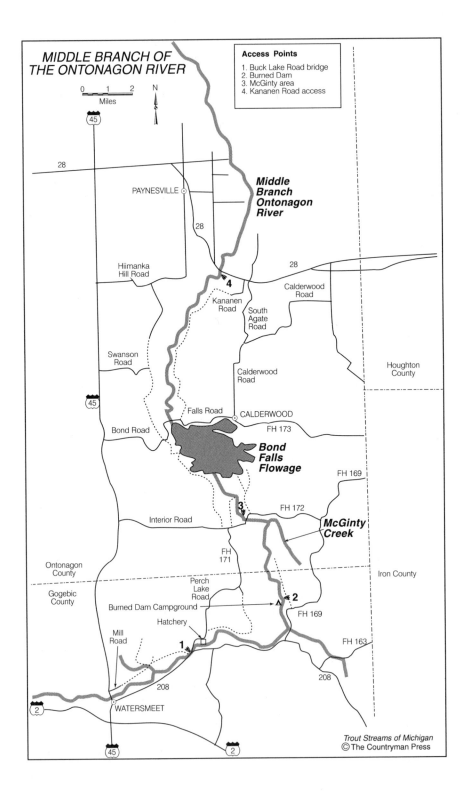

MIDDLE BRANCH OF
THE ONTONAGON RIVER

0   1   2
Miles

N

45

Access Points
1. Buck Lake Road bridge
2. Burned Dam
3. McGinty area
4. Kananen Road access

28

PAYNESVILLE

Middle
Branch
Ontonagon
River

28

Hiimanka
Hill Road

28

4

Calderwood
Road

Kananen
Road

South
Agate
Road

Swanson
Road

Houghton
County

Calderwood
Road

45

Falls Road   CALDERWOOD

Bond Road

FH 173

Bond
Falls
Flowage

FH 169

FH 172

3

McGinty
Creek

Interior Road

FH
171

Ontonagon
County

Perch
Lake
Road

Iron County

Gogebic
County

Burned Dam Campground

2

FH 169

Hatchery

1

FH 163

Mill
Road

208

208

2

WATERSMEET

45

2

Trout Streams of Michigan
© The Countryman Press

Falls, and the scenery, the wilderness impact, is a distinct pleasure. The camp-grounds at both Sparrow Rapids and Lower Dam are exceptional. They are on the water with beautiful surroundings and a strong measure of solitude.

The Middle Branch of the Ontonagon watershed is first approachable by the fly-rodder in the Watersmeet area in southeastern Gogebic County. The Middle Branch system begins near the Watersmeet lookout tower west of town close by Crooked Lake. The Middle Branch flows easterly, crosses US 45, and is joined by Duck Creek within the city limits. At the roadside park in Watersmeet, the Middle Branch is 15 to 20 feet wide with a slow, flat cur-rent flowing over fine gravel, sand, and aquatic grasses.

Heavy hatches are infrequent in the area immediately up- and down-stream from US 45, but when they occur it is necessary to match the emer-gence or spinner fall closely in order to take the rising trout. General attractors are in order most of the time and, due to the streamside grassy banks, general cricket, ant, and beetle imitations work well. An especially good fish attractor in the Middle Branch is the SRB (Secret Rubber Bug—fully described in appendix A) in sizes 12 and 14, and a "double" version of this pattern in sizes 8 or 10 is a real killer.

East of Watersmeet the river closely parallels the railroad and CR 208 (Old US 2) to the Watersmeet trout hatchery. Just past the hatchery it jogs northward toward Perch Lake, then back eastward curving slowly to the north and the Burned Dam area. From Burned Dam the Middle Branch flows north into Ontonagon County.

Just 3.0 miles east of Watersmeet, Buck Lake Road intersects with CR 208. Take Buck Lake Road north just a few yards and you will cross the river in a very fishable location. Park on either side of the one-lane bridge and fish upstream or downstream as your heart desires. The Middle Branch at this spot is 1 to 3-plus feet deep and 20 to 25 feet wide. It flows smoothly through the brush and the riffles, and undercut banks hold some decent fish. The casting is a bit tight and roll casts are the order of the day.

This stretch of river between Watersmeet and Burned Dam on FS 169 is heavily fed by springs and feeder creeks, and the Middle Branch at the Burned Dam campground is 50-plus-feet wide with heavy riffles, rapids, deep holes, and long pools. The bottom is a combination of rock, gravel, and muck. There are brook, brown, and rainbow trout in attendance and they will smack a reasonably presented wet fly, nymph, or small streamer with abandon. The Grizzly Spruce in size 10, lightly weighted, is a favorite near Burned Dam. Soft-hackle wets, as popularized by Sylvester Nemes, should be fished before and after a hatch, and popular patterns are the same as used elsewhere in the Upper Peninsula.

Proceeding north, the Middle Branch continues through the Ottawa National Forest on its way to Bond Falls Flowage, a major boating, fishing, and general tourist attraction just east of US 45. Near Interior Road (FS 172) the Middle Branch is enlarged by McGinty Creek and must be waded with care.

The Middle Branch leaves Bond Falls Flowage in majestic splendor in the form of a spectacular, two-section, stair-step waterfall, and in controversy in the debate over the water volume released and its effect on the downstream fishery. The river has been drastically altered by the dam and diversions of flow, and the question of acceptable volume for the Middle Branch below Bond Flowage is forefront in the minds of dedicated trout anglers and other conservationists. At this writing the issue is not fully resolved to the trout's benefit, but some progress is seemingly being made.

Below Bond Falls and the town of Paulding, access to the river is difficult but not impossible. Current maps show poor dirt-road access at various points from both east and west sides of the river. Some of these approaches will actually get you close enough for a short hike to the fishing. Most will dead-end at the cabin driveway, with the creek temptingly visible.

The river is flowing through a steeply cut, narrow valley in this section. It is characterized as fast water with some deep holes at the hard-turning bends. Whirlpools, back eddies, midstream riffles, and the cover afforded by downed timber hold sizable brook trout and a few browns and rainbows. Woolly Buggers with Flashabou or Krystal Flash applied sparingly to the black marabou tail are very effective. The Silver Hilton, Pass Lake, Llama, Muddler, Grizzly Spruce, and Light Spruce streamers produce fish regularly. A local favorite is the Bucktail Royal Coachman, heavily weighted and fished with rapid, cross-stream jerks.

Effective nymphs include the Black Girdle Bug in size 10, the June Wiggler (simply a Clark Lynn or Spring's Wiggler nymph with the addition of two pairs of fine, white rubber legs) in sizes 8–12, the Hare's Ear in size 12 and 14, and various shades of the Latex Caddis larvae in sizes 10–14. Dry patterns should be tied in the western style with stiff bushy hackles and lots of deer hair. The Irresistible, Humpy, and all the Wulff variations in sizes 10–14 will bring strikes.

The only relatively easy access to this part of the Middle Branch is near the bridge on MI 28 west of the village of Trout Creek. The first road east of the bridge on MI 28 is Kananen Road, which leads south. Take this road, winding through a large meadow, to a two-track and a weathered wooden sign that directs you along a rough two-track to a small, open parking area. You will need a vehicle with sufficient clearance to navigate deep potholes and ruts; a four-wheel drive is good insurance. From the parking area a narrow path descends the hill to the river and from there follows the river on its south bank in both upstream and downstream directions.

This is lively and lovely fishing. The water pours over rocks and into small pools and bankside cuts. Averaging 1 to 3 feet deep with a high oxygen content, the stream is rich in aquatic insects and the brook trout are quite aggressive. Deer-hair dry patterns like the Goddard Caddis float very well and pull the trout to the surface like trained pigs to a trough. The deeper holes and smooth glides beneath bankside willows occasionally produce brown trout and, rarely, a rainbow will be taken on a bright streamer. The dominant fish, however, is the brook trout, and the streamers, wets, and dries mentioned earlier will all produce strikes with regularity.

Upstream from the point where the footpath first reaches the river's bank there is an active beaver family with most of their engineering work taking place near the tail-out of a large, deep pool. Some local anglers periodically remove the construction work and then the beavers rebuild. So far, the fishing has not been adversely affected.

Farther upstream about 200 yards there is a long deep run, almost a chute, with fairly heavy current coursing hard against the left-hand bank. The overhanging foliage and deeper water is ideal cover for larger fish, and there is at least one magnum in residence most of the time.

The pattern of riffle, pool, and pocket water, repeated time and again, presents a variety of water types and angling challenges to the fly-rodder. The lightly tea-stained flow is clear enough to require fine tippets and careful presentation, but not so crystalline as to demand ultralong leaders tapered finer than 5X.

About 50 yards downstream past the footpath from the parking area, the river makes a 90-degree turn to the right, and the resultant hole is deep and enticing. It is crisscrossed at varying depths with old logs, and the trout can strike out from just about anywhere. Small, soft-hackled emergers, Hare's Ears, and Woolly Buggers will bring strikes if allowed to sink and then pulsed slowly against the current. High-riding Humpys and Irresistibles, and the Secret Rubber Bug bring the brook trout to the surface. Downstream from this hole the river flattens for a way and then resumes an alternating posture of pool, riffle, pocket water. The rough path follows the stream's edge for quite a distance, and it is best to walk down for a selected distance and then fish back upstream to your vehicle.

The bridge at the highway is not a place to consider as a fishing access point. This is a large, well-maintained roadside park with picnic tables, dog runs, and a highly traveled path to the scenic (and dangerous) Agate Falls just a short distance downstream.

Anglers can and do follow the path to the viewing area at the base of the falls, and it's a great place to be photographed at the very least. Downstream from the falls the fishing is fair for a distance, but this is primarily an anadromous fishery with excitement peaking in the spring and fall as the big fish stack up at the base of the overpowering waterfall.

In summary, the Middle Branch is the center of controversy, the subject of continuing debate over the quality of the fishery downstream from Bond Falls Flowage. Despite the barroom and media attention and the limited access, it is definitely worth the effort to explore and fish. Wild brook, brown, and rainbow trout are in residence, and their willingness to take a properly presented fly make a hike through the woods a worthwhile exercise.

Notes:

- Watersmeet has a full Las Vegas–style casino that is clean, fair, and well managed.
- The campgrounds at Burned Dam, Marion Lake, and Taylor Lake are first-rate.
- Visit the Sylvania Recreation area south and west of Watersmeet. Some of the highest points and grandest vistas in the state are in this area.
- Drive east of Paulding 3.5 miles and view Bond Falls—truly spectacular but dangerous; stick to the paths and keep small children in hand.
- Agate Falls on MI 28 is a short but steep walk from the roadside park, and very beautiful. Bring a camera.
- The "Mystery Light" of Watersmeet has various explanations. Some believe it is a ghost, others insist on UFO activity. Whatever kind of phenomenon it is remains a mystery. The "light" is usually visible at dark off Robins Lake Road north and west of town.
- Ajibikoka Falls at Brush Lake 5.0 miles northwest of Watersmeet is worth the drive.

II | VEILED TREASURES

10 | The Northern Highlands

Clare, Gladwin, Roscommon, Oscoda, Alcona, Iosco, Arenac, Ogemaw, and Crawford Counties offer diverse and pleasing vistas, friendly people, and excellent trout fishing. Gladwin, Clare, and Arenac Counties are at the extreme southern edge of the "highlands" and are a blend of rich agricultural lands gradually ceding territory to mixed hardwood and pine forests. These counties do have national and state lands, but the larger share is in private ownership. If in doubt, an angler should seek permission to fish.

Roscommon, Ogemaw, and Iosco Counties form a psychological gateway to northern Michigan. There are fewer farms, the forested areas are more vast, and the proportionate share of acreage held in the public trust is much greater than to the south. This is a peak summer tourist area; lakeside cottages, festivals, numerous campgrounds and parks, and glorious fishing for both warm- and cold-water species attract vacationers from Michigan's urban centers and from neighboring states.

Crawford, Oscoda, and Alcona Counties have an even higher percentage of state and federally owned lands. The soil is mostly sand, and vast forests of pine have replaced early farming ventures. This sand spelled financial disaster for farming but, in part, assured the survival of the area's cold-water resources. The rivers are continually filtered and fed by abundant springs.

Major commercial centers complete with fine restaurants, first-rate golf courses, shopping, and health-care facilities include Gladwin and Clare in the south, Houghton Lake, West Branch, and Tawas City in the center, and Grayling in the north.

RIFLE RIVER
Ogemaw County

The Rifle River is the main artery of a river system that covers more than 70 miles between Lupton and Lake Huron. In the spring it hosts a sizable steel-

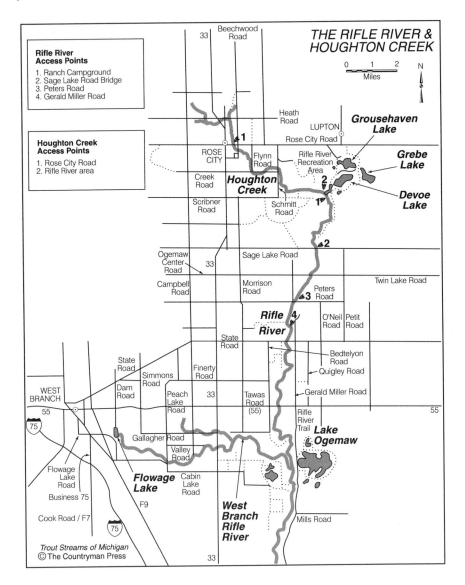

THE RIFLE RIVER & HOUGHTON CREEK

Rifle River Access Points
1. Ranch Campground
2. Sage Lake Road Bridge
3. Peters Road
4. Gerald Miller Road

Houghton Creek Access Points
1. Rose City Road
2. Rifle River area

Trout Streams of Michigan
© The Countryman Press

head and sucker run, and in October it receives chinook salmon in respectable numbers. Both of these anadromous species spread throughout the main river and its branches and tributaries, and provide quality angling for trophy fish.

Overshadowed by the world-famous Au Sable a few miles to the north, the Rifle River receives only sporadic fishing pressure throughout the trout season. Despite its easy access, scenic beauty, and dependable hatches, it has been largely ignored by visiting anglers. From the headwaters at Devoe Lake in the Rifle River Recreation Area near Lupton, downstream to its merger with the West Branch south of the intersection of highways MI 55 and MI 33, the Rifle River is a beautiful, challenging, and productive trout stream.

Within the boundaries of the recreation area, from Devoe Lake to the footbridge downstream from the Spruce and Ranch Campgrounds, the stream averages 18 to 25 feet wide. It is largely composed of a sand and gravel bottom with marl edges and is dominated by a near-wilderness aura complete with downed cedars, drumming grouse, and the secretive white-tailed deer.

About 1 mile below the bridge at Devoe Lake, the access road passes through a large open area and the Ranch Campground. This is a good place to park and fish back upstream to the Houghton Creek junction, or farther to the Birch Cabin and beyond. Downstream from the Ranch Campground there is an excellent access point at the footbridge turnaround. It will take you the better part of a morning or afternoon to cover the water past Clear Creek back upstream to the Spruce Campground. Downstream from the footbridge turnaround there is a canoe-launching site, and fishing below this point can be a high-traffic consideration during peak summer months or on weekends.

Hare's Ears, Prince, Caddis Creeper, and Pheasant Tail nymphs are mainstays in this upper section of the Rifle. Adams and Cream Variants, olive

The Rifle River near Selkirk

Elk-Hair Caddis, and black ants are productive dries. Smallish Muddler Minnows, olive Woolly Buggers, and white or yellow marabou streamers regularly take fish here and in the smaller tributaries throughout the recreation area.

Between the recreation area boundary and the MI 55 bridge there are major access points at Sage Lake Road, Peters Road, State Road, and upstream from State Road, off Gerald Miller Road. This is bigger, heavier water and, although the bottom is easy to negotiate, caution is urged, particularly if one is fishing in the late evening and nighttime hours. There is relatively heavy canoe activity here. For the most part the "aluminum-hatch" people are courteous and try to stay out of your way, but the occasional boatload of slobs can leave you angry and frustrated with humanity at large. Fish this stretch in the early morning and late evening and you will eliminate the problem.

The middle and lower sections of the Rifle River hold resident and migratory fish that seek a substantial meal. A yellow-bodied Au Sable Skunk or a clipped Deer-Hair Mouse is a good choice for dry-fly probing in the early morning or evening periods. The Michigan Caddis *(Hexagenia limbata)* patterns are productive during June and early July, and a standard assortment of Adams, Elk-Hair Caddis, variants, and terrestrials will cover your dry-fly needs throughout the season. Small dark stonefly nymphs (size 10 and 12), caddis larvae (green and cream), soft-hackle wets, and the Halfback pattern produce when fished patiently and deep. Larger streamers will sometimes entice a late holdover steelhead or a brown the size of an otter, so a few casts with heavy metal in the size 2 and 4 variety can be worthwhile. A gray marabou leech or a brown sculpin are overachievers at dawn and dusk in this section of the Rifle River.

Special mention is due the West Branch of the Rifle River if only for the grand opportunity it provides young anglers. There is a stretch of this stream, within the city limits of the town of West Branch, with reserved trout fishing for children aged 16 and younger. This water is not overly easy to fish but the trout are there and more than willing to take a fly. The community and its anglers are to be commended for their foresight and restraint in reserving water for our beginning trouters. It's a great way to "infect" tomorrow's conservationists.

In addition to the restricted water, the West Branch and its many feeder creeks offer scenic, uncomplicated fishing to the general public. Rifle Creek, Woods Creek, Ogemaw Creek, and Brewery Creek flow through town and join at Flowage Lake to form the West Branch. All of this is trout water, and the West Branch from Flowage Lake Road downstream to the MI 33 bridge is lovely brown trout water with scattered "hot spots" of small rainbows.

Small Humpys and Irresistibles along with the Royal Trude are favorite dries. The Prince, Zug Bug, and Hare's Ear are all that is needed in a nymph box, and a small Woolly Bugger or Pass Lake streamer will complete the fly selection for this fishery.

Notes:

- The town of West Branch is a full-service community with many fine restaurants and motels. The local golf course has some interesting hazards—pumping oil wells.
- The Rifle River Recreation Area has excellent camping facilities and beautiful hiking trails. Nearby Lupton has the Sunrise Cafe for hearty food and a smile.
- In this area just about every ditch with moving water has trout in it. Explore!
- There is a small but well-stocked fly shop, Bachelder's Spool and Fly, on State Road near the bridge.

HOUGHTON CREEK
Ogemaw County

Houghton Creek is a major tributary of the Rifle River and, throughout its roughly 4½-mile flow from Rose City to its confluence with the Rifle at the Rifle River Research Area near Lupton, provides very good fishing for brown trout.

And this is as true today as it was when the first edition of this book was published, but since that time the little river has been more heavily "posted." Fewer sections are readily accessible without specific permission. This is particularly nettlesome upstream from Flynn Road. Still, the fishing is good and worth the effort to put on a smile and ask politely. In the unlikely event that charm fails, try the water just upstream from the junction with the Rifle River in the Rifle River Recreation Area. It is excellent and is rarely fished.

An angler's first impression would likely be that the stream is too small for fly-fishing, particularly if that angler's initial view of Houghton Creek is from MI 33 just a few yards north of the Rose City town center. Here the stream is 5 to 6 feet across and thick with bankside vegetation. From this highway vantage point it is only about 100 yards to the Rose City Park, where the Houghton is joined by another branch and doubles in size. From the park downstream to the research area, Houghton Creek is a good fishery with dependable mayfly and caddis hatches and wary but not finicky browns. It remains, however, a small stream, and short roll casts are most often required.

For our purposes here, the first section to examine is from the bridge at Rose City Road just west of Rose City, upstream to the park. This is very "skinny" water, and a low-profile approach is best suited to the cramped quarters. Here the stream is quite narrow with many twisting turns and shallow gravel- and sand-bottomed runs diving into deeper bends and holes. You will see the decaying evidence of CCC-installed shelters and cribs and, occasionally, the remnants of aged erosion-control structures. Be watchful! The large protruding nails used to assemble these decades-old projects have snagged many waders.

Though the streambed is primarily sand and fine gravel, occasionally the angler will find sections of extremely slick clay, usually in the deep bends just downstream from this first bridge. I've taken an unwanted (and I thought unneeded) bath more than once in this stretch.

In general, the fish in this stretch are not overly large, but I have taken several browns over 15 inches from the edges of the deeper bends. My best fish ever was a 17-inch hook-jawed male brown in full spawning regalia that munched a size-8 crayfish during a cold evening drizzle. Upstream from

Both Houghton Creek and the Rifle River have sections reserved for anglers under age 16.

Rose City Road, Houghton Creek twists through an orchard-edged meadow for about 150 yards, then there is a fairly straight and slow, heavily wooded stretch before the creek ends in the park. There are solid, healthy fish throughout this stretch and they are fairly generous with their forgiveness of imprecise fly selection. Turnabout is fair play, and catch-and-release is always a sensible move.

If you wade and fish cautiously you can plan on approximately 2 hours to thoroughly cover this part of Houghton Creek. From the park it will take you about 10 minutes to walk back to a car parked at the Beachwood Road bridge. A 7- or 7½-foot rod for a 4-weight line and 7½-foot leaders tapered to 5X are all that is needed.

Just below the intersection of Flynn Road and Houghton Creek Road southwest of town, Wilkins Creek joins the Houghton and considerably increases the flow. There is a washed-out bridge (barely visible now) just upstream from this juncture and it is a good place to park a vehicle. Downstream from the confluence, Houghton Creek flows through a meadow for quite a distance, and a good place to start to fish back upstream is about 300 yards below the washed-out bridge.

The creek is wider, slower, and, in the bends and under the sweepers, considerably deeper than upstream, and the fish in this section are generally larger. You will probably notice several ash rings from dead campfires as you negotiate the bank. There are some really serious-sized browns in this stretch, and the late June evening emergences of the Brown Drake duns bring the fish and the night-skulking fly-fisher together.

During August and early September, this is excellent grasshopper water. The meadows and breezes provide just the right combination to condition the trout to the potential of a substantial meal, and a size-10 yellow-bodied Dave's Hopper is a favorite item on the menu.

Throughout the year you will find that the Adams, Light Cahill, and various Elk-Hair Caddis patterns (both tan and olive) are very productive here. Cricket and ant imitations receive considerable attention in the wooded stretches upstream from the Wilkins-Houghton junction and, if there has been a light rain producing slightly off-colored water, or an overcast sky, a weighted Woolly Bugger fished deep with slow twitches will get your blood pumping.

Fished methodically, with a short diversion up Wilkins Creek for a few yards, this stretch can take from 2 to 4 hours to cover. The timing depends on whether or not an angler decides to pass by some of the tighter, fly-snatching cover and concentrate on more open opportunities. An 8- or 8½-foot rod, 5- or 6-weight with a 9-foot leader, will cover every situation in this section.

Downstream from this point Houghton Creek widens and slows. It meanders through excellent woodcock and grouse coverts on its way through private forest and farmland before joining the Rifle River at the Rifle River Research Area near Lupton.

The water is bigger here, deeper in the bends, and a wading angler needs to exercise prudent judgment. The silt and marl edges provide ideal habitat for large burrowing nymphs, and late evening fishing in June and July can be very exciting. Until the river enters the research area it is primarily surrounded by private property, and access should be at the county road bridges or with landowner permission.

There are fewer trout in this stretch, but they are generally large and exceptionally robust on light to medium rods. An 8½-foot rod for a 6-weight line will supply enough muscle to keep fish out of the logjams and sweepers and allow you to land and release them quickly enough to avoid unduly stressing the fish.

It is worth noting that there are many big fish in the lower reaches of Houghton Creek. Late in the evening you'll be standing on the bank listening, watching, and testing your leader knot. A bat darts to the left and swoops low to take a large emerging dun. A small trout rises next to the rotted stump near your feet. Something large crosses downstream a few yards, and you can just make out the dim shape and white flick of the tail. Two decent fish start rising at midstream and then, back in the slick under the birch on the far bank, there is a sound not unlike a large pot hitting and scooping water at the same time. You will be pleased to be fishing Houghton Creek.

Notes:

- A 17-pound, 5-ounce brown trout has been taken from Houghton Creek.
- The Rose City bars have great pizza.
- Bring a camera. Wild turkey and deer are plentiful.

THE BIG CREEKS
Oscoda County, Crawford County

Feeding the majestic Au Sable between the towns of Grayling and Mio are two separate and distinct Big Creek systems (see the Au Sable River System map in chapter 3). The southward-flowing Big Creek headwaters are near the Oscoda-Crawford county line south of Lewiston and east of Lovells. It comprises the West, Middle, and East branches that course through the Au Sable State Forest and join near North Down River Road and Big Creek Trail. From this point it is only a short distance before Big Creek meets the North Branch of the Au Sable just a few river miles from the big river.

Big Creek is a smallish stream with relatively close quarters for the fly-fisher. It is manageable with a short rod and careful casting and is well worth the time and effort to explore. It is lightly fished (comparatively speaking), due largely to its close proximity to its glamorous, superstar neighbor and the requirement for accurate casting with light rods and fine tippets. Numerous county roads and forest service fire trails access all branches, and a quick tour will put you on the stretch that has the type of water you most enjoy fishing.

The fish are eager, plentiful, and opportunistic feeders. An angler could get by with only the Adams and Elk-Hair Caddis dry fly, Gold-Ribbed Hare's Ear and Caddis Creeper nymphs, and the Olive Woolly Bugger in size 10 as a complete day's assortment unless there is a hatch or spinner fall in progress.

What Big Creek's trout lack in size (average is about 10 inches) they make up for in beauty and wildness. They are pure and delicate and belong in their stream.

Northward-flowing Big Creek is home to some critical and demanding trout. Its gin-clear water and sophisticated residents will not tolerate poor presentation and careless wading. Long leaders, fine tippets, and stealth are the keys to success.

The village of Luzerne on MI 72 in Oscoda County is the center for operations on this fishery. Just downstream from Luzerne near CR 489 and north of Randall Road, the two arteries form Big Creek proper, which then journeys approximately 3½ river miles northward to the Au Sable. This is excellent water for the fly-rodder. Pools and riffles with sweeping curves and attendant deep-water holes are enhanced with tree stumps, logjams, and the cooling umbrella of tall trees. In this lower and larger section, Big Creek hosts mostly browns and rainbows. Although the average fish is about 12 inches, many much larger fish are caught each season, usually during the Brown Drake or Hex hatches or with a streamer fly-fished methodically through the darkness.

Upstream from Luzerne the West and East branches are both worth exploring. County roads and fire trails reach right to the headwaters of both stems of Big Creek and will take the angler to fish (now brook trout) that may never have seen an artificial fly. This is near-wilderness fishing and the joys and sorrows of the wilderness are in attendance. The fish are wild and generally gullible. The mosquitoes are wild and gluttonous.

Try the East Branch off Galloway Road north of Mapes Road. Start with a Royal Wulff or McGinty Bee and lather up with bug repellent. Just south of MI 72, Marble Road and CR 490 join close to the West Branch, and the fishing is very good either upstream or downstream from the bridge on CR 490.

You will quickly notice that this is not country-club angling. There are no amenities, nor is there present the blare of horns or streamside litter. The trails are made by deer and bear and the only sound you hear is the stream.

Notes:

- Black bears are reasonably plentiful here. It is unlikely you will see one but you might see tracks.
- Big Creek Preserve is located on Zimowske Road just west of MI 33. They have a superb, challenging sporting-clays course, a private lake for fishing, complete facilities for a bird hunt, and a 3-D archery range for a change of pace. Call Steve Basl at 517-826-3606.
- Have a beer or a soda at Ma Deeter's historic saloon in Luzerne.

SOUTH BRANCH RIVER
Ogemaw County, Iosco County

This is primarily a brown-trout fishery with long, placid, sand-bottomed stretches bordered by willow-lined bogs. The South Branch River is wild and pure with exceptionally clear water and little evidence of man-made stream improvements.

The entire river, from its merger with Harper Creek just west of Branch Road between the villages of Long Lake and South Branch to its mouth at the Au Sable River upstream from Loud Dam Pond, is easily fly-fished. Its width varies from 20 to 35 feet and its firm sand and gravel bottom allows slip-free wading.

From the bridge at Branch Road, looking eastward (downstream), the river flows relatively straight through a soft-edged bog. Your first look might convey the impression of barren water—little cover and very few fish. This is not the case. Selective browns hug the banks and edges from this bridge downstream to a large pond. This is a tricky area with mud and silt and very difficult bankside walking. Because of this difficulty this section is lightly fished.

After the South Branch flows beneath Wickert Road and through another short series of ponds, it follows a gentle northeasterly course roughly parallel to Liberty Road for about 4 miles before crossing Rollaway Road and descending to the Au Sable. This part of the river is accessible via several two-track fire trails cutting north from Liberty Road and is an interesting fishery with wide, open flats interspersed with tight curves, pools, and riffles. The average brown trout from this stretch of river will be 11 to 12 inches with some fish up to 15 inches and a rare find in the 18-inch class.

Mayfly and caddis populations are numerous and reliable. Hendricksons, Sulphurs, Olives, and Brown Drakes make their appearance predictably, and

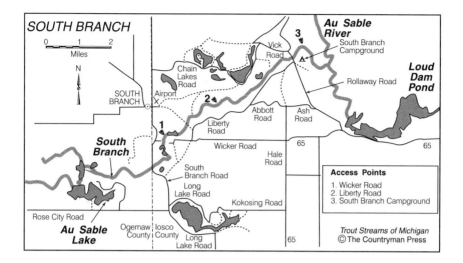

the Little Black Caddis is an entertaining and productive early season hatch. Terrestrials are very abundant, and cricket and ant (both cinnamon and black) artificials are productive throughout the season. Grasshoppers are a must from late July through September, and a dark Deer-Hair Mouse will bring coronary excitement in the evening hours all season long. The South Branch can be very generous to an angler fishing a 2- to 3-inch grayish tan marabou leech pattern under an overcast sky, and the Clouser minnow in various colors is effective in the deeper holes throughout the day. Favorite nymphs are just what you would expect to work on a wild stream. Gold-Ribbed Hare's Ears, Prince, Zug Bug, and the Halfback are attractors that you should carry along with Hendrickson, Brown Drake, and floating Blue-Winged Olive nymphs. Green and cream Latex Caddis larvae and pupae will complete your fly book for this stream, and an 8- or 9-foot rod balanced with a 5-weight line will handle all the requirements.

Notes:

- The biscuits and gravy at the Sunrise Cafe in nearby Lupton are fabulous and for the serious appetite.
- The Timbers Steak House in South Branch has very good food and a friendly smile.
- Drive slowly with a watchful eye on the roadside ditches. Deer cross at all times of the day.
- There are two very nice public campgrounds in the area. One is on the South Branch at Rollaway Road and another is on the Au Sable just 2 miles south.

EAST BRANCH AU GRES RIVER
Iosco County

Hale Creek and Smith Creek join forces south and east of the town of Hale near the intersection of MI 65 and Old State Road. At this junction the East Branch of the Au Gres is formed, and from this point downstream to Whittemore Road the angler is presented with firm-bottomed riffles and pools, wide and sunlighted runs with room for casting, and very obvious holding lies. The East Branch seems to have been created especially for the fly-rodder.

From the junction of Hale and Smith Creeks to Old State Road the East Branch of the Au Gres is lightly fished, averages 25 feet wide, and flows over a rock, gravel, and sand bottom. The oxygen-rich habitat is ideal and supports a healthy population of stoneflies, mayflies, caddis, midges, and dragonflies. The streamside vegetation and grasses contribute to the trout's food source in the form of ants and beetles throughout the season, and grasshoppers are abundant in the more open areas from mid-July through September.

Easiest access is from the bridge at Old State Road, and the fishing is pleasurable in either upstream or downstream directions. Mitchell Creek enters the East Branch just a few yards up from this bridge, and many casual anglers stop at this point and return to their cars. It's definitely worth pushing onward from here, and, if there is no visible hatch in progress, casting to the obvious cover with smallish attractor dries such as the Trude patterns in size 16, female Adams in size 18, or the tan or brown Bivisible in 14 and 16. Stonefly nymphs will produce throughout the season in this river, and lightly weighted black and brown patterns in size 10 and 12 should be tried in the deeper runs and shaded riffles. The trout in this section seem to favor brightly colored streamers and the Pass Lake and Spruce Fly in size 10 work well. An olive-tailed and -hackled, peacock-herl-bodied Woolly Bugger is an excellent choice as a general searching pattern.

Continuing downstream from Old State Road to MI 55, several creeks empty into the East Branch and increase its flow volume and width. This is a prime spawning area for steelhead in the spring and salmon in the fall. The Lake Huron–raised rainbows are in attendance until early May, so the fly-fisher should carry some Micro-Egg and stonefly nymph patterns and keep on the alert for spawning redds. The fish will generally hold in the closest heavy run or deeper hole immediately up- or downstream from a spawning redd, and these areas should be probed thoroughly. A dark mink, Zonker-style leech pattern seems to agitate the big fish and can provide some memorable moments on a light rod.

There are excellent caddis hatches in this stretch of water, and the early

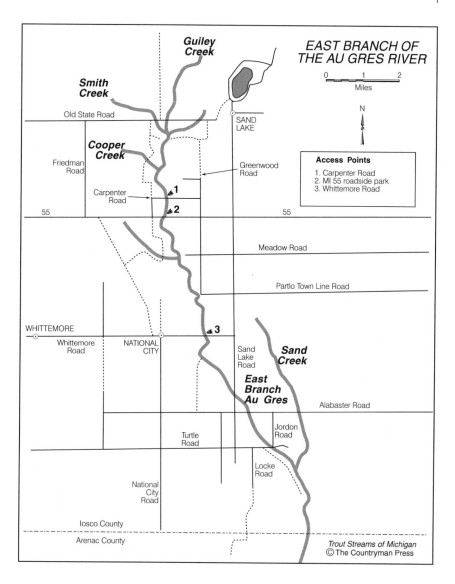

white caddis can be effectively matched with a size-16 light cream elk-hair pattern. Stonefly nymphs, Gold-Ribbed Hare's Ears, Emerging Caddis in cream, brown, and olive, and the Pheasant Tail in sizes 12, 14, and 16 will provide a well-rounded selection for this river. Small streamers are effective, and dark sculpin imitations are top producers. The dry-fly enthusiast can do very well with Dun and Cream Variants in sizes 14 and 16 in addition to the patterns listed earlier. Terrestrials are more and more in evidence as the river nears and crosses Carpenter Road. This section has many streamside homes and cottages and the lawns seem to encourage the ant, beetle, and grasshopper populations.

From Carpenter Road downstream to MI 55 the angler will fish through another prime spawning area for steelhead. The river is 35 to 45 feet wide in most places and bottomed with the fine gravel that is ideal for both steelhead and salmon. A black Woolly Bugger with a bright, lime-green head has produced some fine fish in the vicinity of Carpenter Road.

At the MI 55 crossing there is a very nice state-maintained roadside park with wooden stairs descending to the river and its wide gravel bed. This area of the river is easy to wade and there is ample room for longer back casts. Downstream to Whittemore Road the river has its highest density of anadromous fish and, of course, there is significantly early- and late-season pressure until the steelhead have returned to the lake and the salmon have died. From MI 55 to the mouth at Lake Huron, the East Branch has been open all year to facilitate the harvest of the big fish, and even if you are not interested in a cartwheeling, 20-pound king salmon, the late fall experience is rewarding. The colors are spectacular, the river is low and clear, and the resident trout are gorging on salmon eggs.

During midseason this stretch of the river is fished surprisingly little. It is easy wading and casting and the trout are eager for attractor dries, terrestrials, and slowly fished streamers. The light Spruce Fly is an excellent pattern in this water and, in the late evening, a Deer-Hair Mouse or large moth imitation will produce some hair-raising moments. The flow is heavier in these lower reaches and the bends have some spots that will soak a careless wader. Use common sense. If you are going to fish at or after dark, familiarize yourself with your selected fishing area in the daylight and do not stray.

Overall, the East Branch of the Au Gres is easy to navigate, and requires only moderate casting skill. It is a beautiful river with a naturally reproducing, wild-trout population and sizable runs of spawning steelhead and salmon. The surrounding hillsides abound with game and the river valley itself is very scenic. Do not forget to bring a camera.

Notes:

- Fly-tiers should keep an eye on the ground. There is a very good chance of finding turkey wing and tail feathers.
- East Tawas is a bustling, full-service town with a good fly shop, Nordic Sports.
- Tawas City and Oscoda have scenic vistas of the big lake, good restaurants, golf, tennis, and a wide range of attractions that will prove interesting to the tourist.

CEDAR RIVER
Gladwin County, Clare County

Gladwin and Clare Counties border Roscommon County to the south, and the city of Gladwin is approximately 20 minutes from the tourist mecca of Houghton Lake. Just west and a bit north of Gladwin, the Cedar River is a first-class brown trout stream with the best water beginning at and continuing upstream from Eagleson Road.

The bridge at Eagleson is a good starting point. The river here is 30 to 40 feet wide. Clear and cold, the Cedar has something for everyone. Its bottom of coarse and fine gravel, edged with sand and marl, harbors dense aquatic insect life. Its lively riffles and runs feed oxygen-rich water to the deep holes at the bends and, sweeping beneath overhanging vegetation and undercut banks, to the full-bodied and richly colored resident brown trout.

The stretch from Eagleson upstream to the bridge at Bard Road is a pleasant way to spend a leisurely morning or afternoon. It is about a 3-hour fishing episode at a casual pace and there is a reasonable chance of moving one or two very big fish with either weighted sculpin or crayfish imitations (light olive or sand colored), fished slowly in the deeper water and around tree stumps and snags. This part of the Cedar has quite a few backwater pockets and eddies with upcurrent swirls next to the banks. These are very often passed by without a cast, and it is definitely worth the minimal risk of losing a fly to drop an enticing streamer or large nymph into these big-fish refuges.

At Bard Road the river averages 30 to 35 feet wide with dense streamside foliage. This is an excellent piece of water for attractor dry-fly patterns and, in the morning, meaty streamer flies (such as the Spruce in size 8 or olive Woolly Bugger in size 10) fished up and across with a quick, darting retrieve. The crayfish pattern is also a good selection in this stretch.

Probably the best access point for this part of the Cedar is at Clarwin Road (also called County Line Road). Take Eagleson Road west 1.0 mile and the road turns into a narrow two-track descending a steep, rutted hill to the river. It's best to park at the top and off to the side; even a good, high-riding four-wheel drive is in jeopardy here. At the foot of the hill facing north, the river flows from left to right and there is very good fishing in either direction. Upstream about 40 yards, there is a deep hole where the river cuts a hard bend on your left side. The tail of this pool is quite productive during a mayfly or caddis emergence and should be approached with stealth under any condition as there are large fish in residence.

As mentioned earlier, the Cedar has prolific hatches, and dry-fly and nymph boxes should carry a complete seasonal selection. Mahogany duns and white caddis provide good sport in May, and March Browns and Brown

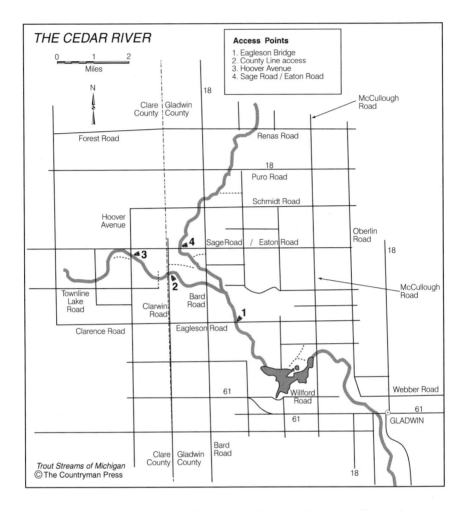

THE CEDAR RIVER

0   1   2
Miles

N

Access Points
1. Eagleson Bridge
2. County Line access
3. Hoover Avenue
4. Sage Road / Eaton Road

Clare County | Gladwin County

Forest Road

18

McCullough Road

Renas Road

18

Puro Road

Schmidt Road

Hoover Avenue

Oberlin Road

18

Sage Road / Eaton Road

≰4

≰3

≰2

Townline Lake Road

Clarwin Road

Bard Road

McCullough Road

Clarence Road

Eagleson Road

1

61

Willford Road

Webber Road

61

GLADWIN

Bard Road

Clare County | Gladwin County

Trout Streams of Michigan
© The Countryman Press

18

Drakes activate the fish throughout June. Terrestrials, especially crickets, are effective throughout the season in this section of the river system.

Hare's Ears, Pheasant Tails, and small dark stonefly nymphs fish well, and sculpin patterns (yellow Marabou Muddler is effective), Woolly Buggers, Light Spruce, and crayfish patterns are all that the Cedar requires.

Farther upstream at the bridge on Hoover Avenue (Clare County), the river is about 30 feet wide and very fishable for the fly-rodder up to the confluence of Cranberry Creek and the Middle Branch. This is still predominantly brown trout water although an occasional brook trout with wanderlust is found in the shaded side pockets. Fish the heads of riffles and bankside runs with weighted Hare's Ears or a small (size 10 or 12) rubber-legged pattern such as the Girdle Bug. If there is a hatch in progress you must match it fairly closely; otherwise the Adams or Elk-Hair Caddis will bring the fish to the surface.

The North Branch of the Cedar holds some very nice fish and is easily accessible at Eaton Road. Just east of the bridge there is a two-track heading north and this will take you to convenient streamside parking. The North Branch is 15 to 25 feet wide with dense vegetation streamside and very heavy beaver activity. You will not want to fish a rod much longer than 8 feet, and a 7- or 7½-footer for a 4-weight line is probably ideal.

In general, the fish here are not superselective or terribly sophisticated, but they are not foolish either. Royal and Grizzly Wulffs in size 12 along with the Adams and Elk-Hair Caddis will suffice unless there is an active hatch in progress. The Zug Bug and Prince nymphs work well along with the Hare's Ear and Caddis Creeper nymphs. Streamer patterns to carry include the Mickey Finn, Black Ghost, Woolly Bugger, and Muddler Minnow.

The Cedar River and its North Branch are beautiful, gentle, accommodating fisheries. They carry a healthy population of wild fish and are worthy of a day or more of your time.

Notes:

- Gladwin, Beaverton, and Harrison are all nearby and are full-service communities.
- Lost Arrow Resort north of Gladwin has an excellent restaurant and bar.

THE PINE RIVER
Iosco County, Alcona County

The Pine River and its many smaller tributaries are largely overlooked by visitors to Michigan's scenic Highlands. Trout fishing in this area is centered—riveted is perhaps a better word—on the Au Sable, and so many miles of fishable water go essentially untouched throughout the season.

Backus Creek, Gimlet Creek, McGillis Creek, Kurtz Creek, and Wallace Creek, among others, join in the Huron National Forest in southeastern Alcona County in the general vicinity of County Roads F 30 and F 41 to form the Pine River. South and continuing slightly eastward from the bridge on F 41 about 5 miles from the Lake Huron shore, the Pine crosses into Iosco County, flows into Van Etten Lake near Oscoda, and then into the Au Sable near its mouth.

Like the Au Sable, the lower Pine hosts steelhead and salmon runs in season, but save this point any reasonable comparison ceases. The Au Sable is famous and majestic while the Pine flows in anonymous quietude with only light fishing pressure and hiking traffic.

In its upper reaches the Pine is nearly deserted throughout the trout season. Many of its trout have rarely seen an artificial fly, and the prospect of bumping into another angler, particularly on a weekday, is very remote. At

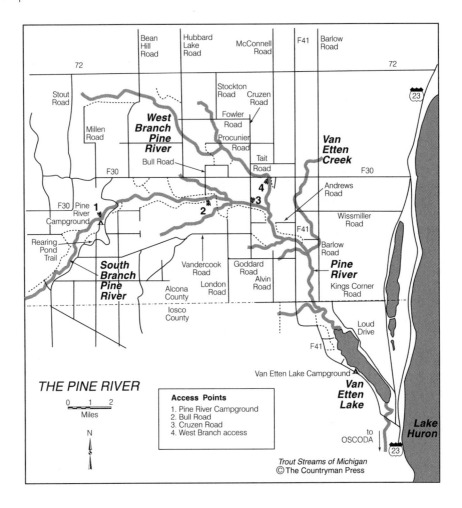

THE PINE RIVER

0   1   2
Miles

N

Access Points
1. Pine River Campground
2. Bull Road
3. Cruzen Road
4. West Branch access

Trout Streams of Michigan
©The Countryman Press

the upper end of the fly-fishable water is the Pine River Campground, which is just downstream from the junctions of Kurtz Creek and Wallace Creek, and south of F 30 (Mikado-Glennie Road), and east 0.75 mile from Adams Road. This national forest campground is small (only 11 rustic sites) with stately Norway pines, a log pavilion for sheltered picnics, and best of all, immediate access to the stream via a short downhill path from the pavilion. The Pine is 10 to 12 feet wide here with consistent bankside cover in the form of logs, overhanging limbs, and undercuts. The current is lively, the water is clear, and the fish are wild, brightly hued, and eager. Short rods and accurate, upstream spot fishing with roll casts are necessary to take fish from the campground area downstream to Bull Road near the national forest boundary and the influx of water from McGillis Creek and McDonald Creek. Throughout this stretch the Pine (and its tributaries) supports brook, brown, and rainbow trout, all eager for a chance at dry or wet fly.

The West Branch of the Pine River joins the South Branch south of Mikado Road and east of Cruzen Road and there is a significant size increase below this junction pool. The West Branch supports trout into its upper reaches near MI 72 and Stout Road, but the best fly-fishing is in a relatively short stretch upstream from the bridge on Cruzen Road to its merger with the South Branch and the formation of the main stream of the Pine River. As in the South Branch, brook, brown, and rainbow trout are found throughout the West Branch. Generally speaking, the Adams, Elk-Hair Caddis, and an attractor pattern such as a Royal Wulff or Renegade will bring fish topside. A Prince nymph, or Gold-Ribbed Hare's Ear, and a small Muddler or Mickey Finn will complete wet-fly needs.

The view from the bridge over the Pine River at F 41 in southern Alcona County shows a stream of 25 to 30 feet in width flowing slowly over a sand and fine-gravel bottom. The river bends through well-shaded, wadable reaches to its meeting with Duval and Van Etten creeks. From here the Pine crosses King's Corner Road and flows south to Van Etten Lake, the Au Sable, and mighty Lake Huron. This lower stretch of the Pine holds some very respectable brown trout and not a few rainbows. An occasional brook trout may be caught but their presence diminishes downstream from Andrews Road. The Pine produces excellent caddis hatches and its trout seem to be always on the lookout for wind-blown terrestrials. Grasshopper imitations in August and crickets and ants from June to September are very effective. Fishing the lower reaches of the Pine can produce some surprises on large nymphs and streamers. A 9-foot rod for a 6-weight line is a good choice, and a 3X dropper knotted to a small egg pattern is a thoughtful approach to taking a trophy.

Notes:

- The surrounding countryside is very scenic throughout the summer, and the fall is spectacular. Bring color film.
- Oscoda is a full-service community that gladly caters to tourists.
- Harrisville, a few miles to the southeast of the Pine River valley, has several good restaurants and a friendly atmosphere and hosts one of the largest art festivals in the state.

11 Thunder Bay Territory

The extreme northeastern lower peninsula is the pride of the "Sunrise Side." Cheboygan, Presque Isle, Alpena, Montmorency, and Otsego Counties are blessed with rolling hills, deep, clear lakes, abundant wildlife including the majestic elk, cold and clear trout streams, and compelling vistas. The major cities of Cheboygan, Alpena, and Gaylord are large enough to support fine restaurants, ski resorts, antiques dealers, and luxurious golf clubs, but small enough to remain relaxed, friendly, and comfortable.

Interstate 75 cuts the western edge of Thunder Bay Territory, and US 23 follows the scenic shoreline of Lake Huron. Either avenue can deliver an angler to the heart of the region from the airport in Detroit in about 3½ hours. Tourist accommodations are plentiful and range from small, homey, backcountry, lakeshore cabins to the fine wine and Victorian elegance of the Grand Hotel on Mackinac Island.

There are numerous festivals, art shows, band concerts, and boat races throughout the summer months. The conclusion of the Mackinac Island yacht races is worth a special boat ride to the finish line. While you are waiting for the commencement of the general hoopla surrounding the leading boats, take a cab ride (horse drawn—no motorized vehicles are allowed) and try a piece of the world's best fudge.

PIGEON RIVER
Otsego County, Cheboygan County

Most of the flow of the Pigeon River is nestled within the 98,000 acres that constitute the Pigeon River State Forest. Northeast of Gaylord and directly east of Vanderbilt and Wolverine, this forest is home to Michigan's thriving elk herd, the reintroduced pine marten, bear, bobcat, and bald eagle.

The Pigeon River enters the forest boundaries just upstream from Stur-

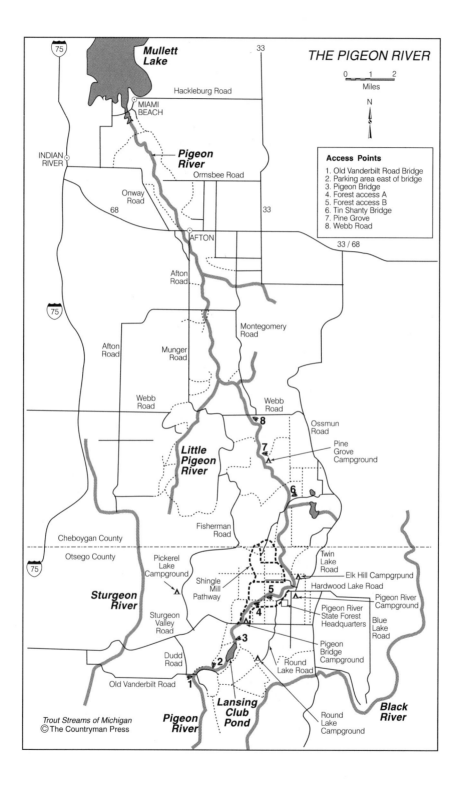

THE PIGEON RIVER

0   1   2
Miles

N

Access Points
1. Old Vanderbilt Road Bridge
2. Parking area east of bridge
3. Pigeon Bridge
4. Forest access A
5. Forest access B
6. Tin Shanty Bridge
7. Pine Grove
8. Webb Road

Mullett Lake

75

Hackleburg Road

MIAMI BEACH

INDIAN RIVER

Pigeon River

Ormsbee Road

Onway Road

68

33

33

AFTON

Afton Road

33 / 68

Montegomery Road

75

Afton Road

Munger Road

Afton Road

Webb Road

Webb Road

8

Ossmun Road

Pine Grove Campground

7

Little Pigeon River

6

Fisherman Road

Cheboygan County

Otsego County

75

Pickerel Lake Campground

Twin Lake Road

Elk Hill Campgrund

Hardwood Lake Road

Shingle Mill Pathway

Sturgeon River

5

Pigeon River Campground

Pigeon River State Forest Headquarters

Blue Lake Road

Sturgeon Valley Road

4

Dudd Road

3

Pigeon Bridge Campground

2

Round Lake Road

Old Vanderbilt Road

1

Trout Streams of Michigan
© The Countryman Press

Pigeon River

Lansing Club Pond

Round Lake Campground

Black River

geon Valley Road approximately 7 miles east of Vanderbilt. The first fly-fishable area is located in the area of the Old Vanderbilt Road Bridge off Dudd Road to the south of Sturgeon Valley Road. Here the river ranges from 25 to 30 feet wide with room to fly-cast in most cases. The bottom is firm sand mixed with some fine to medium-sized gravel. The clear, cold flow averages between 1 and 3-plus feet in depth, and the downed cedar logs, stumps, and banks provide shelter for the resident brook trout.

An 8-foot rod for a 4- or 5-weight line is ideal for fishing in the general vicinity of the Old Vanderbilt Road Bridge. Roll casts are sometimes required due to overhanging tree limbs and brush, and a 4 or 5-weight has enough muscle to deliver a 25-foot roll cast to a lively run and still settle the fly with some delicacy.

Very small olive Woolly Buggers with a single strand of black Krystal Flash in the body will bring fish out of the stumps and from under the banks. A size-10 or -12 Light Spruce is another effective streamer, and the Beaman's Ghost is always a top brook trout producer. Hare's Ears, tied extra spiky and in different shades, are the only nymphs required. Topside patterns can be limited to the egg-sac Irresistible, Lime Trude, and Royal Wulff.

Just a bit farther east (0.4 mile) from the bridge there is a small parking area on the north side of the road. A path leads from the parking area directly to the river, a distance of about 50 yards. At this site, the river has a slower, smoother surface, depths reaching 4 feet, and some heavy cover for larger-than-average fish. The bottom is fine gravel and sand, which makes for generally easy wading, but despite the first impression, this is not hip-boot water. Minimally, waist-high waders are in order and chest high is a better choice. Just upstream from the point where the path reaches the river there is a slow, gentle curve and, at the outside edge of this curve, the bank is heavily undercut with a depth in the 4-foot range. With a careful approach, a dead-drift with a Hare's Ear, or a slow retrieve with a Woolly Bugger, there is a good possibility of a solid take from a very respectable brook trout. If the wind is blowing even a little in late summer the fish seem to be ever watchful for unfortunate terrestrials, and a large, yellow-bodied hopper is the fly to use. Alternatively, sipping rises next to the grass beg for coverage with a size-18 or -20 black ant.

The Shingle Mill Pathway begins at the Pigeon Bridge Campground on Sturgeon Valley Road 8.0 miles east of Vanderbilt. This pathway has several "loops" of varying distance and difficulty and some of these loops follow the course of the Pigeon River for several miles. By starting at the Pigeon Bridge a hiking angler can follow the downstream course of the river through very lightly fished territory all the way to the Cheboygan County line.

The river at the bridge on Sturgeon Valley Road is fairly heavily fished but still worth the time to make a few casts. It is 30 to 35 feet wide with a sand and gravel bottom and depths ranging from 1 to 4 feet. The wading is generally easy and the obvious holding areas will usually produce fish if approached carefully. Brown trout and a few rainbows join with the brookies to add a measure of diversity to the fly-fishing near the campground and in the immediate bridge vicinity.

If you are not a backpacker or hiker, it is possible to reach some of the Pigeon's most lightly fished stretches via automobile. It will help greatly (at least with peace of mind) if your vehicle is a high-clearance, four-wheel drive. The first such downstream access can be reached by turning left (north) just 0.4 mile east of the bridge on Sturgeon Valley Road. The two-track road is centered between two large trees with painted yellow spots on their trunks. This two-track parallels a power line and runs 0.8 mile through some deep, heavily rutted spots, to a dead end at the river.

Fishing upstream from this spot will take the angler through some very tight cover and very heavy streamside foliage. Roll casts are usually necessary to present the fly fairly to the eager brook trout. About 300 yards upstream, the river flows through a very large open meadow with some deep pools and exciting runs near the banks. There are large brown trout alongside the brookies in this meadow area and occasionally a respectable rainbow will take your streamer or nymph.

About 200 yards downstream from the parking spot there is a fairly large, recent beaver dam on the river. The dammed-up water is almost impossible to fly-fish but the water immediately upstream and downstream can be very productive. This section of the Pigeon has some very dense caddis populations, and the Elk-Hair Caddis in olive, brown, and cream and in sizes 12–16 is a very productive fly. Similarly, the Caddis Creeper nymph is a good pattern just about anytime.

The next two-track heading north from Sturgeon Valley Road is also open to motor vehicles and will take you right to the river's bank. Another 0.5 mile farther east on Sturgeon Valley Road brings you to a dirt road marked as number 80. This road heads due north for 1.0 mile to its dead end at the Pigeon and a small parking area deep in the woods.

This spot is downstream several hundred yards from the beaver-dam site mentioned earlier. It is typified by a sandy-edged, gravel bottom and a 25-foot-wide flow ranging to 3 feet in depth. Heavy, overhanging trees provide shade and the lively current shelters a good population of brook trout in the deeper runs and holes.

Attractor patterns are productive unless there is a hatch in progress. Look for Blue-Winged Olives throughout the season as a supplement to the prolific caddis. Small gray leech patterns and the Light Spruce Fly entice fish in hatchless periods, and a small Woolly Bugger is always worth trying for a few casts.

A short distance farther east on Sturgeon Valley Road there is an intersection with Twin Lakes Road. Drive north on Twin Lakes Road to the forest headquarters building and pick up a copy of the Pigeon River Country State Forest Access Map and a copy of the Shingle Mill Pathway Map. These two will be invaluable guides as you further pursue access to the Pigeon River's trout, either by foot or by vehicle.

Two extremely high-traffic areas on the Pigeon River are at the Pigeon River Campground north of the forest area headquarters building and the Elk Hill Camp farther downstream and north off Twin Lakes Road. The river in both camping areas holds brook, brown, and rainbow trout and is quite lovely, but the popularity and the subsequent liveliness of both spots are not conducive to the contemplative aspects of angling.

At the Otsego-Cheboyan county line, Twin Lakes Road changes its name to Osmun Road. Just about 1.0 mile north of the county line, or 1.2 miles south (on Osmun Road) from the sign for the Cornwall Creek Flooding, there is an unnamed, dirt county road angling to the southwest. If you have a dependable four-wheel drive the following route will take you to a very lightly fished and highly productive stretch of the Pigeon River. Take this road southwest for 0.5 mile to a left-hand turn and follow this left fork for 0.4 mile to a poor two-track headed due west. This two-track is Forest Road 47 and is marked on the Forest Access Map you picked up at the headquarters building. Follow FR 47 westward for 0.9 mile, to a perpendicular intersection with another two-track, then continue on, straight west, to the sand barricades at the end of FR 47.

From the small parking spot at the sand barricades the two-track continues for nearly 200 yards to a very small, meadowlike opening in the forest. This meadow is on the east bank of the river and there is premium fly-fishing for brook, brown, and rainbow trout in both upstream and downstream venues. The river averages 35 feet wide in this area with a gravel and rock bottom and a depth ranging from 1 to 4 feet.

One late August day was abnormally cold with gusting winds and scattered clouds. The river was low and crystalline and showed splashy rises every minute or so in both directions. Grasshoppers, a bit stiff with cold, were being blown into the stream from both banks. A size-12 Dave's Hopper produced several rainbows and one brook trout on the upstream foray, and the same-sized Clark Lynn nymph hooked fish on a downstream swing of 200 yards or so. Proceeding downstream into a less open area, the Grizzly Spruce brought several short strikes and one large brookie of 13 inches to hand. There was no evidence of other vehicular traffic on the two-tracks and the only footprints on the bank were of elk, deer, and raccoon.

The bridge on Tin Shanty Road can be reached by proceeding north on Osmun Road to the sign for the Cornwall Flooding area. This is 1.2 miles

PIGEON RIVER COUNTRY FOREST

POLICY: TO MANAGE THE PIGEON RIVER COUNTRY TO PROTECT AND MAINTAIN THE NATURAL BEAUTY OF ITS FORESTS AND WATERS, AND TO SUSTAIN A HEALTHY ELK HERD AND WILDLIFE POPULATIONS.

OBJECTIVES ARE: 1. TO PROVIDE FAVORABLE HABITAT FOR ELK. 2. TO PROVIDE NEEDED FOOD, COVER AND SECLUSION FOR WILDLIFE. 3. TO PROVIDE RECREATION IN KEEPING WITH THE WILD CHARACTER OF THE AREA. 4. TO MANAGE GAME SPECIES FOR HUNTING AND VIEWING OPPORTUNITIES. 5. TO PROTECT THE WATER QUALITY AND TO MANAGE STREAMS AND LAKES FOR A NATURAL FISHERY. 6. TO MANAGE, HARVEST, AND USE THE TIMBER AND MINERAL RESOURCES OF THE AREA FOR THE GOOD OF MAN. 7. TO PROTECT THE PIGEON RIVER COUNTRY FROM OVER-USE AND OVER-DEVELOPMENT WHICH WOULD DESTROY ITS WILD CHARACTER.

BOB LINSENMAN

north of the turnoff to the immediately preceding locale. Turn left at the Cornwall Flooding sign and drive west 2.1 miles to the bridge. There is parking on both sides of this older bridge. The current here is slow with a smooth, glassy surface flowing over a sand bottom with stretches of fine gravel. The depth ranges from 1 to 3 feet, deeper in a few holes at the edges of turns, in the 40- to 45-foot-wide stream. Bankside overhangs, sunken logs, aquatic grasses, and undercuts hold the fish.

The trout at Tin Shanty are a balanced population of browns, brooks, and rainbows and all three are insistent on careful casting with long leaders and fine tippets. The smooth surface and slow current allow careful inspection and only the dead of night or a very dark overcast will cover mistakes. The same flies described elsewhere work in the vicinity of Tin Shanty, but smaller sizes are recommended as a rule.

Farther downstream the Pine Grove Campground sits tight on the banks of the river. Proceed north on Osmun Road about 3 miles to the sign indicating the direction to the campground. This left turn is onto Webb Road, then another quick left leads 2-plus miles downhill to Pine Grove. The campsites are within a very short walk down a small hill to the Pigeon. Trails follow the stream's course throughout this area and it is an easy matter to follow them back to camp. Campsite number one has a short trail that leads directly to the bank of the river at the tail of a very deep hole.

Although the bottom is visible, the water is deep enough to fill the waders of an NBA center, and the slick clay edges provide additional hazards to safety.

The river affords ideal cover for large trout throughout the Pine Grove area. It has dense, overhanging vegetation, deep runs, holes, and undercut banks, and enough sunken timber to build several barns. The stream ranges from 25 to 35 feet wide with a depth exceeding 4 feet in places. Roll casts are often necessary to put a fly on the water instead of in a tree or bush. Brook, brown, and rainbow trout are present in good numbers and some reach hefty proportions. Look for the larger fish in the very deepest holes and under the darkest banks. Fish a long line downstream (wade very carefully and slowly) with a size-10 Hare's Ear as a dropper and a size-6 Woolly Bugger or Marabou Muddler as the point fly.

The next downstream access is very easy to reach from Pine Grove. Drive back north on the campground road to Webb Road and turn left. The bridge on Webb Road is less than 2 miles west.

This is, for the most part, an all-gravel bottom with some large rocks. The current is fast but wadable with felt soles, as the rocks are not terribly slippery and the water is very clear, allowing the angler to see well and pre-select foot placement. The depth ranges from 1 to 3-plus feet and the 40- to 45-foot average width makes for easy casting.

The trout cover is very obvious. Most fish are found ahead of or behind large rocks, under overhanging vegetation at the banks, or near sunken timber in the deeper holes. Downstream 50 yards from the bridge, the river makes a hard left turn and then parallels Webb Road for several yards. The outside, high sand bank is deeply undercut and holds some large browns that will take at dawn or dusk if approached very cautiously. The left-hand bank, facing downstream, is very shallow over hard-packed, dark sand and allows an easy approach to the best water, but a heavy foot will push alarming waves directly into the hole at the foot of the hill.

The river upstream from the bridge holds browns and rainbows and some brook trout. The coarse gravel bottom is easily waded and the stream's general openness affords little difficulty in casting.

Sculpin and crayfish patterns of somber hue in small sizes are often productive near the bridge at Webb Road. Olives and caddis are common and the Pheasant Tail and Caddis Creeper are good nymphs to send into the pockets and runs. The Elk-Hair Caddis, Adams, White Wulff, and Irresistible will raise fish if there is no obvious emergence or spinner fall in progress.

Downstream from Webb Road there are additional access points to the Pigeon. If you have time and the inclination, explore a bit. Pigeon River Road, Afton Road, and MI 68 cross the Pigeon east of Wolverine and Indian River and are easily reached just a few minutes' drive from either town.

Canoes start to become an issue from Webb Road north but generally they are not a nuisance.

The Pigeon is a lovely river flowing through a large, carefully managed state forest with tightly controlled vehicular traffic. The sights, sounds, and smells are nearly all wild and the fishing, with some planned exploration, can be wonderful.

Notes:

- There are several very nice campgrounds in the state forest that are close to fishing, hiking, and elk-viewing areas.
- Some of the best elk-viewing areas include Fontinalis Road near the Cheboygan county line, Pickerel Lake Road near Honey Locust Trail, Range Line Road and Elk Trail, and Sawdust Trail near Tin Shanty Trail.
- The Gateway and Blue Goose restaurants in Vanderbilt have good food, friendly service, and reasonable prices.
- A nature hike along the Shingle Mill Pathway can be planned to fit individual physical conditions and time constraints. Pick up a map at the headquarters building.

BLACK RIVER
Otsego County, Montmorency County, Cheboygan County

The Black is another beautiful trout stream nestled in the heart of Michigan's thriving elk herd. It originates in east-central Otsego County and reaches fly-fishability at the Tin Shanty Bridge about 3 miles southeast of the head-quarters of the Pigeon River State Forest. From there the Black winds through some lovely country with relatively easy access, until it reaches extensive private holdings in western Montmorency County and southeastern Cheboygan County. It exits the Black River Ranch south of Clark Bridge Road and proceeds northeast through the Mackinaw State Forest into Presque Isle County for a few hundred yards, then back into Cheboygan County for an extended northward run into Black Lake and, finally, into the south channel of the Straits of Mackinaw (Lake Huron) at the town of Cheboygan. Overall, the new coldwater regulations are having a postive impact on the average size of the brook trout in the Black.

Historically, the brook trout population of the Black River System has had growth rates significantly above the state average, but has been subject to considerable fluctuation in the sheer number of trout. These fluctuations are not completely understood but are the object of continuing research by the Michigan Department of Natural Resources. Currently, brook trout populations are low but improving for the area around Crockett Bridge and downstream. Anglers should concentrate efforts in the upstream sections between Tin Shanty Bridge and Clark Bridge Road.

Tin Shanty Bridge is found by driving east, past the Pigeon Bridge Forest Campground on Sturgeon Valley Road, for approximately 3 miles. Take a right turn on Tin Shanty Bridge Road and drive south 2.0 miles to the bridge over the Black River.

Upstream from the bridge the river is flat and smooth with a 30-foot-wide channel and relatively slow current flowing over a sand bottom at depths ranging from 1 to 3 feet. The middle of the river is largely barren, with most fish holding near the banks under the considerable cover of the alders. Downstream from the bridge the water is lively and pretty. It flows quickly and dances over gravel and large rocks, through tight bends, and through log tangles. The trout cover here is readily apparent and, although roll casting is often required, it is a relaxing, pleasant area to fish.

The brookies near Tin Shanty are not large, but they are responsive to a fairly presented fly. Dace streamers work very well in sizes 10 and 12 and the Thunder Creek series is effective. Small Muddlers, the Pass Lake, and the Mickey Finn should be tried as well. Nymphs that are impressionistic are the best bet. As always the Hare's Ear is the first choice. Dry patterns should be high-riding and easy to see on the water. The Royal Wulff, Lime Trude, and Irresistible in sizes 12–16 should cover 95 percent of the situations you will likely encounter in this section.

In addition to the limited parking near the bridge, there is an unimproved campsite on the river, downstream from the bridge, that can be reached by driving 0.2 mile north from the bridge to a two-track heading east (right). Follow this trail for 0.3 mile to the campsite on your right. The river is at the foot of the small hill and is 20 to 25 feet wide. It flows over sand and fine gravel with very heavy overhanging cover from the streamside alders. Roll casts are necessary to reach the free-rising brookies, and ants, beetles, crickets, and small grasshopper patterns are your best bets most of the time.

Continuing north past this access point for another 0.2 mile you will come to a good gravel road and a state campground sign. Follow this road east for approximately 1 mile (you will notice a sign indicating a high-country scenic area) and you will come to Forest Road 118. This is a sandy two-track that heads directly to the river and an unimproved campsite after just 0.1 mile. From this campsite a narrow path leads through grass and over downed logs for a 40-yard stroll to the Black.

Your first impression here will be that there is not enough water to provide cover for the fish. At the path's end the river is 45 feet wide and extremely shallow, but immediately upstream and downstream the channel averages only 25 feet wide with a deep enough flow to shelter respectable

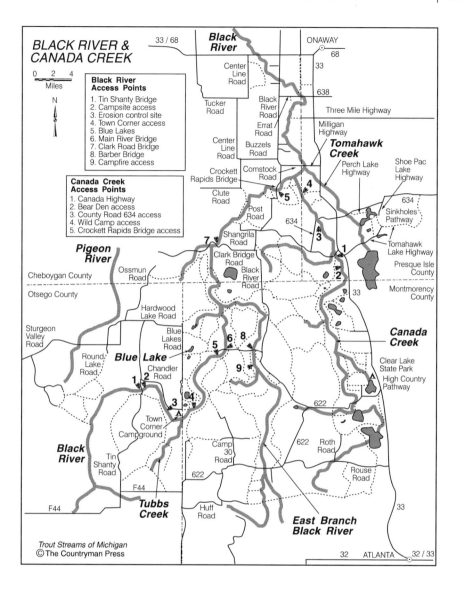

BLACK RIVER & CANADA CREEK

33 / 68

0   2   4
Miles

N

Black River Access Points
1. Tin Shanty Bridge
2. Campsite access
3. Erosion control site
4. Town Corner access
5. Blue Lakes
6. Main River Bridge
7. Clark Road Bridge
8. Barber Bridge
9. Campfire access

Canada Creek Access Points
1. Canada Highway
2. Bear Den access
3. County Road 634 access
4. Wild Camp access
5. Crockett Rapids Bridge access

Pigeon River

Black River

Tubbs Creek

Blue Lake

Tomahawk Creek

Canada Creek

East Branch Black River

Trout Streams of Michigan
© The Countryman Press

fish. This section has depths ranging to 3 feet, a largely gravel bottom, snags, and tight alder overhangs covering some deep, bankside cuts.

Terrestrials, small dace-imitating streamers, and Latex Caddis nymphs should be roll cast into the dark water closest to the banks. This will cause more than a few hookups with brush as well as fish, so patience and a well-stocked fly box will be helpful.

Continuing eastward from this access for an additional 1.2 miles will bring you to another parking spot that is easy to locate and very close to the fishing. It is right at the point that the main gravel road makes a sweep to the left and there is a short trail off to the right. This trail is only a few yards long and ends in a parking area on a hill overlooking the river.

Some erosion-control work has been completed here recently and anglers should take care in approaching the stream from the parking spot. At the very base of the rock control bed there is a fairly deep run that, despite its proximity to the road, usually holds fish. Hare's Ears and Fox Squirrel nymphs work well in this stretch and a small grasshopper with a pale yellow or cream body is a good late-summer selection.

From this access point continue until you see the sign for the Town Corner Lake Campground and follow this road past the campsites and the boat launch. Bear left at the boat-launch sign and follow this trail for about 1 mile to its dead end at private property. This is the Town Corner access.

All along this road, from the boat-launch area to the dead end, you are driving parallel to the Black River. Several trails break off to campsites (no facilities here) along the right. These campsites are on a small hill and the river is directly below them. It is an easy walk to the stream and paths lead along the banks, providing comfortable navigation.

The stream in the campground section is about 30 feet wide with a firm sand and gravel bottom. The depth varies from 1 to 3-plus feet and fly-casting is fairly easy. Dace, sculpin, darters, and a healthy variety of caddis and mayfly populations provide a good forage base for brook trout up to and exceeding 12 inches in length. A small Muddler Minnow with a tiny split shot pinched to the leader right at the hook eye is very effective in this part of the river.

The next downstream access is the Blue Lakes Ranch area, and the Black River borders this private property for a considerable distance. To reach the Blue Lakes area, retrace your route from the Town Corner Lake Campground to the main gravel road and drive north for 3.7 miles to a spot where the road forks. Take the right fork, which will run east, south, and east again, for 3.7 miles. At this point a two-track runs 0.2 mile to the southwest and ends at a large parking area. A well-marked trail leads from this parking area 300 yards to the river.

Another Blue Lakes Ranch access is just a short distance farther east on the main gravel road. Approximately 0.75 mile past the first Blue Lakes access there is a large open parking area on the north side of the road. There is room here for several cars, and a prominently positioned sign displays a map delineating private property and public access along the Black River in this immediate area.

Directly across from the parking area there are two wooden posts marked with blue paint. Between these posts is the beginning of the footpath to the river. This footpath is bordered every 30 yards or so with splashes of blue paint or blue ribbon on the trees and it would be truly difficult to get lost.

At the exact point where the path ends at the water, the river is slow, shallow, and flat over a dark silt bottom, and this is a very unattractive view after a 250-yard walk. Just downstream from this spot, perhaps 15 or 20 yards, the river takes a hard bend to the left and picks up velocity over a clear gravel bottom. From this area on, downstream to the Main River Bridge, the Black has beautiful cover, lively runs, deep holes and cuts, over-hangs, and enough vigorous, shining trout to please the twelve apostles.

About 150 yards below the path from the parking area you will notice a cabin on the far bank. This is the Gaylord Fishing Club property and its holdings extend downstream on both banks to the road (another 250 yards or so). Just downstream from the building there is a deceptively deep hole that needs to be carefully circumnavigated and, following this hole, there are two more about 40 yards apart. Each of these deep covers will be noticed in plenty of time to fish carefully. A weighted Woolly Bugger is a fair choice as a general enticer. A small Muddler or Light Spruce will also create a stir. The Main River Bridge is just a few yards below the last deep spot, and below this point the property is owned by the Black River Ranch. Strictly speaking, one should stay in the river when fishing this area, but it is allow-able to get out of the water to avoid deep water, a snag, or other hazard.

The Black River from the Blue Lakes parking area to the Main River Bridge and below into the Black River Ranch property, ranges from 30 to 35 feet in width and has depths from 1 to 4-plus feet. It is open enough for tra-ditional casting but an occasional roll cast is required. It is beautiful water in a beautiful countryside.

From the Main River Bridge it is a 0.25-mile (uphill) walk back to your automobile at the parking area on the north side of the road. You can reach the next downstream public access by driving east across Main River Bridge and across the East Branch of the Black for about 2.5 miles to Black River Road. If you want to try the Clark Bridge area, turn left (north) and drive approximately 5.0 miles to Clark Bridge Road. Drive west on Clark Bridge Road for 2.25 miles to the bridge. There is parking space at the bridge or you can drive another 0.2 mile to a two-track road headed south. This road fol-lows the river closely for several hundred yards and there is a parking area at the end of the trail.

Further downstream at Crockett Rapids Bridge, a new access is provid-ing some excellent fishing, especially in the spring of the year. Walk south on the road from the bridge to a two-track on the west side. Follow this two-track to its dead end at a fence. You will find a small stairway that descends to the river. There are some nice fish in and near the gravel riffles in this area.

This stretch of river has, over the years, produced good catches of brook trout with an occasional brown trout thrown into the mix. This part of the stream is below the junction with the East Branch and it has greatly increased its width and depth. Very careful wading is required. Muddler Minnows, Light and Grizzly Spruce, Pass Lake, and crayfish imitations produce heavy strikes in the vicinity of Clark Bridge. Grasshoppers, ants, and beetles should be in your box alongside attractors like the Royal Wulff, Lime Trude, and Renegade. Hare's Ears, Pheasant Tails, small Brown and Black Stonefly nymphs, and olive Latex Caddis larvae will make up an adequate nymph selection for the lower Black.

The East Branch of the Black River is best fly-fished in the immediate vicinity of Barber Bridge, which is 1.3 miles east of the Main River Bridge referred to earlier. The East Branch at Barber Bridge ranges from 25 to 30 feet wide. It flows over a sand and gravel bottom at depths ranging from 1 to 4-plus feet. The banks are heavily overgrown with tag alders and, in the bends, hide trout within deep cuts. There are a goodly number of logs and stumps in the stream and trout use these as shelter even in midcurrent.

The silt edges and mud banks support burrowing nymphs, and strong populations of Brown Drake *(simulans)* and Hex *(limbata)* are present. Caddis populate the river along with Brown and Yellow Stoneflies and Sulphurs *(dorothea)*. This rich soup is flavored more with crayfish, dace, and sculpin.

Upstream from the bridge the surface is smooth and slow and the brook trout are typically found tight to or under the banks. Downstream is more vivacious with a livelier current and more pronounced holding and feeding zones. The downstream section is banked by Black River Ranch property and the immediate upstream water flows through private property as well. The fly-fisher must stay in the river in order to be in compliance with the law.

To avoid confusion and a possible long discussion on the nuances of riparian rights, drive east past Barber Bridge for 1.3 miles to a T in the road (this is Black River Road—by turning left you will be heading north toward Clark Bridge Road) and turn right (south). You will shortly pass a two-track with an iron gate on your right, and just a short distance beyond this gate you will observe another two-track headed off to the right. This trail mixes with several others, crosses a shallow ravine, and proceeds 0.2 mile to the river and a parking spot next to a campfire ring. The river is down a fairly sharp but short slope about 40 yards from the parking area. This is state-owned land.

The East Branch in this area is 25 to 30 feet wide and quite deep in spots, certainly over most chest-high waders at the outside of some of the curves. Stumps, logs, heavy foliage, and deep water bring good news and bad news. The bad news is that roll casts and extremely cautious wading are requisite to a rewarding excursion. The good news is that this is exceptionally fine trout water that is not often fished with the methodical precision required to take the much larger-than-average brook trout.

The deep runs and holes should be fished slowly and repeatedly. If a spot looks as though it should hold a 14-inch trout, it probably does. Fish heavily weighted streamers with a slow, pulsing, drop-back retrieve. Cast weighted nymphs, a small Yuk Bug for example, as tight to the bank as possible and give the fly a modest twitch or two on its drift. If there is a good wind on a hot day, this is grasshopper heaven. Make your artificial hit with a hard splat and give it a quick twitch to start the float.

The two-track that brought you to this spot parallels the river for several hundred yards upstream before turning back out to the main gravel road, and there are several convenient places to park and enter the stream along the course. The fishing can be very good in this stretch if you remember to wade cautiously, cast precisely, and fish methodically and with patience.

The fastest way out of this maze is to continue on the main gravel road in a southeasterly direction for about 8 miles to MI 33. You will cross over the headwaters of Canada Creek and pass Clear Lake just before hitting the state highway north of Atlanta.

Notes:

- Elk Ridge Golf Course (Atlanta), Cedar Valley Golf Club (Comins), and the Fairview Golf Club (Fairview) are all pleasant, easy to play, and inexpensive.
- The Country Road House, across from the fairgrounds north of Atlanta, has very good food, fair prices, and warm, friendly service.
- Onaway is a full-service community with golf, good restaurants, and shopping.
- The Redwood Steak House in Lewiston has fresh seafood and first-class beef.

CANADA CREEK
Montmorency County, Presque Isle County

The headwaters of Canada Creek flow from Muskellunge Lake, near the state park at Clear Lake in northern Montmorency County, to the junction with Montague Creek just west of Lake Geneva approximately 3 miles west of MI 33 near Millersburg Road. This is the upstream limit for the classification of blue-ribbon trout stream by the Michigan Department of Natural Resources. A good county map is a real aid in fishing Canada Creek. Montmorency and Presque Isle Counties are not famous for abundant road signs and it is easy to take a wrong turn.

Driving north on MI 33, look for Canada Creek Highway about 1.5 miles into Presque Isle County. Take this road (there is a sharp turn to the left, which is south, then another back to the right) west for a very short distance before crossing a culvert-based bridge over the stream. You can park here or backtrack a few yards to a two-track trail heading north and paralleling the water. This trail dead-ends after a short way and there is room to park at streamside.

At this location Canada Creek is 20 to 25 feet wide, and 1 to 3 feet deep. The fine gravel bottom is firm, and although there are spots that insist on chest-high waders rather than hip boots, it is very easy to navigate. This is wild brook trout water. Clean and cold, Canada Creek's banks provide tempered shade and undercuts for the larger fish. It is relatively easy casting, although in some spots it is good advice to check your back-cast space carefully and, once in a while, a roll cast is required.

There are beautifully marked, vibrant, aggressive trout averaging about 9 inches with some reasonable representation of fish over 12 inches. And, for the careful stalker, there is a chance to take a fish in the midteens from the deeper holes and undercut banks.

These fish are (usually) not at all selective. An Adams, Royal Wulff, or Lime Trude may bring rises all day long, all season long. Small streamers work well if fished deep with erratic twitches or jerks near cover. A size-12 Mickey Finn Clouser or a size-10 olive (black tail) Woolly Bugger will generally do the trick in this stretch of Canada Creek. Just downstream from this culvert at Canada Creek Highway, there is a piece of water that appears at first glance to be flat and barren. Appearances are deceiving in this case as the cover is excellent for large fish, and some brookies in excess of 13 inches are in residence. Fish this area slowly with the Woolly Bugger or with a weighted size-12 Gold-Ribbed Hare's Ear and a strike indicator about 30 inches above the fly. And, please, release these fish.

The next downstream access is a little tricky in that the county road map leads one to believe there is a bridge at CR 634. No such luck. The bridge has been gone for quite a while, and CR 634 dead-ends on both sides of the stream. Both banks are heavily posted, and it is necessary to stay in the water when fishing this part of Canada Creek. The stream here is 25 to 30 feet wide with slow curves over a firm, sand-based bottom. The dark overhanging canopy feeds a banquet of terrestrials into the flow, and ants, beetles, and jassids are on the menu. In addition to land-based imitations, the Irresistible and Renegade patterns should be fished. A small (size 10 or 12) yellow Zonker has produced some handsome fish, and a Pass Lake is always effective.

Bear Den Road cuts off to the south just a few yards west of the access at Canada Creek Highway. Turn left and proceed approximately 0.5 mile to a two-track on the left going up a slight hill. From this point it is 0.4 mile to the stream and ample parking in a beautiful setting. This is just a short way upstream from the culvert, and essentially all the creek's characteristics are the same. About 50 yards upstream from your parking area you will notice a number of downed trees crisscrossing the water at all angles and creating a jungle that is nearly impossible to fish. There are big and neglected brook trout here, and the creepy-crawly approach with a dapping technique can be rewarding. Although "landing" these fish on a fine leader is nearly impossible, the strike and pull of a 12-inch brook trout is reward enough. Just a few more yards upstream from the downed trees there is an active beaver colony whose handiwork is immediately evident. The backwaters of this beaver dam run to a depth of 4 feet, perhaps more, and are home to some very nice fish that rise freely in the late evening and early morning hours. They are inclined, however, to careful inspection of their food.

About 500 yards north of Canada Creek Highway on MI 33 there is a two-track fire trail heading west (this is approximately 150 yards past a two-track driveway protected by a yellow steel gate) that takes you to the river's edge in short order. The water at this spot averages 30 feet wide and with a casual glance appears flat and uninteresting. The upstream view presents a straight flat surface with a moderate to slow current over sand. Immediately downstream, a series of easy bends and curves appear. All of this is worth fishing, although the downstream selection is a little easier and more attractive. There are some very nice fish in this stretch and an occasional brown trout of substance will take your fly.

Farther downstream there is an excellent access off MI 33 about 0.5 mile south of Tomahawk Creek. At the end of the S-curve (if heading north) there is a two-track that angles sharply off the highway and then straightens to the west. This trail winds through the Mackinaw State Forest for about 1.5 miles before taking you past a clear-cut hill on your left. At this point you are within a few yards of the river and a beautiful open camp with easy parking and space to turn the vehicle around. This is a wilderness setting and a lovely spot to spend the day. The current is slow over a sandy bottom and the stream is about 30 feet wide with some deep holes that will overtop waders. Overhanging cedars, wildflowers, and elk sign all contribute to a sense of having been transported back in time.

Slowly fished leech patterns are effective here and a methodical coverage of the obvious lies will be rewarded with larger-than-average brook and brown trout. The Fox Squirrel nymph and the Caddis Creeper are mainstay wets and the Adams, Lime Trude, and Royal Wulff cover dry-fly needs.

If there is a fountain of youth in Michigan, Canada Creek is probably it. This is a beautiful little river with eager fish, beauty, and quietude.

Notes:

- Watch for elk and elk sign in this area.
- Atlanta to the south and Onaway to the north are full-service towns.
- Camping facilities at Shepac Lake, Tomahawk Lake, and Ess Lake are nice.

HUNT CREEK AND GILCHRIST CREEK
Oscoda County, Montmorency County

Approximately 20 minutes north of the town of Mio on MI 33 and 15 minutes east of Lewiston, both Hunt Creek and Gilchrist Creek cross CR 612 flowing northward to a rendezvous with the Thunder Bay River.

Driving from the town of Lewiston, you will find Hunt Creek just east of the turnoff for CR 487. This is a good access point and there is room to park a car at roadside near the bridge. The stream here is about 15 feet wide and requires skillful roll casting to the shadowed pockets near the bank for calculable success. Hunt Creek's firm bottom is largely sand with quite fine gravel and heavily silted edges. It is surrounded by thick brush and overhanging limbs, and while this necessitates a hands-and-knees approach in many spots, the cover keeps the water cool, provides a continual supply of terrestrial menu items, and ensures light fishing pressure.

This wild-trout population is aggressive in pursuit of any reasonable food item. Truly opportunistic, the browns and brookies respond to attractor dries, impressionistic nymphs, and simple, small streamers such as the Pass Lake, Woolly Bugger, and Mickey Finn. A 7- to 8-foot rod balanced to a 2- or 3-weight line is right for the required short, precision casts. Although the water is very clear, the fish are not leader-shy, and tippet diameter is only important as a consideration in balancing fly size. Six- to 7½-foot leaders with a 4X tippet are adequate for all the fishing on Hunt Creek.

As Hunt Creek continues north toward Harwood Road, it is joined by Sugar Creek flowing from west to east. The fishing at Harwood Road, both up- and downstream from the bridge, is excellent. The creek still has very tight cover and continues to demand stealth and careful casting, but the lively current, fine gravel bottom, and deep, undercut banks are haven to wild, brilliantly colored brown and brook trout of 12 inches and more. An occasional rainbow will smack your Royal Wulff in this stretch, but this is more the exception than the rule. From the bridge at Harwood Road to the next access at Schmallers Road it is about a 2.5-mile jaunt. The fishing pressure here is extremely light and some large fish are taken from the deep holes and undercut banks with black marabou streamers and mink leech imitations. The Irresistible, Deer-Hair Cricket, and Royal Humpy are high-floating dries that are meaty enough to bring the larger fish to the table. A size-10 Zug Bug or size-12 Gold-Ribbed Hare's Ear works as well as anything in the nymph category.

Schmallers Road dead-ends into private property at the bridge over Hunt Creek. Just downstream from this bridge and turnaround, the southward-flowing Thunder Bay River absorbs Hunt Creek and, from this junction downstream, you will be fishing bigger water.

Gilchrist Creek's headwaters are just west and a bit north of the town of Comins in Oscoda County. Flowing north to its meeting with the Thunder Bay River in Montmorency County, it is lightly fished and home to a healthy and totally wild brown trout population.

Fed by springs and small unnamed creeks, Gilchrist Creek comes to the edge of fly-fishability at CR 612 about 1.0 mile west of MI 33. Here the creek is shallow with a sand and fine-gravel bottom, tight cover, and inviting undercut banks. From 612 to Harwood Road the fly-fisher needs to apply a studied, cautious approach to each cast. This requirement is not so much for the trout, but more for the preservation of tippet and fly supplies.

Cover and holding lies are totally obvious in Gilchrist Creek. Any reasonable presentation can bring a response from the fish—a follow or flash, if not a deliberate take. Small streamers are effective, and, like Hunt Creek, a large selection is unnecessary. Attractor dries and "near-enough" imitations such as the Adams are a good bet. A Hare's Ear (or perhaps a Soft-Hackled Peacock or Pheasant Tail) is the only nymph pattern needed.

Downstream and northward from Harwood Road, Gilchrist Creek is fed by three smaller streams and gains some volume near Schmallers Road and the bridge on MI 33. There is a grocery and gas station at the intersection of Lockwood Lake Road and MI 33, and Lockwood Lake Road to the west appears to be an access to the stream. It is not. The stream has no access here due to private property and the angler is advised to proceed north to CR 451, then east for 150 yards to the bridge. Facing east, Gilchrist Creek flows from right to left and the first pool, or hole, visible from the bridge on the downstream side has some very healthy brown trout. This spot is more heavily fished than almost any other on Gilchrist Creek and the trout are savvy, but any reasonable hatch will bring them topside. Lacking visible activity, a slow retrieve with a weighted streamer, or crayfish pattern, at dawn or dusk, usually supplies enough action to justify the effort in such an obvious, high-traffic location.

Continuing downstream from CR 451, Gilchrist Creek parallels MI 33 until it joins the Thunder Bay River about 1.5 miles north of CR 451. The property on both banks is private and the angler should stay in the river and respect landowner rights. The fishing is very good in this lowest section of Gilchrist Creek. Some large fish are present and there is a good chance to exercise fish in the 16-inch range if some care is allocated to wading stealth and presentation.

Although the trout are not demanding, the confines of Gilchrist Creek, along with the clear water, require due respect for success. It is a lightly utilized fishery, and with careful treatment, should remain an angler's gem.

Notes:

- Avery Lake Forest Campground and Big Oaks Forest Campground, both on Avery Lake, are centrally located for safaris to the Black River, Canada Creek, Hunt Creek, Gilchrist Creek, and the Thunder Bay River.
- Nearby Atlanta has some good restaurants and very friendly citizens.
- The Hunt Creek Fisheries Research Area, near the Oscoda county line, is home base for some of the nation's leading trout scientists.

THUNDER BAY RIVER
Montmorency County

In recent years the mild winters, warm and early springs, and lower than normal rainfall have warmed the Thunder Bay River and affected the trout fishing during the summer months. It is best to fish it (until weather conditions change) in spring and fall. Warmer temperatures from June through August bring smallmouth bass into the equation. This underrated stream has several miles of productive trout water from the town of Atlanta downstream to the backwaters of the Alpena Power Company dam at Hillman. The Thunder Bay flows in a southeasterly direction from Atlanta to its merger with Hunt Creek near Schmallers Road, and then turns northeast and picks up steam in its progress to the town of Hillman.

Downstream from the dam in Atlanta, the creek is fairly small, but still offers good fly-fishing for the experienced, patient angler with developed roll-casting skills and a short rod. It can be reached at Red Bridge and Eichorn Bridge just southeast of Atlanta. The fly-fishing pressure is very light on this part of the Thunder Bay, and general attractor dries, such as the Royal Trude and Lime Trude, work as well as anything when the fish are inclined toward the surface. Small streamers also produce fish, and the Muddler Minnow, Mickey Finn, and olive Woolly Bugger will do nicely.

From just a few yards north of Schmallers Road, 6.0 miles north of the Montmorency-Oscoda county line, to the bridge at Hall Road, the Thunder Bay weaves a winding, magical path. Twisting and turning, the stream forms deep holes, lively tail-out runs, bankside pockets, and large fish havens in the undercuts. Brook, brown, and rainbow trout are present in good numbers with brown trout making up the bulk of the population.

The best access on this upper section of the Thunder Bay is at the bridge on Hall Road just west of MI 33 between MI 32 and CR 451. Drive west on Hall Road and you will find the river just about 100 yards after the road

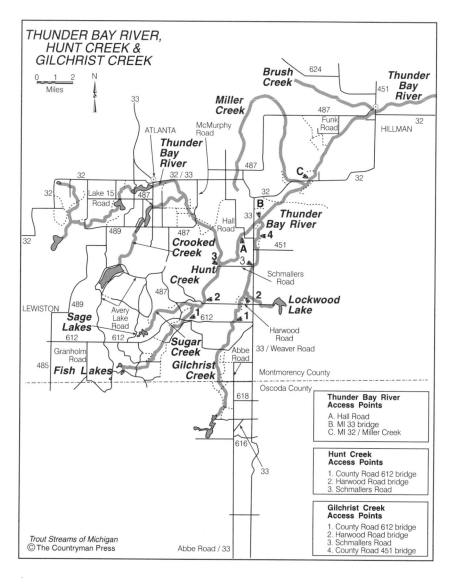

THUNDER BAY RIVER, HUNT CREEK & GILCHRIST CREEK

Brush Creek
Miller Creek
Thunder Bay River
ATLANTA
McMurphy Road
Funk Road
Thunder Bay River
HILLMAN
Lake 15 Road
Thunder Bay River
Crooked Creek
Hunt Creek
Schmallers Road
Lockwood Lake
LEWISTON
Avery Lake Road
Harwood Road
Sage Lakes
Sugar Creek
Gilchrist Creek
Fish Lakes
Granholm Road
Abbe Road
33 / Weaver Road
Montmorency County
Oscoda County

Thunder Bay River Access Points

A. Hall Road
B. MI 33 bridge
C. MI 32 / Miller Creek

Hunt Creek Access Points

1. County Road 612 bridge
2. Harwood Road bridge
3. Schmallers Road

Gilchrist Creek Access Points

1. County Road 612 bridge
2. Harwood Road bridge
3. Schmallers Road
4. County Road 451 bridge

Trout Streams of Michigan
© The Countryman Press
Abbe Road / 33

makes a 90-degree turn to the north. There is room to park a vehicle near the bridge, and either an upstream or downstream fishing approach can be rewarding. At the Hall Road bridge, the river is 25 feet wide and beautiful. The current is moderate and ensures easy wading. The bottom is mostly sand and fine gravel with a mixture of rubble and silt at the edges. The downstream side of the Hall Road bridge features a large "swimming-hole" pool with high prospects for hooking a trophy-size brown at dawn or dusk.

With relatively easy wading and casting in either direction, your decision can be made by considering a preference for upstream dry-fly or indicator-nymph fishing, or quartering downstream streamer or emerger offerings to the banks and runs. Excepting peak mayfly and caddis hatches, the trout are not overly selective and a reasonably careful cast with a presentable fly du jour is sufficient enticement for action.

Downstream from Hall Road to the bridge at MI 33, there is about three-quarters of a mile of excellent cover for larger fish. An olive Woolly Bugger (black tail), with a strand or two of dark flash on each side of the marabou, is very effective when fished with a slow, wide sweep out from the banks on overcast days. Another effective pattern here is a weighted tan crayfish on a size-8, 3X-long hook. As with the Woolly Bugger, the crayfish should be moved in as wide an arc as possible and retrieved with short jerks. Meaty nymphs also take their share of fish, and both the Fox Squirrel nymph and Halfback pattern are effective.

Gilchrist Creek flows into the Thunder Bay downstream from the bridge on MI 33. This increases the flow by about one-third and a bit more wading care is required. From this point, the river proceeds in a northeasterly direction for approximately 4 miles to the bridge on MI 32. Miller Creek flows into the Thunder Bay just a few yards upstream from this bridge, and this junction and the immediate up- and downstream vicinity is a good place to try a few casts with a small Zonker or leech pattern.

From MI 32 the river continues its northeasterly flow toward Hillman and the Alpena Power Company dam. Sucker Creek enters the Thunder Bay near the backwater "pond" formed by this dam, and this is about the downstream limit for trout fishing. Smallmouth bass, walleyes, and even a few northern pike start to appear here, and the dedicated trout angler is advised to concentrate efforts upstream from Sucker Creek. This section is fed by springs and two unnamed creeks, and harbors many large trout in its deeper holes. Large streamers in somber hues are effective during the morning and evening hours and throughout the day during overcast periods. Still more wading care is required in this part of the river, and a daylight scouting trip is recommended before any late evening or nocturnal fishing is attempted.

The Thunder Bay is a lovely river, wild and bright in its upper reaches, large and serene near Hillman. It has a good population of wild trout and the sylvan beauty to make its exploration a memorable event.

Notes:

- Alpena, to the east, is one of the largest cities in northeast Michigan. It features fine restaurants, excellent golf courses, and reasonable accommodations.
- Gaylord, to the west, is a city designed with a Bavarian style. It is famous as a golf mecca and has several superb resorts with fine dining.
- Both Atlanta and Hillman have the necessities for tourists—restaurants, fuel, motels, and proud, friendly folks.

12 | Sleeping Bear

In recent years there has been a tremendous population explosion in this part of Michigan. Still, this is perhaps the most productive trout-fishing district in the state. Bordered to the west by Lake Michigan, the Sleeping Bear area of the northwest lower peninsula has a wide variety of stream types and sizes and a high percentage of the most scenic vistas in the central United States.

Sleeping Bear Dunes National Lakeshore gives the area its name. This national treasure lies west of Traverse City on Lake Michigan at the terminus of MI 72 near the village of Empire. The dunes are easily accessible by the touring angler, family, and friends. Scenic drives, hiking trails, and spectacular beaches make the side trip very worthwhile.

Cherry orchards, lumber, gas and oil, and tourism constitute a large percentage of the economic base for northwest Michigan. Ski resorts, world-class golf, fine hotels, shopping, and, of course, excellent trout fishing make Sleeping Bear a first and repeated choice for anglers and vacationers from around the country.

The district comprises Emmet, Charlevoix, Antrim, Kalkaska, Missaukee, Wexford, Manistee, Benzie, Leelanau, and Grand Traverse Counties. Traverse City, Kalkaska, Manistee, Cadillac, Charlevoix, and Petoskey are the major population centers. All of these elegant and friendly small cities have a full range of services.

BOARDMAN RIVER
Kalkaska County, Grand Traverse County

The headwaters of the Boardman River begin their westerly flow in Kalkaska County. The North Branch starts as a tiny brook northeast of the town of Kalkaska, while the South Branch originates at the outflow of the Mill Pond

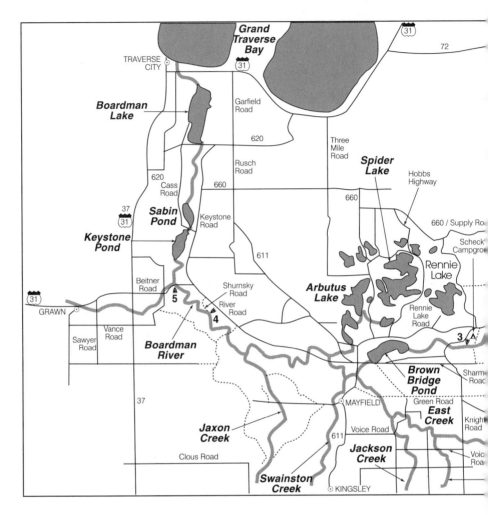

in the village of South Boardman. The two streams meander through private lands and the Pere Marquette State Forest, cross the line into eastern Grand Traverse County, and join forces at Supply Road just upstream from the Forks Campground.

At the Forks, which is on Brown Bridge Road, the Boardman ranges from 25 to 35 feet wide with a depth ranging from 1 to 3 feet (some holes are a good bit deeper), a bottom consisting of fine to medium-sized gravel, and very clear water. The banks are heavy with tag alder and cedar, and roll casting is required on occasion. Fine tippets are usually necessary to seduce these finicky, spooky fish.

This streamside campground is very popular with hikers and canoeists, and during "high T" (peak tourist season) this part of the river is best fished during early morning and late evening hours. From the beginning of the

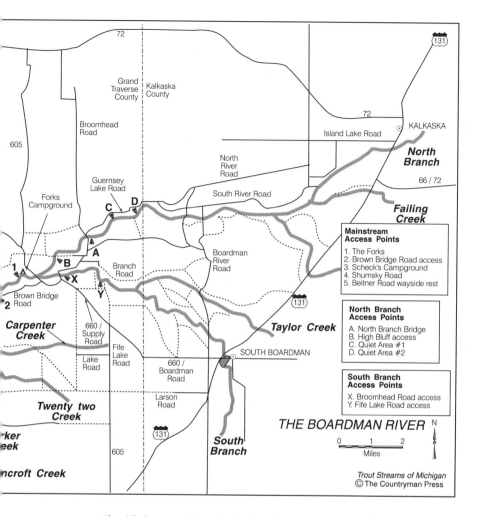

The following labels appear on the map:

72

131

Grand Traverse County | Kalkaska County

605

Broomhead Road

Island Lake Road

72

KALKASKA

North Branch

North River Road

66 / 72

Guernsey Lake Road

South River Road

Failing Creek

Forks Campground

C   D

A

B

1

A

X

Y

Brown Bridge Road

2

Carpenter Creek

Branch Road

Boardman River Road

660 / Supply Road

131

Taylor Creek

Fife Lake Road

Lake Road

SOUTH BOARDMAN

660 / Boardman Road

Twenty two Creek

Larson Road

Mainstream Access Points

1. The Forks
2. Brown Bridge Road access
3. Scheck's Campground
4. Shumsky Road
5. Beitner Road wayside rest

North Branch Access Points

A. North Branch Bridge
B. High Bluff access
C. Quiet Area #1
D. Quiet Area #2

South Branch Access Points

X. Broomhead Road access
Y. Fife Lake Road access

ker eek

ncroft Creek

605

131

South Branch

THE BOARDMAN RIVER N

0   1   2
Miles

Trout Streams of Michigan
© The Countryman Press

season until mid-June, and again during the month of September, the Forks stretch is largely relinquished to the schemes of the angler, and both periods are sparkling times to pursue the Boardman's brook and brown trout.

A very effective streamer for this water is the Woolly Sculpin size 6 or 8. Small Marabou Muddlers and Mickey Finns bring strikes when cast on light tippets and fished through the side pockets and dark runs near the banks. Pheasant Tail nymphs should be tried year-round. Carry a supply of natural, black, and dark olive Hare's Ear nymphs, both weighted and unweighted, in sizes 12 through 16 and your subsurface insect requirements are satisfied. Rusty's Spinner, Borcher, Adams, Lime Trude, and Royal Wulff are usually very productive patterns for the upper Boardman, but various olives abound and their hatches, both emergences and spinner falls, need to be closely matched for consistent success. The fish relish these bugs, and it's wise to carry a selection of duns, floating nymphs, and spinners in sizes 16 through 22.

An angler seeking more solitude than that afforded by a busy campground should explore the water downstream from the Forks. Just 0.4 mile west of the campground entrance you will find the first of three riverside parking spots. All three of these access points are easy to locate just off Brown Bridge Road and are within a few short yards of the river. The stream in this section closely parallels the road and is fished fairly hard on weekends. It has the same characteristics—gravel, sweepers, and very clear water—as the Forks area, and the same rules relative to fine tippets and accurate roll casting apply.

Proceeding farther west another 0.3 mile past the third roadside parking spot, you will notice a sand-based two-track heading toward the river. Follow this trail 0.4 mile down a twisting hill to a quiet parking area on the Boardman's bank. If you do not have a high-clearance, four-wheel-drive vehicle it is probably wise to park as soon as you encounter the deep ruts and walk the last 200 yards to the fishing.

Here the river averages 35 feet in width. It has a firm bottom of fine gravel, sand, and some mud with silt-edged banks. These banks are lined with cedar and pine, and many have toppled to the water, creating sweepers that provide excellent trout cover. Sadly, some of these sweepers have been "groomed" with a chain saw to provide (one suspects) easier passage for canoes. Decent paths lead up- and downstream from this access point, and it's an easy matter to walk and then fish in the direction of your choice.

Both brook and brown trout are abundant in this part of the upper Boardman and they are not overly selective. The Adams and Royal Wulff in size 16 are good attractor patterns most of the time. The Lime Trude or Elk-Hair Caddis will work if the upright-winged patterns fail. A Zug Bug, Woolly Worm, or Gold-Ribbed Hare's Ear is a good choice for a nymph, and the Woolly Bugger in size 10 or a small tan crayfish pattern retrieved with quick snappy jerks will lure some of the larger fish from the deep holes on dark days or at dawn and dusk.

The next major downstream access is by the bridge at Ranch Rudolph about 1.5 miles farther west on Brown Bridge Road. The banks are private property at this location and a respectful angler will stay in the river. The Boardman is narrower here, averaging 25 feet wide, and it is correspondingly deeper with a heavier current so wading is a bit more difficult. The banks are thick with overhanging vegetation that necessitates delivering the fly with a tight-loop roll cast. All of this, combined with the occasional need to deftly sidestep an aluminum flotilla, would usually send the fly-fisher to another locale, but the fish here are larger than average and exceptionally robust on light tackle.

The beautiful, productive Boardman.

Dawn and dusk are peaceful and productive times to fish near Ranch Rudolph. You will not be trampled by horseback riders nor run aground by boaters, and the fishing can be very, very good for muscular, brightly colored brooks and browns. Stonefly nymphs, both black and brown, in sizes 10 and 12 are effective in this water. Weighted crayfish and leech patterns work well, and a large Irresistible is a good searching dry fly.

One mile farther west on Brown Bridge Road brings you to Scheck's Campground, a very popular and lovely camping and picnic area on the banks of the river. In this location the Boardman is 35 to 45 feet wide with depths ranging from 1 to 3 feet at normal to low flows. The bottom is rock and coarse gravel with some finer gravel and sand. The banks are silt-edged and occasionally undercut with overhanging alder, cedar, and pine. The current is fast and it would be very difficult to safely wade this stretch during high-water conditions.

Deer, grouse, and woodcock are plentiful in the area, and upstream from the campground, about 400 yards, there are horse trails interwoven with the deer routes and the fisherman's path. This spot is easily identified from the river by an opening on the left bank (facing upstream) at the tail-out of a very large, dark hole. This hole serves as a watering spot/rest stop for horseback riders and is home to several large brook trout.

In late August the fish seem to respond particularly well to an Elk-Hair Caddis or a pale cream–colored grasshopper in the early evening. Several anglers have told me that throughout the season a rapidly retrieved, weighted crayfish pattern is the single best fly for fish in the 14-inch and better category. Additionally, good-sized fish respond to the Woolly Bugger and Muddler Minnow, and a small Mickey Finn will (almost) always bring strikes from the resident brookies. From Scheck's Place Bridge to Brown Bridge Pond, the Boardman has the same characteristics as at the water at the campground. The float distance of 2 miles is a bit short for most canoeists, but inner-tube floaters have recently found this stretch to be an attractive distance. Most of the surrounding property is private and access is difficult, so an angler, once in, needs to stay in the river. For these reasons the upstream waters are recommended.

Downstream from Brown Bridge Pond, the Boardman is difficult to access except at the obvious bridges on public roads. It is always possible, if not probable, that permission will be granted to venture onto private property. The cut of your jib will need to be trim and proper and the approach tack very courteous for success.

Steve caught his first-ever trout on a fly, a 15-inch brown on a size-10 Gray Bivisible, near the bridge on Beitner Road many years ago. There is a wayside rest at this lovely spot just a few miles straight south of Traverse City near Chums Corner on MI 37. Here the river is 40 to 45 feet wide with a fast clear current flowing over medium-sized gravel. This is a high-traffic area with picnic tables and canoe launch, but the river is lovely and there are plenty of trout available to the patient angler.

There is another well-marked public access to this section of the Boardman off Shumsky Road about 2 miles southeast on River Road from the intersection of Beitner and Keystone Roads. Again, this is a high-traffic area with day hikers, canoeists, and, occasionally, freezing swimmers. Still, there are fish present and, if you are willing to hike a bit to escape the hoopla, they can be enticed to take a well-cast fly on a fine tippet. It's a worthy investment of time to try the fishing at Shumsky Road, and upstream from Beitner Park, at dawn or dusk.

Between Beitner and Keystone Pond there are pathways and easy access to the stream. The fishing below Beitner is truly excellent with prolific hatches and selective trout. All of the popular mayflies bring trout to the surface for dun and spinner feeding, but you may find late-season Olives and tricos particularly rewarding. Check in with the folks at The Troutsman in Traverse City for an accurate appraisal of the fishing and for the most productive fly patterns.

Within the city limit, the fishing below Sabin Dam is very good during the Hex hatch. This is deep, flat water that needs to be respected by wading carefully. This stretch holds very large brown trout and, seasonally, steelhead.

KELLY GALLOUP

There is easy access and good fly-fishing in this section of the Boardman.

THE NORTH BRANCH OF THE BOARDMAN RIVER

The North Branch is a clear, cold, sand-and-gravel-based beauty that ranges from 10 to 25 feet wide. It has depths to 3 feet and more, but averages from 6 inches to 2 feet in most stretches. In general, the casting lanes are tight due to the confines created by heavy vegetation and limbs overhanging from the banks of a narrow stream channel.

The stream is fly-fishable for the patient, careful caster, from just upstream of the confluence pool with the South Branch to the outskirts of the town of Kalkaska, below the entrance of Crafton Creek off South River Road in western Kalkaska County. It varies greatly in its "friendliness" to the fly-rodder, with impenetrable jungles of crisscrossed logs, tag alder, and muck-bottomed beaver-dam backwaters. These heavy brush areas are interspersed with pleasing, semiopen channels with clear casting lanes that allow effective fly presentation to the wild, native brook trout.

As one proceeds upstream from the confluence with the South Branch, the first convenient access is at North Branch Bridge on Broomhead Road. Broomhead Road runs into Supply Road about 0.25 mile east of the Supply Road–Brown Bridge Road intersection. Take Broomhead Road north and you will cross the South Branch of the Boardman almost immediately. Continue for approximately 2 miles to the culvert under Broomhead Road that is known as North Branch Bridge.

The downstream outflow of the culvert has created a wide, deep hole and sandy, flat tail-out that narrows into a brushy, overgrown channel with a casting lane approximately 15 feet wide. There are good numbers of brown trout in this part of the North Branch, and the angling is quite good due to fairly light fishing pressure. Upstream from the culvert, the river offers casting lanes as confined as 10 feet, but the willingness of the trout to take a fly make the necessity for stealthy wading and very precise roll casting well worth the effort.

A rod of 7 to 8 feet in length and balanced to a 3- or 4-weight line is ideal for the close quarters of the North Branch. During normal or low flows, the water is exceptionally clear, and fine tippets are necessary even though the fish are not unduly shy or selective. Generally, attractor dries or small, dark streamers are sufficient fare, but if a hatch is in progress it should be matched closely. The fish seem to scrutinize Blue-Winged Olives with a very critical eye to size, hue, and drag-free float.

Driving south from North Branch Bridge you will notice a graded road headed west after 0.3 mile. This road continues westward for 0.7 mile and ends at a parking area on a high bluff graced with stately Norway and majestic white pines. The parking area overlooks the stream in one of its most beautiful and productive stretches. The flow ranges from 15 to 25 feet wide and the crystalline water covers a sand and fine-gravel bottom with downed cedars and pines, stumps, and undercut banks for trout cover. Good paths lead in both directions from the parking spot and it's an easy walk back to your vehicle after time on the river.

Trude flies, Henryville Caddis, Adams, and Variants consistently produce fish. The Mickey Finn and Royal Coachman streamers are effective in sizes 8 and 10 and, seasonally, grasshopper and cricket patterns are practical offerings.

Upstream from North Branch Bridge there are numerous access points in the Sand Lakes Quiet Area off Guernsey Lake Road and South River Road. The first graded road headed to the right, after heading north from North

Branch Bridge, is Guernsey Lake Road, which parallels the river for about 3 miles. After 1.0 mile on this road you will come to a parking area with wooden stairs descending to the river, which, at this spot, is 1 to 3 feet deep and 20 feet wide with a sand and gravel bottom. The stream here is tight for fly-casting but it is manageable. There is a healthy population of brook and brown trout, and the light fishing pressure allows them to be nonselective, opportunistic feeders.

After another 1.8 miles on Guernsey Lake Road there is a firm two-track headed to the river on your right. This trail is 0.2 mile in length and ends in a very picturesque grove of tall trees at the river's edge. There is heavy beaver activity in this area, with a succession of fresh dams just upstream from the parking/camping spot. The bottom is mostly sand and silt with undercuts and jackstrawed logs providing trout cover. The banks are lined with cedars and alders and the casting is tight, but the fish are wild and eager and well worth courtship.

Guernsey Lake Road forks into South River Road (the right fork) just a short distance from the beaver dam area and South River Road then parallels the North Branch right into the city limits of Kalkalska. Much of the waterfront property in this section is in private stewardship and access is more difficult. The river is in most places too brushy and narrow to fly-fish here, so it is best to concentrate efforts downstream from South River Road.

THE SOUTH BRANCH OF THE BOARDMAN RIVER

Much of the South Branch flows through private property and affords very limited public access between its junction with the North Branch near Supply Road and its upper limit as a fly-fishing stream near the Grand Traverse–Kalkaska county line. The South Branch does have a very stable and healthy population of brook trout (and some browns) and can be sampled at two public entry points.

The first, and most downstream, of these accesses is at the bridge on Broomhead Road just 0.2 mile north of Supply Road near the Forks Campground on the main river. Here the South Branch is about 20 feet wide and the river channel is effectively reduced for the fly-fisher by the thick overhanging trees and shrubs. Still, effective presentations can be made by roll casting with a lightweight rod and fine-tippet leaders. The resident brookies in this area seem to have a decided preference for deer-hair floaters such as the Irresistible and Goddard Caddis. Gaudier offerings like the Royal Wulff and Lime Trude are somewhat less effective, but worth trying if the deer-hair bugs do not produce.

Our favorite stretch of the South Branch is reached by driving southeast on Supply Road to the intersection with Fife Lake Road (about 2 miles). At this spot Fife Lake Road heads directly south (to your right) and a sand two-track runs due north from Supply Road. Take this two-track 1.0 mile to its end at a small, very tight circular parking spot at the top of a high hill overlooking the stream.

This hill is steep and sandy, but is negotiable with a careful sidestep descent, and you may need to hold on to a sapling or two on the trip to prevent an ungainly entrance to the water. At the base of this hill the river is flowing from right to left and there is a path of sorts that follows its course. On your right you will notice a beaver dam and on your left (downstream) there is an area where the stream breaks into several channels close to the base of the hill.

The stream is 20 to 25 feet wide in this area, but because of the channels it varies greatly. The bottom is a mixture of sand, silt, and small fine gravel, and is crisscrossed with log tangles and downed trees every few yards. This calls for a studied approach to the fishing, as much to prevent a twisted ankle as to make an effective cast.

The fish here are seldom bothered and are wild to the core. They dart quickly from the lively current at the edge of a bank and take your Adams or Trude with an audible smack. You'll often see the flash of a fish before you feel its pull when fishing streamers. There are a few browns in this area, but this is a true domain of the native brook trout. They are brilliantly colored, especially in late September, hungry and guileless, and all should be carefully released.

Notes:

- Traverse City has been called the San Francisco of the Great Lakes. It has gourmet dining, exquisite shops, beautiful scenery, and friendly people with civic pride.
- The Grand Traverse Resort in Acme boasts superb golf, tennis, shops, and more.
- Winery tours are available nearby, and a sight-seeing trip to the Leelanau Peninsula will present several tasting opportunities.
- Sailing and motor yacht charters tour the sheltered waters of Grand Traverse Bay.

JORDAN RIVER
Antrim County, Charlevoix County

Surrounded by a forest of northern hardwoods, the Jordan River watershed drains over 100,000 acres on its journey from its headwaters near the intersection of US 131 and MI 32 in northeastern Antrim County to its mouth at

MATT SUPINSKI

The Hex hatch generates high passion on area rivers.

the South Arm of Lake Charlevoix in the town of East Jordan. American beech, white ash, American elm, maple, oak, and basswood are the dominant species, and they are joined by aspen (popple), white birch, pine, spruce, and cedar as you leave the hillsides and approach the river's edge.

Dedicated in 1972 as Michigan's first National Scenic River, the Jordan is managed primarily as a wild brook-trout stream, but it does receive a sizable run of steelhead in the spring and it supports a population of naturally reproducing brown trout as well.

The Jordan River Pathway was first established as a hiking and backpacking trail. It covers 18 miles and follows the river's course in a large loop from Dead Man's Hill Road (about 1 mile south of the US 131 and MI 32 intersection) to Pinney Bridge and back to Dead Man's Hill. For the backpacking angler this trail is the ultimate way to explore the upper Jordan River. The hike-in campground near Pinney Bridge is a restful spot to spend the evening or, alternatively, it can be used as a convenient pickup location. (A map of the Jordan River Pathway is available from the Department of Natural Resources.)

The more customary approach by automobile should be started by turning west onto Jordan River Road (also called Old State Road) just south of the US 131 and eastbound MI 32 intersection. From this point it is 3.1 miles to the first "bridge" over the headwaters of the Jordan. The river is small here, and the brook trout, though numerous, are also quite small. A wooden stairway leads to the water's edge and you will notice a wide, shallow flat with a clean sand bottom and dark, silted banks. The stream at this location is perhaps 20 to 25 feet wide and ranges from 1 to 2 feet deep. Downstream from the culvert the stream is narrower, perhaps 15 feet, and it features some good pocket and riffle water that is well shaded by overhanging brush.

About 0.5 mile farther on this road will bring you to the next access, which offers some soft-bottom areas and an open, marshy terrain. The fish-

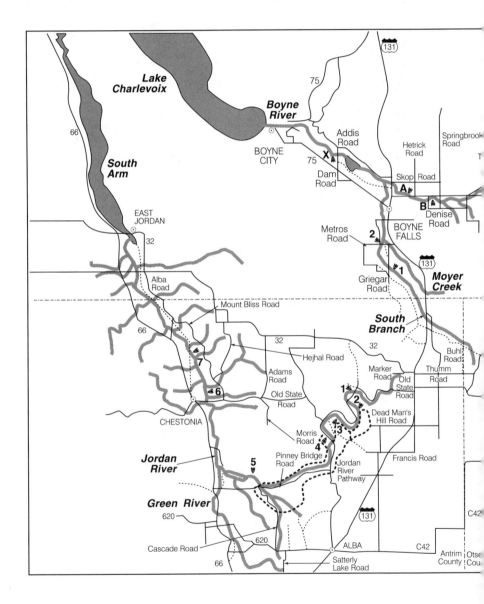

ing is much better farther downstream, and if you drive another 1.2 miles you will come to a pull-off spot with a foot trail that leads directly to the stream and the impoundment behind an old beaver dam. The water is very clear and quite deep in spots. The soft silt bottom and spongy banks make wading difficult, but the sight of cruising brook trout in their early teens will rivet your attention for more than a few casts.

Downstream from the dam, the road closely parallels the river for more than a mile. The stream rushes over a milky white sand bottom, around

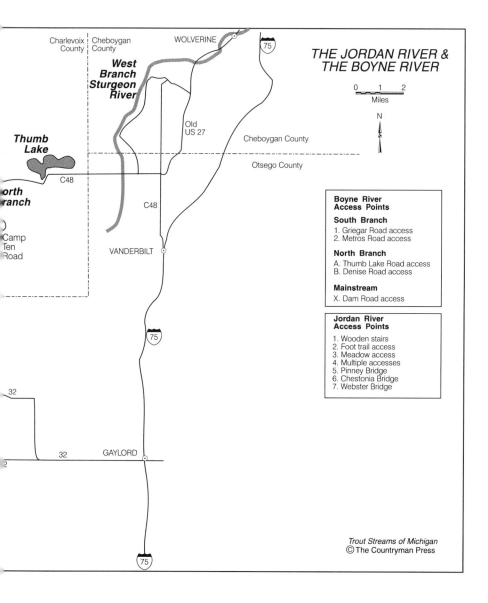

THE JORDAN RIVER & THE BOYNE RIVER

Boyne River Access Points

South Branch
1. Griegar Road access
2. Metros Road access

North Branch
A. Thumb Lake Road access
B. Denise Road access

Mainstream
X. Dam Road access

Jordan River Access Points
1. Wooden stairs
2. Foot trail access
3. Meadow access
4. Multiple accesses
5. Pinney Bridge
6. Chestonia Bridge
7. Webster Bridge

Trout Streams of Michigan
© The Countryman Press

downed cedars and pine stumps, and under moss-covered banks. All of this is perfect brook trout habitat, wild, cold, and clean. The flow has grown stronger, deeper, and wider in this stretch, but it is still an easy river to wade and fish. The trout are anxious and will eagerly smack just about any seasonal offering, and the only trick to the wading is to watch the log tangles.

Two miles downstream from the old beaver dam area there is a pull-off trail to the left. This trail leads to an open meadow that sits on the upstream edge of the next beaver dam (about 200 yards downstream). The river here is banked by sheltering cedars and pines on one side and a terrestrial-producing meadow on the other. There is ample room to cast to cruising fish in this area. The shallow stream is about 30 feet wide, and the very clear water is uniform in its moderate flow. The water is, in fact, just about as clear as water can get, and even the usually carefree brook trout will insist on a light touch and a fine tippet. Griffith's Gnats and Krystal Flash–bodied midge pupae worked very well one recent day in late September, but only after the leader had been lengthened to 14 feet and refined to 7X.

As you continue downstream the road crosses the river again and they follow each other closely from this point to Pinney Bridge. This stretch of the Jordan is just about as lovely as a trout stream can ever be. The crystalline water belies the increased depth, flowing smoothly over long-dead blowdowns, stumps, and the pale white sand. The trout are just about anywhere and everywhere. There are so many pockets, runs, cuts, and stump-side hiding holes that it takes time and a considerable number of casts to effectively cover the water.

An 8- or 8½-foot rod balanced to a 4- or 5-weight line is perfect for the stretch of the Jordan between the second beaver dam and Pinney Bridge. This outfit will provide the delicacy needed to protect a light tippet and produce enough reserve power to punch out an extra 5 feet of line when it is required. The current is faster now and the fish don't have the luxury of a slow, smooth flow that allows supercritical inspection of your fly. Small-sized attractors, size 16, are a good choice for starters, and the Secret Rubber Bug, Royal Wulff, or Irresistible will bring most fish to the surface. Deeper runs and holes near stumps may require a drift or two with an olive-shaded Gold-Ribbed Hare's Ear or a Zug Bug to bring a strike. The deepest runs and holes will surrender their treasures to a weighted Mickey Finn, Pass Lake, or Light Spruce. The olive-bodied Woolly Bugger and a black Marabou Muddler will both produce strikes if fished quartering downstream, with quick, erratic jerks, on an overcast day.

Downstream from Pinney Bridge, the river is heavily braided, broken into many meandering side channels that wander off, regroup, and rewander. This area is lightly fished, due largely, one supposes, to the profusion of tangled deadfalls and the surprisingly deep pockets around stumps. It is absolutely mandatory that the wading angler take each step with great care. A twisted ankle, or worse, would make for a miserable trip back to the vehicle, and it is unlikely that there would be anyone nearby to lend assistance.

Pinney Bridge Road leads west from the dead-end parking area at the bridge to MI 66. The Jordan has now turned north and gathered steam from the added flows of Landslide Creek and the Green River, both respectable trout streams on their own merits. Turn right on MI 66 and drive north for a little more than 1 mile to the sign for Graves Crossing, then turn right to the bridge over the river or into the campground at the water's edge.

The river at the bridge and campground site is a more formidable venture than the peaceful, meandering ribbon of water along the upper pathway. It is now more than 40 feet wide with a fast, heavy current sliding over a sand and gravel bottom, and the jackstrawed logs and stumps add more elements to the safe-wading equation. This is fine pocket water for the experienced angler who is also a strong and cautious wader. A 9-foot rod for a 5- or 6-weight line will have muscle enough to deliver bigger, weighted flies and still allow a delicate dry-fly delivery when required.

Stonefly nymphs, both black and brown, in sizes 8, 10, and 12 are effective throughout the year and are particularly favored early in the season when steelhead may be holding in the darker runs and deep holes. The Hare's Ear in olive and natural shades is widely used throughout the Jordan's watershed, and rubber-legged critters such as the Yuk Bug, Girdle Bug, and June Wiggler produce well when the water is slightly roiled and high. The favorite streamer for this bigger water seems to be the Muddler Minnow, with the Woolly Bugger a close second.

The next downstream access of note is at the Chestonia Bridge on Old State Road about 1.5 miles north on MI 66 from Graves Crossing. Twin culverts funnel the water under the road and into a very deep hole with a beautiful, long tail-out pool. This spot has back eddies, swirls, crosscurrents, and heavy, deep water. It is home to large and worldly brown trout and, in season, it is a temporary resting place for migrating steelhead. This hole demands time and respect to fish properly. Time is needed to thoroughly probe the depths with nymph or streamer, and respect is necessary to avoid an unwelcome bath. Any dunking could become very serious very quickly.

The river, both up- and downstream from Chestonia Bridge, is open enough for back casts, but due to the current strength and depth, the angler is often confined to a narrow, bankside slot for safe wading, and the foliage will necessitate some well-timed, powerful roll casts to reach active fish. A 9-foot rod pushing a weight-forward 6-weight will get the job done handsomely.

Approximately 1.5 miles farther north on MI 66, Webster Bridge Road angles off to the northeast and crosses the river after 0.3 mile. Fifty yards past the bridge there is a turnoff into a large parking area that is often used as a canoe-staging and rendezvous point. The Jordan has flattened a bit in this stretch and it is definitely less threatening in appearance. Cautious wading is still mandatory, however, as this smooth current is deep and deceptively strong.

The river averages 40 to 45 feet wide near Webster Bridge. Its bottom is sand, gravel, and large rocks. The fish rest ahead of and behind the larger rocks, in deep midstream runs, and under overhangs at the banks. Streamers can be very effective at dawn or dusk (unless one is very familiar with the lower Jordan, wading at night would be far too dangerous), particularly Marabou Muddlers with dark wings and heads. This is also excellent nymphing water and a small, weighted Pheasant Tail or dark Hare's Ear will earn takes during hatchless periods. Attractor dries in the heavily hackled western style are fine in the rough pocket water, but these flat, calmer flows demand more precise imitations. Parachute-style Olives are effective throughout the year. Griffith's Gnats, foam ants, hoppers and beetles, and tiny midge pupae will also take these critical fish.

There are more access points farther downstream, right into the town of East Jordan, and fish are regularly caught at all of them, but the canoe traffic and civilized commotion are bothersome after the upstream experience. It is a more soothing move to drive back upstream to some point along the pathway, perhaps the lovely, braided channels near Pinney Bridge, and start over.

The Jordan Valley has some of the loveliest scenery in Michigan. The river is cold, bright, and so clear it defies adequate description. The trout are brash, gaudy, and small in the headwaters and wise, sullen, and large in the lower river. Sparkling, trout-rich tributaries flow through stands of hardwoods and dense, new-growth aspen to feed the system on its way to the big water. The river and its surroundings epitomize one of the reasons we fish for trout—because the country is so beautiful.

Notes:

- Angler or not, the Jordan River Pathway is a beautiful trail. You do not need to hike the entire 18 miles to enjoy the countryside. Several loop options are available, some as short as 3 miles.
- East Jordan has several good restaurants, antiques shops, and picturesque vistas.
- A drive around Lake Charlevoix will take you through East Jordan, Charlevoix, and Boyne City. On the way you will see some pricey real estate, some nifty boats (ships, yachts), and you will pass a golf course or two and more than a few tennis courts.

- Fisherman's Island State Park, just south of Charlevoix on the shore of Lake Michigan, is a beautiful spot to take a stroll.

BOYNE RIVER
Charlevoix County

Two fairly small streams, the South and North branches of the Boyne River, come together northwest of the town of Boyne Falls to form the mainstream, itself a short but very productive river for larger-than-average brown trout. Exiting the impoundment upstream from Dam Road, the Boyne proceeds on a northwesterly course to Boyne City and Lake Charlevoix. These mingled waters ultimately meet with Lake Michigan at the town of Charlevoix.

Although small, both the South Branch and the North Branch provide good fishing for brown trout. The South Branch begins its flow near the Antrim-Otsego county line and cuts a small corner of extreme northeastern Antrim County before entering Charlevoix County near US 131 about 4 miles south of Boyne Falls. This land area, although enclosed in the Mackinaw State Forest, is largely in private ownership, and many signs proclaim an obvious dislike for unannounced, wader-clad visitors. Access is possible, and the stream is fly-fishable, at three points south of Boyne Falls and just west of US 131.

About 1.5 miles south of Boyne Falls, Metros Road enters US 131 from the west. Drive west on Metros Road for about 300 yards to Greigar Road and turn left (south). Greigar Road crosses the South Branch 0.8 mile south of Metros Road. Here the stream is 12 to 15 feet wide and 1 to 2½ feet deep. It has a bottom mixture of sand and fine gravel with silt on the edges in those areas with a slower current. All of this is excellent habitat for mayflies, caddis, and forage fish. Roll casts are required most of the time; in fact only a few spots allow enough room for even a tight, short back cast, but the fish are where they should be and will typically smack a fairly presented fly du jour.

Small streamers work wonders in the South Branch. The Light and Dark Spruce Fly, Llama, Pass Lake, Woolly Bugger (very small, size 12), and Muddler will produce strikes if fished upstream into the pockets and bankside cuts. This is difficult water to effectively nymph-fish, at least in the classical manner, but the old reliables will catch fish for you. If the trout won't eat a size-12 Hare's Ear though, it's probably wise to switch to attractor dry patterns. The Royal Wulff, Adams, Irresistible, and Elk-Hair Caddis are all you should need on most days.

The South Branch also crosses Metros Road just a bit farther west (another 200 yards or so) from Greigar Road. The conditions at this spot are pretty much the same as upstream, where there are cedar, spruce, and pine confusions to dramatize your casting. The stream is small, delicate even, and the fish are in the pockets and under the banks or logs. Downstream from Metros Road the land is aggressively posted, but at this writing, there is no such narrow-minded animosity toward the angler expressed on the upstream side.

Upstream from Metros Road, the stream ranges from 12 to 15 feet in width with a significantly narrower channel for casting. Roll casts need to be fairly precise or you will spend a lot of time disengaging fly from bough, or breaking off and reassembling tippets. The fish run up to 12 inches or so, and anything in the 14-inch class is justification for an all-out swagger. This is pretty water and a lot of fun to fish.

Just upstream from the pond on the South Branch there is a long, flat stretch that can be accessed at the dead end of Cherry Hill Road, just south of Boyne Falls on US 131. The water here is clear, wide, and slow and the fish have a very skittish demeanor. Downstream from the dead-end barricade there are the usual postings promising dismemberment for evil intruders. Upstream, no one seems to care if some fly-rod-waving innocent scares a few fish.

The North Branch of the Boyne gurgles along through some pretty country east of Boyne Falls. It generally parallels Thumb Lake Road and joins the South Branch after crossing US 131 just north of town. In its uppermost run, above the junctures with Kuzmick and Licks creeks, near Denise Road, it is too small to consider attacking with a fly rod. This is kid and worm territory, so save your energy and your flies.

It is possible, though, to fly-fish the North Branch for someone blessed with patience and skill and possessed with the love of small water. Take a look at the stream where it crosses US 131 just north of town. If this is to your liking, the creek can be fished near the highway, or just a bit farther upstream where it crosses Thumb Lake Road near Hetrick Road, or at two crossings on Denise Road, a U-shaped road about 1.5 miles east of 131 off Thumb Lake Road.

There are plenty of hungry, wild, opportunistic trout in the North Branch. The only real trick to catching them is getting a fly on the water for a short, clean drift. The flies that work on the South Branch will do the job on this lovely little creek as well.

Easy access to the main stream of the Boyne is no less problematic than on its branches. The one reliable location for the visitor is at the bridge on Dam Road about 2 miles northwest of Boyne Falls or 2.5 miles downstream from Boyne City. Both Addis Road and MI 75 intersect Dam Road about 0.5 mile, either north or south, from the river. Parking is only allowed on the east side of the road, but there is plenty of space for several vehicles.

The river has a solid, strong current below the dam and all the way to Boyne City, but is wadable with moderate care under any but the most radical water conditions. Averaging 1 to 4 feet in depth (with many holes, thankfully obvious, well above your wader tops), the water is quite clear and flows over a mixed sand and gravel bottom. Silt edges and mud runs accommodate a healthy population of Brown Drake *(E. simulans)* and Michigan Caddis *(H. limbata)* nymphs, and their heralded emergences in June and early July are media events with neoprene-clad specters and large trout dancing in the moonlight.

The stream ranges from 30 to 40 feet wide in most places, wider in some flats and bends and narrower, with a greater force, in some of the channels. Footing is firm and there is plenty of room (most of the time) for lengthy back casts. Well-worn paths lead in both directions from the bridge but, sadly, you will notice the discarded trash of subhuman bipeds. During late September and October, the rush of spawning salmon attracts fish-gatherers (never use the term *angler*) with 4-ounce weights, large hooks, and 50-pound-test mono. Some, but not all, of these have little interest in the sights and sounds of the stream. Empty bait containers, potato chip bags, Styrofoam cooler parts, and crumpled beer cans attest to their style and concern. Still the river is a beautiful and bountiful host and during most of the season is generally well cared for by concerned local and visiting fishermen.

The river is fishable with your choice of armament. Fly rods from 7½ to 9 feet pushing line weights from 2 to 7 can be put to good use on the Boyne. Depending on time of year and stream conditions, anything from 30-inch, 6X tippets and size-22 midge pupae to 3X leaders loaded with weighted streamers could be in order. There are some real trophies in this river. Very large brown trout activate near dusk throughout the season and, in the spring, steelhead appear on the spawning redds near Dam Road. Atlantic salmon still visit the lower Boyne and several are taken each year, usually during the pursuit of brown trout.

The Boyne is a short, very productive river with strong, wild fish. It is fairly easy to fish, if not to access, just about anywhere and should be on your itinerary for at least a day or two.

Notes:

- Boyne Falls is a neat place to hang out. There are lots of good restaurants, and the Brown Trout Motel will appreciate your business. There is a nice antiques shop and art gallery in town.
- Boyne Mountain ski area is just south of town. Superb golfing is available.
- Charlevoix, Boyne City, and Petoskey are nearby communities with golf, scenic tours, hiking trails, theaters, and the impending wood-smoke glitz of a midwestern Vail.

BETSIE RIVER
Benzie County

If one ponders the etymology of "Betsie" (the name of that popular river emptying into Betsie Lake and then Lake Michigan between Frankfort and Elberta in Benzie County), romantic scenarios of a coureur de bois's femme fatale, a sturdy lumberjack's lost love, or a pioneer farmer's beloved may cross the mind.

How about a duck? A merganser, to be exact. It appears the early French took note of the large numbers of this fish duck living thereabouts and called the river *Aux Bec Scies* (River of the Sawbill Ducks), and we Michiganders, who can shorten *Hexagenia limbata* to "big bug," cranked her down to a simpler "Betsie," and so it remains.

Still, it's a pretty name for a most beautiful river, and the prognosis for the Betsie staying so attractive is excellent; the Natural Rivers Management Plan has established it as a natural river, and development will be limited in coming years. The fact that much of its 50-mile flow is through state land is another plus.

If you begin in Grand Traverse County, you can pick up the Betsie as it exits Green Lake. It is generally held that river temperature in this upper reach is too warm to be ideal trout habitat. However, don't discount the area if spring has been cold; if not, a short jaunt down into Benzie County below the Grass Lake Flooding puts you into water cooled by springs, and you can usually depend on midsummer, daytime water temperatures that will not exceed the low 60s—an ideal trout condition.

A recent trip to the shallows around World's Bridge put us in 56-degree water—in the sun at 3 PM in August. Encouraged, we moved down to one of our favored stretches where the river crosses the east-west running Wallin Road. A two-track on the southwest side leads back through state land for 0.25 mile or so to a picturesque, meadowy, pine-planted area bordering extremely inviting water. Here the Betsie flows clear and cold over lots of gravel. It is shallow, running from 1 to 3 feet, but there are abundant deep runs and cuts along the sand banks. We have done well on caddis in July and small hopper patterns in August. Browns and rainbows are the rule and they usually aren't overly shy.

Elk-Hair Caddis in olive, tan, and brown body shades, and in sizes 14, 16, and 18, will cover your needs here. Small yellow- or pale cream–bodied hoppers are the most effective. The Lime Trude is particularly effective as a general searching pattern in this stretch, and the Griffith's Gnat is probably the only midge you will need.

The river flows southwest from here, and there are several bridge crossings where one can access before hitting the Thompsonville Road. One spot well worth trying can be easily reached by driving a mile west of Thompsonville to Haze Road, then heading north 0.3 mile to the old one-lane "Black Bridge." There is a state land pull-off on the southeast side of the river, and just 50 yards northwest of the bridge is a high-ground overlook where we've tented comfortably on occasion.

This is a scenic and productive area for the fly-fisherman. The Little Betsie has emptied in about a mile above, adding more cold, fish-sustaining water. (By the way, the Little Betsie contains smallish rainbows of remarkable color, but it is a devil to fly-fish unless you are willing to poke and dap or bust a lot of brush to find the few open pools.) The Betsie itself is still easily waded both up and down from the bridge, with a nice alternation of pools and runs. Cover is plentiful and the remains of man-made structure from MDNR work a couple of decades back are still in evidence. In fact, if you wade tight against or clamber over some of these old creations, watch out for foot-long spikes that have loosened and become exposed. They're still sharp and nothing you want to snuggle up to.

Hatches have been varied and dependable just about every time we've hit this location, and we've sparred with decent fish more than once. To cover a variety of hatch possibilities with a minimum of patterns, carry the Adams in 12, 14, and 16; Rusty's Spinner in the same sizes; Borcher's Special in 10, 12, and 14; parachute Olives in 16 and 18; and an assortment of the standard attractors such as the Lime Trude, Royal Wulff, and Irresistible. If you fish the Betsie in late May or early June be sure to carry Sulphur patterns and some light cream caddis dries in 14 and 16.

An added bonus: The resident strolling minstrel may provide a musical interlude, as fell to our lot one summer's eve. We were parked on the high ground west of the river preparing dinner when the only vehicle we'd seen or heard that day chugged up and stopped on the bridge. The driver got out, stared into the river for a few moments, kicked around some rocks, then glanced up and saw us at our camp. He froze for a second, then as if galvanized by sudden inspiration, dashed to his car, pulled out . . . (we weren't sure what at first in the fast-fading light), advanced in our direction several more yards, and stopped.

A discordant but enthusiastic rendition of "Good Old Mountain Dew" ruptured the sylvan silence. Apparently taking our bemused inaction for encouragement, he came closer and whanged out another chorus of the same.

"Holy Joseph," Bob whispered, "a third-string banjo player way out here. Hey, don't invite him for dinner."

"Not to worry. But you know, I think that's a mandolin. Doesn't that put him higher in the ranks of riparian rhapsodists? Bet he fishes trout—dry, on 6X."

"Bet he uses a spear," came Bob's cynical murmur. "Oh great, here he comes."

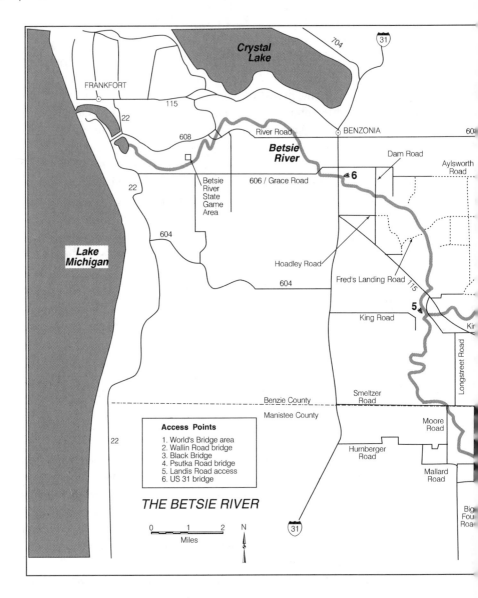

We were cordial, of course, and he gave us a slurry, medium-length version of his life history, then departed, perhaps for brighter lights and bigger crowds. We were left to our head-shaking fireside conversation, much of which dealt with where this ranked on the ever-lengthening "d—est things happen to us" list. Pretty high, we concluded.

After leaving Opry-land north, follow the Betsie south from the Thompsonville environs and you'll see it hook southwesterly into Manistee County for a few miles before flowing north into Benzie once again. You'll pass

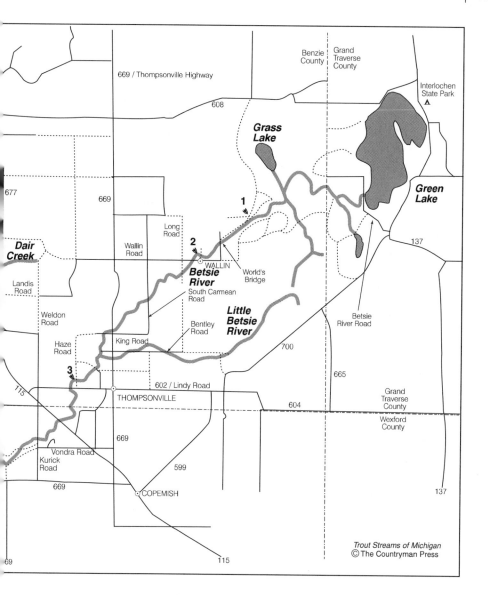

Trout Streams of Michigan
© The Countryman Press

Kurick Road, the traditional upstream limit of the stretch of the Betsie that is open to year-round fishing.

According to Jeff Bower, the owner of Aries Tackle in Thompsonville, the Betsie doesn't get fished as much down in this loop, and he recommended it for large browns. I used to fish this a bit years ago, and I can't imagine why it doesn't receive more angling pressure. There is easy access at several crossings, and we've taken fish all through here, as have numerous friends.

Try taking Smeltzer Road (County Line Road) west from MI 115 to about a mile shy of the County Line Bridge (not a bad spot itself) where you can duck south on Psutka Road to the rustic bridge on a scenic and wooded bend in the narrow gravel road. Pull well off the shoulders.

The water is compelling both above and below, a mix of sand, gravel, marl, and silt edges. There is plenty of log cover, cress, and deep pools for fish holds, and wading is still easy when conditions are normal. Try the long deep slicks that glide below some of the high sand banks. If caddis or mayflies aren't active, work a crayfish imitation of some sort through the slower portions of the graveled runs. Two browns we recently kept for a camp meal contained intact crayfish and remnants of others. And if you are around in early June, the Brown Drake hatches can be as good as anywhere.

As you progress downstream, the river flows northward for a few miles and crosses MI 115 again. There really isn't enough room to park safely on MI 115, but it's easy to slide just south of the highway bridge and park at the Landis Road–Dair Mill junction and walk the shoulder to the river.

This is a good spot to move a large brown—and/or float your bonnet if careless. Dair Creek has contributed more water, and pools and runs are deeper and darker, fraught with promise for that throbber you know has to be skulking and brooding . . .

The width of the river here varies from 40 to 60 feet, the depth from 1 to 6 feet (deeper in several pools), and the bottom is mostly sand. However, there are enough gravel riffles to provide for varied aquatic forms; most hatches you would expect are in evidence. You may find yourself leaving the river more often due to obstructions and depth, but the extra work keeps the casual traffic down, and who reaps the benefits?

Case in point. Bob recently test-fished a "Silver-Gray," touted by the earlier-mentioned Aries shop prop as a dynamite steelhead fly, and he promptly lost it on a "sizable" brown just downstream from, still in sight of, the highway bridge. We have since, needless to say, tried variations of this pattern, namely the Critter, a fly that looks like a modified, slimmed-down Hornberg, with good success.

Other patterns that will move big trout in this venue are the various marabou leeches, the Woolly Bugger, Marabou Muddler, the dragonfly nymph, and a tan and olive crayfish (weighted). A dry-fly purist will do well to fish large deer-hair patterns at dusk. Try a bushy Irresistible or a salmon-sized Humpy on a stout leader.

As you move down to the more touristy Beulah/Benzonia/Crystal Lake part of Benzie County, don't despair. You may encounter more people, but river conditions offset this psychological inconvenience. A big plus is the ease of access at a clearly marked MDNR parking lot bordering a popular, yet ever-fruitful piece of water just northeast of the US 31 (Benzie Highway) bridge.

The many twists and turns and narrowings and widenings of the Betsie here, particularly upstream from the highway, result in as intriguing a potpourri of pleasing trout habitat as could ever be desired in a populated area.

You especially won't lack company if you are here for the spring or fall steelhead extravaganza (the more recent midsummer Skamania runs aren't even drawing crowds—yet), but that leaves a big chunk of time for traditional trout fishing with little competition. Your only reminders of earlier traffic will be the easily discernible streamside paths—and assorted steelhead rigs dredged up on your weighed nymphs. Canoeists can, of course, be the minor fly in the line dressing, though they aren't a big problem on the Betsie, especially if arrival and departure times are given logical consideration.

There is still quite a bit of river from US 31 to the mouth, with best access to be had from the two River Road bridges. The first of these is only a mile west of US 31, and what you will find above and below this crossing is a pretty fair indicator of what's left of the Betsie. There is still the narrowing and widening alternation, but more sand and clay shows up and color is prevalent even in low water. Gravel patches show here and there, the current is slower, overhanging brush and marshy edges abound, as do submerged deadheads and log tangles. Wade carefully as usual.

The last 2 miles of the lower river run through the Betsie State Game Area, but unlike many state-owned river properties, there isn't much access—perhaps a good thing, since this is intended to be a sanctuary.

We have drifted a canoe down to Betsie Lake from the last River Road bridge, stopping to wade and cast in likely looking water. This is a relaxing way to cover a lot of river, but of course has the attendant problems of carspotting, more fooling around with boating paraphernalia, and so forth. Yet when the water is high and you want to hit more than one or two pools, this is a worthwhile endeavor and will put you over some good fish (canoes are easily found in Benzonia if you don't have your own).

Another point to keep in mind is that this lower run of the Betsie harbors steelhead, salmon, and large browns for several months out of the year. It is entirely possible that you could be in for a round or two with a heavyweight champion if you fish your nymphs and streamers near the bottom.

Dedicated Betsie River anglers are very fond of their river and particularly supportive of the steelhead program. They are raising and releasing steelhead through the efforts of the Northwest Michigan Hatchery and Trout Rearing Project. This is supported by the private donations of area businesses, various fishing organizations from around the country, and individuals. Look for donation jars and drop in a dollar or two.

Notes:

- Crystal Mountain Resort has golf, biking, skiing, gift shops, restaurants, and special children's programs.
- If you are interested in soaring (taking a ride in a glider), check out the service at the Frankfort airport.
- Petoskey is the state stone. It is found only in the Sleeping Bear area. Try searching the Lake Michigan beaches for these and other treasures.
- Benzie County is the center of a thriving artists' colony with a wide variety of sculpture, wood carvings, paintings, photographs, and jewelry available. You might consider attending the art fair and antique-auto show, which is traditionally held in late August.

PLATTE RIVER
Benzie County

The beautiful Platte River in northeastern Benzie County has been most famous in recent years for its heavy runs of anadromous fish, and it gets a lot of pressure during spring runs of steelhead and the fall runs of coho and chinook salmon. Taking these brutes on the light tippets necessitated by the crystal-clear water is a real test of one's mettle.

Please grant us permission to wax anecdotal for a moment. This river has particularly fond memories for both authors as it was here that we took our first-ever steelhead in the early 1960s, hardly knowing what the silver torpedos were, but being imprinted forever with their allure. It was here that we were casually wading in 1966 and suddenly found ourselves surrounded by literally thousands of troutlike fingerlings that nailed everything we put in the water. Bewildered, it took a bit of inquiry before we ascertained we had been on hand (in river) for the first release of (coho) salmon in Michigan. Perhaps we were the first to catch one of what changed the course of Michigan's fishery as dramatically as anything in history. Even before the salmon runs, the Platte had a reputation as a top-notch trout stream and is still worth your attention throughout the trout season.

The headwaters are particularly picturesque and less pressured. This uppermost fishable fly-water is easily reached by going 4.0 miles east of Honor, to Maple City Highway, north a mile to Fewins Road, east 2.0 miles to Burnt Mill Road, then 0.75 mile to the bridge. You can try fishing upstream from here, but it's really tight with lots of wading and casting obstructions. The downstream segment flowing west to cross Maple City Road is a more pleasant stretch to wade. The depth goes from a shallow 1 to 3 feet and holding cover is easy to spot. There is a varied mix of sand and gravel throughout, with the width fluctuating from 20 to 40 feet.

It is easy to sample short chunks of this upper water by taking the unmarked but abundant two-tracks on both sides of the river between Maple Road Highway and Burnt Mill Road. Old fire rings testify to the primitive camping that can be had in this area of beech ridges, cedar bottoms, meadows, and pine plantings. This is also above canoe country, another plus for the seeker of solitude.

After the river crosses Maple City Road, it parallels the road closely on the west side down to the Platte River State Anadromous Fish Hatchery off US 31. Brundage Creek enters here and adds considerably to the volume of water in the Platte. As long as you don't fish within 300 feet above or below the weir (and their limit signs aren't always there) you can park in the visitor lot and access the river up or down from this sprawling facility. It's also easy to access at the US 31 bridge at the Veterans Memorial Campground on the south side of the highway (canoe liveries launch their "long" floats here).

As you head west toward Honor, about 1 mile from the campground you will notice Goose Road turning southwest to parallel the river. There is a tempting two-track heading riverward on state land right after you enter Goose Road but it turns sour quickly. Better access is available at the state campground (a mile farther down). There is a day-use area across from site 25 as you exit the campground, and a path gets you to the upstream stretch and away from camp activity. Equally as good is Case Bridge on Pioneer Road, the next crossing after the campground. There is some roadside parking here and on a short two-track 100 feet to the northeast of the river. While trout cover is occasionally lacking, the water upstream and downstream from the state campground and Pioneer Road bridge can be impressive and productive. It ranges from 30 to 60 feet in width, maintaining that 1- to 3-foot average depth with a gravel bed, but there are more large pools to skirt in the narrow spots. An abundance of in-stream cress, streamer vegetation, and sunken timbers make nymphing tricky, but dries are a joy. Caddis always seem to be around and terrestrials from midsummer on can summon up nice fish.

Upriver and down—headwaters to the big lake—you will find certain dry, nymph, and streamer patterns produce Platte River trout throughout the season. As mentioned, terrestrials are always present. Ants (both black and cinnamon), beetles, crickets, and hoppers are effective and especially so if there is breeze enough to give the bugs a push into the stream. Caddis patterns work very well, and the low silhouette of the Henryville Special is sometimes necessary in the crystal-clear, calm stretches of the upper river. The Platte supports a variety of Olives, and an astute angler will carry slate-wing, parachute-tied Olives in sizes 16 through 22. The Brown Drake and Hex stimulate large fish in June and July (try the runs and holes next to stretches of silted banks) and a large night moth or Deer-Hair Mouse should be

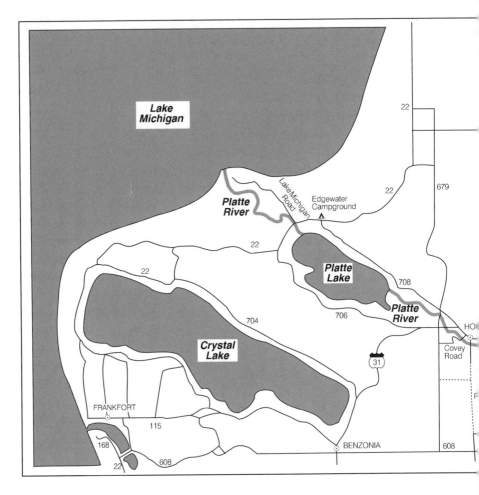

tried late in the evening. Streamers should be a little flashy, if only to interest a migrant Lake Michigan gorilla. Try the Light Spruce, Pass Lake, Llama,
and an assortment of Marabou Muddlers.

As you leave the Goose Road loop there is a white, natural-gas pumping facility 0.3 mile before you hit US 31. A trail behind this leads to a nice
section of river. Up on 31, just west of Honor, you'll see the township hall
on the side of the road. Directly across from it a marshy, faint footpath
alongside a small motel goes south a couple of hundred yards to the water.
If you fancy deep holes, there are a couple of dandies back there. And don't
count out the bridge access you can see directly south of downtown Honor.
It's a bit more cottage-cluttered here, but there is plenty of holding water
and some good stretches of spawning gravel. Collison Creek has added more
volume to the flow by this juncture.

The Platte then flows northwesterly out of Honor toward the 3-mile-

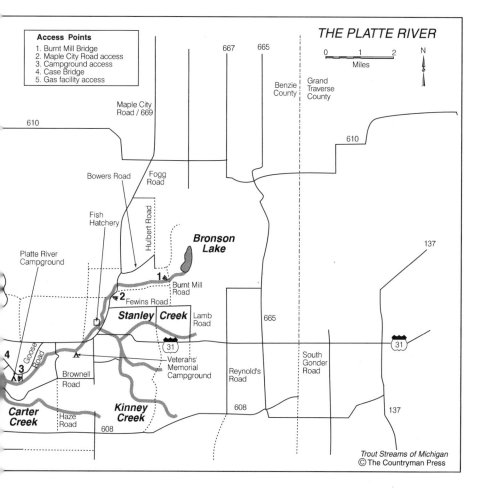

THE PLATTE RIVER

Access Points
1. Burnt Mill Bridge
2. Maple City Road access
3. Campground access
4. Case Bridge
5. Gas facility access

667   665

0   1   2   N
          Miles

Benzie | Grand
County | Traverse
       | County

Maple City
Road / 669

610

610

Bowers Road   Fogg
               Road

Fish
Hatchery

Hulbert Road

**Bronson
Lake**   137

Platte River
Campground

1 Burnt Mill
   Road

2 Fewins Road

Stanley Creek   Lamb
                     Road   665

31   31

Veterans'
Memorial
Campground   South
                    Gonder
Reynold's   Road
Road

4 Goose Road

3

Brownell
Road

**Carter   Haze   Kinney
Creek**   Road   **Creek**

608   608   137

Trout Streams of Michigan
© The Countryman Press

long Platte Lake paralleled by Deadstream Road. Wading in the Deadstream swamp is a chancy proposition (it even sounds ominous) due to muck and depth. Hex come off hereabouts, but a float tube is advised. Below Platte Lake the river warms, there isn't much current, and cover is sparse. For a wading fly-fisher, this section of the Platte, with the exception of a big pool or two off Lake Michigan Road below MI 22, might be better left to the canoeists and tubers. And they are not sparse. If you want to see a three-ring circus, check out things at the MI 22 bridge some warm summer weekend. It will send you back to the headwaters posthaste.

Notes:

- The hatchery operation in Honor is open to the public and it is an interesting diversion from fishing.

- Nearby Interlochen, as mentioned elsewhere, is a world-famous music and art academy with an extensive summer program.
- The mouth of the Platte is in the Sleeping Bear National Lakeshore and worth the short drive for a beachside stroll.
- Honor is a small village, but has all the required services.

BEAR CREEK
Manistee County

Most of the attention directed to Bear Creek comes during the spring steelhead and fall salmon runs, but it won't take many conversations with local anglers to discern that Bear Creek is a lightly fished and very productive full-season trout stream.

You probably won't be overly impressed if you first look at the Bear where it empties into the north side of the Manistee at the public-access site on River Road. This is a low, marshy area where the creek runs slowly through twisting, convoluting bends and usually carries some color to add to the overall "mirkwood" impression. However, many deep, fishy-looking holes form in these bends and around the abundant stumps and fallen trees.

There is a faint path going up the left side of the creek as you move upstream from River Road. Quite a bit of the land here is federal property, but if you fish upstream for some distance, you will probably be wiser to take the river back downstream rather than try a bankside stroll. The banks and hillsides are a tangled jungle and very rough going.

Casting room is adequate through this stretch with the river averaging 30-plus feet in width. The bottom is primarily sand, silt, and muck, but is mostly firm. Wade with caution, particularly if the water color is up, and be very watchful around the stumps and snags.

This lowest section of the Bear has very good habitat for the large, burrowing muck dwellers, the nymphs of the large Brown Drake and the larger *Hexagenia limbata*. Late June evenings will find very large fish chomping the duns and spinners until well after dark. Throughout the season a Woolly Bugger is a good pattern to swim through the deepest holes and runs.

Expect browns and rainbows as a general rule, but since the Bear empties into the Manistee well below Tippy Dam, steelhead and salmon can be skulking in any of the deeper runs and holes.

You may want to explore a bit and try accessing the Bear as it runs through federal land parallel to and north of River Road. There are some old service trails in this area that close in on the stream, but these are rough and tight. If you feel adventurous you might consider a foray or two in a rugged vehicle.

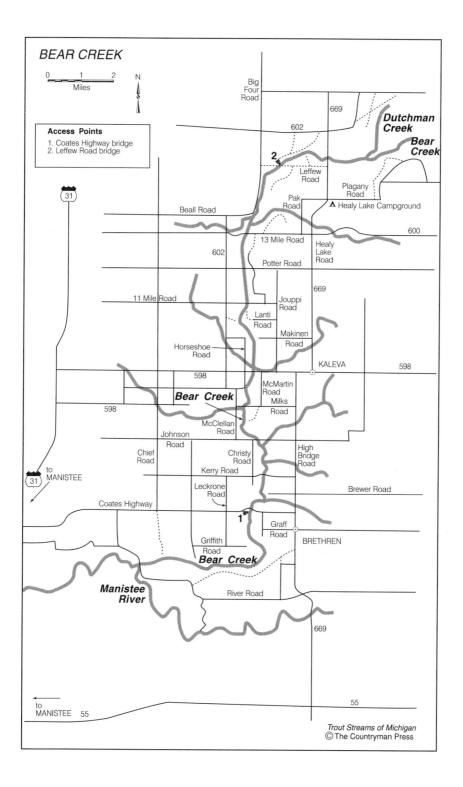

BEAR CREEK

0 1 2
Miles
N

Access Points
1. Coates Highway bridge
2. Leffew Road bridge

31

Big Four Road
669
602
Dutchman Creek
Bear Creek
2
Leffew Road
Plagany Road
Pak Road
Beall Road
Healy Lake Campground
600
13 Mile Road
Healy Lake Road
602
Potter Road
11 Mile Road
669
Jouppi Road
Lanti Road
Makinen Road
Horseshoe Road
KALEVA
598
598
McMartin Road
Bear Creek
Milks Road
598
McClellan Road
Johnson Road
Chief Road
Christy Road
High Bridge Road
Kerry Road
Brewer Road
Leckrone Road
Coates Highway
1
Graff Road
BRETHREN
Griffith Road
Bear Creek
Manistee River
River Road
669
to MANISTEE
31
to MANISTEE 55
55

Trout Streams of Michigan
©The Countryman Press

Perhaps the best way to fish this lower stretch is to go north on High Bridge Road and then cut west on Coates Highway to the bridge. There is a small, off-road parking area on the west side of the Bear, and much of the downstream run is through federal land. Here you get a true picture of Bear Creek's charm; the bottom is mainly sand, but there is a decent mix of gravel and even some large boulders. There are plenty of logs and over-hanging vegetation to provide fish cover, and the occasional big bend creates those large holes and dark slicks one always approaches eagerly and hopefully. The width of the stream varies from 25 to 45 feet and wading is not difficult. The Bear makes a couple of large curls near the highway, and if you take the little dead-end road just east of the stream, you can see the water from the road's end.

Generally speaking, the resident trout of lower Bear Creek are not overly picky eaters. Standard attractor dries will work on most days. A Royal Trude, Lime Trude, Adams, or Irresistible will bring fish to the surface. Olive and dark shades of the Hare's-Ear nymph are effective and the Spring's Wiggler, or Clark Lynn nymph, will excite both the resident trout and the tourists from Lake Michigan. Woolly Buggers, Muddlers, the Light Spruce, and the Pass Lake will cover streamer requirements.

A quick look at the map will illustrate Bear Creek's north to south flow from its headwaters above the hamlet of Kaleva. As you drive north from the Brethren area an abundance of east-west roads cross the stream. The twin cul-verts below the high bank at the Kerry Road crossing steer the downstream flow into a deep pool below the road. This stretch has a sand bottom (some silt on the edges) with the usual mix of logs, sweepers, and other fish cover. This bottom configuration prevails up to and through the Johnson Road bridge area, although above Johnson Road more gravel begins to appear.

If you decide to access the Bear a bit farther north at the Nine Mile Road bridge, park well off the shoulder as this road has a fairly heavy flow of traffic. There are several homes close upon the initial upstream and down-stream stretches here with the occasional footbridge. The stream is open enough for easy casting and presents no real wading difficulty. In the sum-mer months, the lawns of the streamside homes pour a lot of ants, crickets, and hoppers into the flow. Carry a terrestrial assortment.

Jumping upstream to the Eleven Mile Road access shows the river still fairly wide at 25 to 35 feet on the average. If you need to get out of the water to circumnavigate a snag or hole, be cognizant of the heavy mud edges and muck sinks here and there. These, and the very heavy brush, will make you want to keep to the river. The streambed in this section is a mix-ture of sand and fine gravel and is easy to wade. These general conditions prevail upstream through the Thirteen Mile Road area, where the depth aver-ages 1 to 3 feet with a smooth, even flow.

One of our favorite spots on the Bear is what probably, depending on your ability and patience, should be termed the upstream limit for fly-fishing. Drive north on Healy Lake Road from Kaleva for about 5 miles to Leffew Road and go west until you hit the narrow bridge across the stream. Logging trails, some quite fresh, provide pull-off areas for your vehicle. You will find yourself in a pretty, wild region of public forest both upstream and downstream from the bridge. Have a compass handy if you intend to cut cross-country to the stream, or keep the water course well in focus as you navigate the thick brush on the banks.

There are many places with extremely tight casting channels, and only a well-executed roll cast will do. If you have a 7-foot rod, use it here. In some spots, the foliage completely covers the 15- to 20-foot-wide stream and only a "dap" will get your fly on the water. Thankfully, these inconveniences are few and well worth suffering. There is a beautiful mix of sand and fine-to-medium gravel with some marl edges under these crystal-clear, cold waters. The 1- to 2-foot depth provides very easy wading as you creep along probing for the plentiful rainbows and brookies.

The trout here are numerous and far from shy. If you note a spot that should hold a trout, it's an even-money bet that it will hold two or three. Try small Goofus Bugs, Adams, and Royal Wulffs just about any time. One memorable 9-inch brook trout grabbed a size-8 olive Woolly Bugger here, in spite of having a fresh 5-inch baby rainbow still protruding an inch from his lips.

Notes:

- Wellston and Brethren have limited services, but you can find accommodations, gas for the car, good food, and tackle.
- The Stockade Bar, west of Wellston, has good Mexican food and friendly advice for the itinerant angler.
- Manistee is the major city in the area. It has a full range of services and amenities.
- Schmidt Outfitters, in Wellston, has a complete fly shop, guide service, and excellent accommodations.

A straight, trout-filled run on the Big Sable

13 | Wine Country

Mason, Lake, and Osceola Counties form the northern border of wine country and the southern border is the Michigan-Indiana state line. This is the largest geographic district represented in our book. Michigan's wine country actually extends to the tip of Leelanau County in the north, with concentrations of vineyards interspersed throughout the region. The area near Paw Paw, west of Kalamazoo, is representative, with both the Warner Vineyards and the St. Julian Wine Company in vigorous operation.

Grand Rapids and Kalamazoo are the largest cities in the region and Grand Rapids is one of the largest metropolitan areas in the state. Throughout wine country you will be close to all the amenities of civilization. Human clusters have their drawbacks of course, but if you are in the region on business, or visiting relatives, or whatever, you can quickly escape to a lovely stream with willing trout. We have often picked up visiting friends at the Grand Rapids airport and have been fishing the Rogue 40 minutes later. You can be on the White River in 90 minutes, and casting to a promising run in the flies-only stretch of the Pere Marquette in 2 hours. From Kalamazoo you can be knee-deep in Augusta Creek in 30 minutes or less, and the Coldwater River by Hastings is only an hour's drive.

THE BIG SABLE
Lake County, Mason County

Mention the Big Sable River to a trout fisherman and you'll likely get one of two responses, either a confused look with perhaps a "Don't you mean the Au Sable?" or a quick shift of the eyes and a smile that says, "Ahh, you know about that one, too . . ."

Beginning in northwest Lake County, arcing across all of northerly Mason County, and ending in Hamlin Lake by Ludington, this unsung river is known variously as the Great Sauble, the Big Sauble, Big Sable, or just Sauble. Call it whichever you prefer, just fish it a time or two when conditions are right, and you will go back.

Perhaps it receives short shrift because it flows between the more famous Pere Marquette to the south and the close-by Little Manistee to the north. A dam just up from the mouth below Hamlin Lake prevents anadromous fish runs, eliminating pressure from salmon and steelhead aficionados. Also, there are a fair number of warm-water fish in this river, mostly small perch and the occasional pike, the latter not always so small. Full of myself this past July for having played and released an 18-inch brown, I was 2 minutes thereafter left slack-jawed and shaken at having my streamer mowed off by the take and turn of a logjam-dwelling behemoth of a . . . well, pike, I have since consoled myself (dubiously).

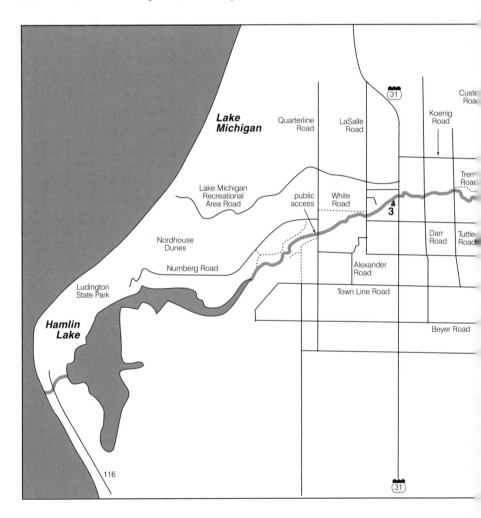

Regardless of these "interlopers," the browns predominate and they are some of the healthiest and feistiest around. Mixed in with them is a thriving population of brook trout, and these guys have some heft to them too. It is not uncommon to pick off a couple in the 12- to 14-inch range. Locals say that you can find brookies only in this stretch or that stretch, but I have encountered them in upper, mid-, and lower sections at various times.

Rarely will you encounter another fisherman on the Big Sable, except maybe during the Hex hatch. From late June into July, locals and in-the-know *limbata* chasers from all around skulk near chosen pools and runs waiting for action. However, there are so many good spots that you'll never run across the elbow-to-elbow situations that can occur on certain stretches of, say, the Pere Marquette or Au Sable during this favorite hatch.

If your preference is for small, easily waded water, take a look at the Big

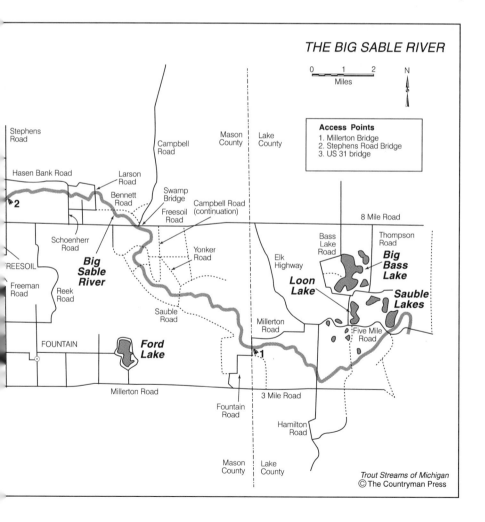

THE BIG SABLE RIVER

Access Points
1. Millerton Bridge
2. Stephens Road Bridge
3. US 31 bridge

Trout Streams of Michigan
© The Countryman Press

Sable where it crosses Five Mile Road near its headwaters by the Sauble Lakes in Lake County. If you like the appearance of this slow, clear stream, a good spot to access it is Mack Road, which goes south from Five Mile Road (aka Loon Lake Road) just southwest of the Sauble Lakes. Mack Road ends in a Y at a popple grove (cottages to left and right), and there is a short path between the forks of the Y right to the stream. You will find the stream to be about 20 feet wide, very shallow, predominantly sand-bottomed with watercress beds scattered throughout and providing cover. Tight casts are called for, but there aren't many serious obstructions to fly-fishing.

As you move west you can pick up the river at Spurgis Bridge where it crosses Hamilton Road just north of Sauble Station. It is "cottagey" along here, with lots of private land bordering the stream. Maps denoting state and federal land might tempt you to explore for access west of the river on the public land two-tracks. The river can be reached from these, but the trails are unmarked and maintenance-free and "can get a mite juicy," a local landowner advised. Classic understatement. These tracks don't lead directly to the river, requiring some compass orienting and moist hiking. Four-wheel drive is advised, with emergency rations a consideration.

An easier way to fish comparable water is to go a bit farther west to Millerton Bridge. Take Three Mile Road 1.5 miles west from its intersection with Hamilton Road south of the river and you'll find an unmarked dirt road angling north. Take this 1.2 miles to a yield sign, turn right, and you'll hit the bridge 0.2 mile north.

The water here is still very clear and shallow for long stretches up or down, but bigger holes, some 3 or 4 feet deep even in midstream, appear more frequently. There are lots of logs in the stream, and the current has washed out holding lies under nearly every obstruction. There is not the sterility here one sometimes associates with a sandy riverbed; a rich variation of aquatic growth in and along the silt/muck edges and cattail marshes provides plenty of insect habitat. We have frequently encountered midday hatches with rising fish willing to take small dries on long, light leaders. Slow, quiet wading and lengthy casts are de rigueur, for the trout are easily spooked in this clear slow current. This section of the river is very reminiscent of a western spring creek; along with sizable hatches, terrestrials form an important percentage of the trout diet. Ants and beetles are effective.

Try walking the left bank downstream for as far as you choose and work your way back to the bridge. It's a pleasant and productive piece of water, and while we haven't taken big trout here, there are reports of 20-inchers and up residing in this general area.

As you move northwesterly with the downstream flow, you can access at several points of public land visible from the road around Pole Bridge just before the Big Sauble comes across Eight Mile (Freesoil) Road, the area's primary east-west highway. Decent fishing can be found both up and down from Swamp Bridge off this highway, but one of the most engaging areas hereabouts can be reached as follows: Campbell Road (Forest Service 5206) intersects Eight Mile Road 0.8 mile east of Swamp Bridge. Go south on Campbell for 1.0 mile to where it becomes a two-track (Forest Service 5178) and continue 0.5 mile south, bending a bit left when the trail forks to the dead end. A faint path takes you 100 yards to the river. If you take the right fork a few hundred yards through the pine planting, you'll also come to the river at an attractive overlook.

This is bigger water with more of those bottomless-looking dark holes at bends and around snags, but it is still easy wading under normal conditions. Good cover abounds, though there are those occasional "flat" stretches one hastens through. The water takes on a more tannic or coppery hue down here, particularly after rain, and submerged snags are not always as easy to see when nymph and streamer fishing. My Hare's Ear supply is usually lighter after fishing this stretch.

In addition to the Hare's Ear nymph try Pheasant Tails in size 16 and be sure to have some Latex Caddis larvae and emerging-pupae patterns available. The best streamers seem to be small, bright Clouser Minnows and Mickey Finns for the brookies and olive Woolly Buggers and dark Muddler Minnows for the browns. A Light Spruce in sizes 8 and 10 will satisfy both.

There is a clearly marked public access to this general area on the other side of the river, which can be reached by going west about 1 mile from Swamp Bridge on Eight Mile to Reid Road, then following MDNR signs south. However, this becomes a bumpy two-track with blind curves, and you are more likely to run into (literally) picnickers and even campers, in spite of posted rules to the contrary. The aforementioned Campbell Road access gets my nod.

North of Freesoil Road the river runs east and west for several miles before it curves south to empty into Hamlin Lake, and there is a vast amount of lightly fished, very good water waiting here. Several north-south secondary roads hit the river as you move west, and access is easy at most of them.

Some of my best catches north of the highway have been made upstream and down from the bridge on Stephens Road, the first road east of the village of Freesoil. The water in this section has a good mix of sand, gravel, the occasional clay shelf, fast riffles alternating with deep, slow bends—lots of variety as it winds through rustic farm country and woods. There is adequate room to park on the road, and there is also a sandy two-track just south of the bridge, which parallels the downstream flow for a few hundred yards. Both browns and brooks can be found, and when conditions are right, the action can rival that on any river. I once took a night-feeding brown of 20 inches below this road on a Goofus Bug, of all things, right beside what sounded like his big brother. On another occasion an hour's fishing above Stephens Road bridge one hot afternoon produced a 15-inch brookie along with several good browns.

Crayfish patterns are very effective in this part of the river. The simple versions produce as many strikes as the more elaborate ties and, since you will lose several to snags and logs, it's a good idea to economize on hooks, materials, and time. Complement the crayfish offerings with the Silver Hilton, Pass Lake, and some Marabou Muddlers. Large, "spikey" nymphs work wonders early and late in the day, and a Wiggle Hex nymph is effective most of the time. Attractor dries will produce when active hatches are not evident. Try the Royal Wulff, Goofus Bug (Humpy), Irresistible, and Lime Trude. Ants, beetles, crickets, hoppers, and the Griffith's Gnat often take fish.

Equally attractive water can be found around the Freesoil Bridge on Custer Road just a mile north of the village. It is easy wading upstream for as far as you care to fish, but downstream from this bridge for a fair distance the river narrows, the brush grows tight, and wading can be a hat floater. The banks are mostly private, but if the water level is low enough, the downstream wade will eventually take you through some beautiful holding water. I have moved some real sharks in here, and once commiserated streamside with a local who had there hooked and lost "an 8- or 10-pounder, by gar," in that same log-infested pool by which we stood. I believe.

Between Freesoil and MI 31 to the west lies Tuttle Road, a dead-end gravel track going north off Eight Mile. It terminates at the remains of an old bridge. Stop when the gravel ends and the downhill two-track continues; it's pretty dicey driving down and turning around again, so the short walk is advised. The river curves through a mix of heavy woods, swamp, and farmland above and below the old pilings, and once again there is every conceivable kind of fish cover awaiting you. On occasion, a heavily weighted fly is necessary to penetrate quickly to the feeding zone of the fish. Try a dark tan Woolly Bugger (which, by the way, is a passable crayfish), a rubber-leg nymph such as the June Wiggler or Yuk Bug, or a Clouser Minnow. The standard dry-fly patterns mentioned earlier are appropriate for this part of the river, and you might consider trying a Deer-Hair Mouse (on a stout tippet) in the twilight hours.

If you don't mind a bit of traffic noise while you fish, head a couple of miles farther west on Freesoil Road to the US 31 bridge just north of Orchard Market Corners. The upstream jaunt from the highway provides wide, easily fished water, lots of sand, but a seemingly higher population of "rough" fish, perch in particular. Suggestion: Ask the friendly folks at the Sauble River Inn about accessing downstream below their motel (good place to stay even; it's inexpensive, clean, and right on the river). One can high-bank the right-hand (north) side down through some pine plantings to some quintessential trout water. It amazes me how frequently I move, and occasionally hook, at least one or two heavy fish in any 2-hour foray. The river is mostly wide down here with a gentle current and firm sand bottom, but be careful of the gooey muck edges here and there.

"It hardly gets fished," the motel proprietor once told me, "except during the 'bug thing.'" Even then it's not all that crowded, and the infrequent fellow "bug" (Hex) chaser can provide interesting diversions. Witness a recent July: I reached "my spot" on the river shortly after dark and stood streamside for several minutes perched at the top edge of a 6-foot bank. I was hoping for a few emergers and listening intently for a decent feeder, when a noncommittal voice from the darkness asked, "How ya doin?"

An unexpected nearby voice in the dark usually makes me start, and the fact that this one came from directly beneath my feet added an inch or two to my standing-high-jump record. The owner of the voice had his feet in the water and had been reclining against the bank, his camo hat just an inch or so from my muddy wader toes. I caught my breath, we exchanged the usual amenities, and I asked if he'd mind if I moved above him about 50 yards. "No problem," he assured me.

Ten minutes later this short remove provided a ringside seat for the next event. It began with strange muffled voices, clankings, swishing of brush, and the like, and culminated in the launching of a canoe directly over my newfound, reclusive friend's now twice-abused hat. (All this by another angler and his nonfishing distaff companion, I was shortly to learn.) It was kind of fun mentally picturing what could be heard but not seen.

When the "yikes!" and low mutterings and apologies died down, I could hear the now-stealthy paddler heading upstream against the gentle current toward my "hold" in the stygian stillness of the brushy shadows.

"How ya doin?" I asked as they glided 5 feet in front of me in the gloom. "Aacck!!" the girl responded with a respectable sitting high jump. "Jeez!" the guy exhaled as he semideftly shifted and back-paddled to avoid capsizing. Then, apologetically, "We'll get well above you."

"No problem. Have a nice evening." I grinned archly, which they couldn't see, and waited for things to settle.

As I got my "night senses" going again, I thought idly (but seriously) of what an exciting experience any novitiate to this sport could have on such a night, and hoped they'd hit some active fish so she would see what drives an angler during "Hex season."

A scant 15 minutes later, about the time a good trout might regain his equanimity and feed again, there came the sound of that dipping paddle.

"Sorry again," the guy said.

"I just got too scared," the young lady declared in the firm and forthright manner of one who had made the only practical decision, and no alternatives could even be considered.

"That happens," I offered lamely. They left, as did the much beleaguered hat man below, leaving me to fish in peace (to no rises) and ponder the vicissitudes and vagaries of romance during the major hatches.

Notes:

- The Ludington State Park along Lake Michigan at the outlet of the Big Sable through Hamlin Lake is a neat place. It has miles of beach, all facilities, hiking trails, and beautiful lakeside scenery. Nordhouse Dunes lie just to the north of Hamlin Lake for other recreational pursuits.
- The Sauble River Inn and the Orchard Market Restaurant on US 31 near the river have always had good food. As you move west toward Freesoil, accommodations become scarce.
- The Heidi Hof bar and restaurant at the east edge of Freesoil has good food also—fortunately, since it is the only eatery in town. There are no nearby tackle shops.
- If you are up near the Big Sable's headwaters, try the Na-Tah-Ka Tavern by Big Bass Lake. Friendly atmosphere and impressive fish mounts make for a pleasant visit. There are some rental cottages in this lake-dominated area.

WHITE RIVER
Newaygo County, Oceana County, Muskegon County

While it may not be quite the same "Waubishsippi" that the early Michigan Indians knew, the White River still holds a semiprimitive charm along much of its course—enough to earn it a "Country Scenic River" designation from the state.

The headwaters of the White are formed by small feeders 8 to 10 miles northeast of White Cloud in Newaygo County. After flowing south to the town of White Cloud, the river turns west to Hesperia, then southwest across Oceana County into Muskegon County, on through White Lake, and finally it empties into Lake Michigan.

The White has a moderate current, an average fall of around 6 feet per mile, a tremendous abundance of wildlife and waterfowl in its varied surroundings, and best of all, there are a lot of trout to be had, particularly in the upper reaches and in its north branch.

Since the White is only a short half-hour from Muskegon and less than 60 miles from Grand Rapids, one might think "Uh-oh. Pressure." Not so. While it does get some canoe traffic in the summer, most of the fishing pressure occurs during the early spring and late fall steelhead and the mid-autumn salmon runs. Its charm as a year-round trout producer isn't as well known. A lot of people are familiar with the lower White: big, sluggish water, often silty and dark, something the wading angler looks at with trepidation. Yet just above and below Hesperia and particularly above White Cloud, this river is a lively and productive, mixed-bag trout fishery.

Consider the uppermost reaches first. If you take MI 37 north out of White Cloud, you can turn east and access at several nearby bridges. Where MI 20 leads east from MI 37, it's less than a mile to the MI 20 bridge that spans pretty water both upstream and down. The banks are private and parking is tight along the busy road, but it is fly-fishable, though small like much of this upper river.

A more wild area can be easily reached by going north of MI 20 to Three Mile Road, then east to an iron bridge with a small adjacent parking area. (The road does cross the bridge, but ends abruptly at a private hunt club.) The river averages 15 to 20 feet across here, is easily waded, and has lots of trout—not all small, either. It is also pleasant to note the extensive habitat improvement and erosion-control work done in past years: stone diversion wings, log "cribs" paralleling the flow, pine stumps strategically and scenically placed. The number of small trout seen on recent trips suggests natural reproduction in progress, an excellent indication for the future.

We have done well here on dries, particularly terrestrials in the waning days of summer. Small black and cinnamon ants most often produce fish in the upper White. Crickets and beetle imitations are received nearly as well, and a Dave's Hopper pulled from the grass into a bankside run will usually entice the larger fish. Other dry patterns worth trying include the flashy Trudes, various shades of Elk-Hair Caddis, and the Adams. Additionally, a selection of Variants in cream, dun, and brown will serve as hatch matchers for these noncritical trout.

Subsurface work can be handled by an assortment of spiky Hare's Ears in natural and olive tones. You might throw in a few small (size 18) Pheasant Tail nymphs, a few Woolly Buggers, and a White Zonker for a change of pace.

If you don't mind a 5-minute walk (and who would when cradling a fly rod on the way to new territory), another beautiful section of the upper White can be reached by going north on MI 37 to Whitford's Corner (where MI 37 makes its big swing west) and taking Jackson Road east for 0.5 mile. Head north on Walnut Avenue for 0.3 mile. A trailhead sign welcoming foot travel across public land can be seen on the east side of Walnut at this point, and the ¼-mile hike to the disused forest service campground puts you on the river. Foot trails parallel the White both up and down through pine groves, aspen stands, hardwoods, and considerable streamside fly-eating,

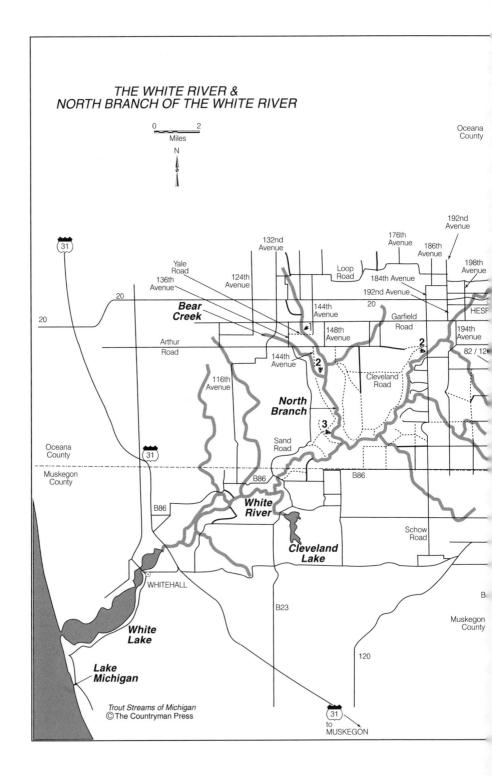

THE WHITE RIVER &
NORTH BRANCH OF THE WHITE RIVER

0   2
Miles

N

Oceana
County

192nd
Avenue

176th
Avenue

186th
Avenue

198th
Avenue

31

Loop
Road

184th Avenue

132nd
Avenue

124th
Avenue

Yale
Road

136th
Avenue

20

20

Bear
Creek

192nd Avenue

20

Garfield
Road

HESP

194th
Avenue

144th
Avenue

148th
Avenue

82 / 12

Arthur
Road

144th
Avenue

2

Cleveland
Road

2

North
Branch

116th
Avenue

3

Sand
Road

Oceana
County

31

Muskegon
County

B86

B86

B86

B86

White
River

Schow
Road

Cleveland
Lake

WHITEHALL

B23

Muskegon
County

White
Lake

120

Lake
Michigan

Trout Streams of Michigan
© The Countryman Press

31
to
MUSKEGON

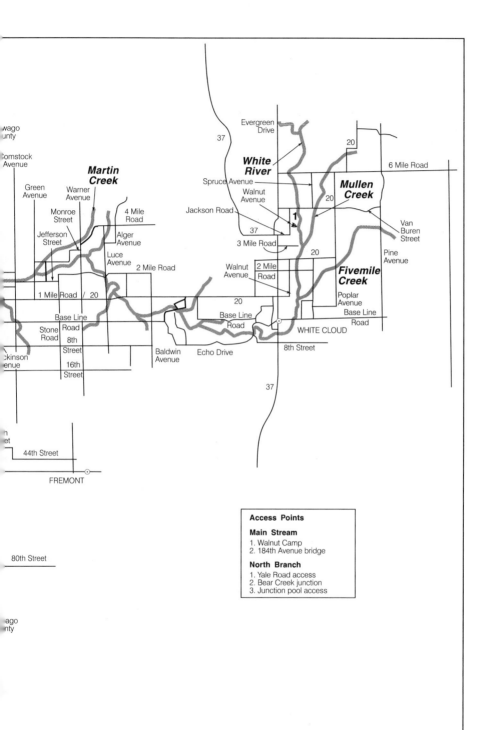

Martin **Creek**

White **River**

Mullen **Creek**

Fivemile **Creek**

Evergreen Drive

Spruce Avenue
Walnut Avenue
Jackson Road

6 Mile Road

Van Buren Street

Pine Avenue

Comstock Avenue

Green Avenue
Warner Avenue
Monroe Street
Jefferson Street
4 Mile Road
Alger Avenue
Luce Avenue
2 Mile Road

37

37

3 Mile Road

Walnut Avenue
2 Mile Road

20

20

Poplar Avenue

Base Line Road

1 Mile Road / 20

20

Base Line Road

Base Line Road

WHITE CLOUD

Stone Road
8th Street
16th Street
Baldwin Avenue
Echo Drive
8th Street

wago unty

ckinson enue

n et
44th Street

FREMONT

37

80th Street

ago nty

Access Points

Main Stream
1. Walnut Camp
2. 184th Avenue bridge

North Branch
1. Yale Road access
2. Bear Creek junction
3. Junction pool access

tippet-busting brush. Roll casting becomes more of a necessity in these increasingly close quarters.

This heavy streamside salad harbors bugs and small critters (mice!) that end up as trout protein. Be sure to try a large cricket pattern near the banks and stumps during any midday lull. A Deer-Hair Mouse, fished dead-drift with only an infrequent twitch, can bring the largest fish to surface at dawn and dusk.

Fly-fishing north of this point is up to one's discretion and ability, but it's worth a look to drive up to the "pool" area, particularly in the spring. (Take Evergreen Road straight north from the MI 37 curve to Six Mile Road, then go east about 1 mile to the bridge.) Wading is tough in the immediate area due to the soft bottom and marshy terrain, but the springs bubbling through the silty sand bespeak the high quality of the water. Insect life is abundant, and judicious wading or belly-boating can put you amidst some good hatches, especially in the pooled areas upstream from the bridge.

As the White River leaves the White Cloud area and flows west below and then above MI 20 toward Hesperia, it broadens and loses that true trout stream character. One is presented with long expanses of sterile-looking sand, bankside brush, and only an occasional snag or rock for fish cover. There are segments of quality water interspersed along this 13 miles of river, and several road crossings north and south of MI 20 provide an easy way to look for what you want.

By exploring the "middle river" in this fashion, we have had some good fishing in the Aetna vicinity on caddis in June. It was here one evening that I convinced Bob that the western-style Goddard Caddis tie could be used to good effect, though he still contends that even though I caught more fish (many more), the *one* he caught was bigger, therefore smarter, therefore pickier, and thus, since the "greatest fish in the river" took his favored Henryville, the best-pattern argument was moot. The fish *are* pickier in this stretch and artificials need to closely ape the naturals. Thorax and Compara Dun ties are recommended for the mayfly hatches and, if fishing in June, be sure you have a supply of Brown Drake patterns in your vest. Olives, Sulphurs, Gray Drakes, and the White Fly *(leukon)* are representative hatches throughout the season, and the Compara Dun versions will rarely fail you. Caddis are abundant. Carry a variety of shades and sizes in the Elk-Hair, a few Goddards in natural and black, and some small Henryville Caddis for those extracritical fish.

This is one of those areas where the White regains some personality: there are broken currents, more rocks and gravel, varieties of slicks and runs. The river maintains this diversity, in varying degrees, up to and a bit below Pinchtown Bridge, which is a mile north of MI 20 on Luce Road.

Attractive water can also be found along several stretches below the dam in Hesperia, the barrier halting the upstream migration of anadromous fish. Along with the occasional big brown, you can, depending on the time of year, look for salmon and steelhead—straggler steelies sometimes hang in our Michigan rivers on into June. The MI 20 bridge and roadside stretches just west of Hesperia aren't a bad bet for the fly-fisherman in a hurry.

Taylor Bridge on Garfield Road just north of town is mostly bounded by private holdings, but a quick 0.25-mile drive south on 194th Street puts you at an access point on public land. The gravel riffle water typical of this area can be fished easily from here.

An even prettier segment of the White flows just a bit southwest of here at the end of 184th Street coming in from the north off Garfield. The road terminates at a scenic overlook where a gaggle of two-tracks meander downstream allowing access at several promising bends. You can also access this area from the south, where several two-tracks go west off 184th Street (which, incidentally, does not cross the river). However you reach it, this portion of the White has everything: wide cobblestone flats, narrow chutes, rapids, big pools, sand, gravel, stream vegetation, and plenty of bug habitat and hatches. This gets a lot of traffic in salmon season, and canoeing is popular, but there is only moderate fishing pressure otherwise. And while the White is an even bigger river farther down, a note of caution is made here too: Bank paths bordering deep chutes or pools have been known to crumble, loose rocks and sand can put a careless high-banker in the river, and slick rocks abound in the stream.

The reasonable downstream limit for the wading fly-fisherman should probably be put at Pines Point and a few more miles downstream. This USFS recreation and camping area can be reached by going 3.25 miles west of Taylor Bridge on Garfield to 168th Street. Signs then direct you south and east 2.5 miles to the site. You can conveniently fish around a big loop by the campground and end up near your starting point, and there are still decent proportions of lively water, cover, and pools.

There are high banks, hardwood forest, and lots of wild territory to the south and west of Pines Point. To better utilize this scenic tract, the forest service has marked a trailhead in the Pines Point campground that starts you down a hiking path southwest along the White for more than 6 miles. Plans are to continue the trail all the way to and up along the North Branch of the White. The trail currently provides walking access to a lot of wide, clear, well-graveled trout water. The bulk of this region has been closed to off-road vehicles so the *quiet* backcountry experience is definitely enhanced.

It isn't uncommon to pick up more chubs downstream here, and while lunker-brown stories circulate occasionally, the White becomes, as you move even farther down, more the realm of northern pike, smallmouth bass, and in recent years, home to a burgeoning walleye fishery. This big slow water

Steve works on a soft-hackle wet on the upper White.

gets real tough to wade even in low-water conditions, especially as you get into the muck farm and marsh regions near White Lake.

In this written ramble along the White River, I have alluded once or twice to a branch coming in from the north. If called on to choose just one of the two, the main White (south) or the North Branch, my nod would go to the North Branch in southern Oceana County. This decision is based primarily on the success of recent excursions, but there is a good deal of nostalgia involved too.

This was the river where in the early 1960s I took my first really good brown, and it was along these banks and in these bottoms that I first stalked deer in the infancy of bowhunting when a recurve was something new. My father-in-law, Glenn Snook, and my wife's uncle, Jim Scott, both of Whitehall, knew these waters well and here taught me many of the intricacies of taking trout and finding cold beer.

I still return to this stream several times a year, now mainly to pursue steelhead in early April, but also to see if I can hit one of those blizzard Brown Drake hatches during June. Big browns are still around, and I hope one day to top Jim Scott's 6-pounder.

When (okay, *if* . . .) this happens, it may well be between Arthur Road and Garfield Road where, due to a paucity of gravel and a late opening, steelheaders don't pound it as heavily. (Above Garfield fly-fishing is *really* tough due to brush-choked casting lanes.) Watch for one of those pastoral little one-lane bridges that looks so isolated you just know no one else has hit it for years. Go south off Garfield on 144th Street for a half-mile. The road bends west to the river, becoming Yale Road, and extends through to 136th Street.

At this bridge there are a couple of pull-offs for parking, and a rough two-track follows the east bank upstream. The bottom is almost exclusively sand with an occasional scatter of fine gravel. Most of the cover is from overhanging vegetation. The casting channel is not generous though the river averages 25 feet in width. It is easily waded most of the time, but remember that the North Branch is quick to rise after a good spell of rain. Fortunately, it lowers and clears quickly also. I hear of brook trout being taken here, but have personally only taken browns. Brooks are also known to be in some of the tributaries feeding into the North Branch, but those feeders I've checked are tough to fly-fish.

A large block of federal land lies below Arthur Bridge. It is a popular but still very productive area of the North Branch and can be easily reached by coming in from the west on Arthur Road and then turning south (right) when Arthur Road meets 144th Street. At 0.3 mile take the smaller left fork and you'll soon see the river from a high overlook. The two-track continues south along the river for a mile, providing many access points before it runs into another trail. A left turn will take you to a parking area at the juncture of Bear Creek and the North Branch.

This is a remarkably beautiful area, and fishing is pretty reliable just about any time of year. The river averages 20 to 30 feet wide and 1 to 4 feet deep, and its myriad twists, bends, and jams create some deep pools with attendant slicks and tailwater, the looks of which will get the juices going in the most jaded of river critics. The bottom has a good mix of sand and clay with silty "burrowing" mud along the edges in plenty of spots. Springs trickle in from slick clay banks here and there, and several tributaries other than Bear Creek also cool the waters.

Gravel bars and graveled runs abound, so anadromous fish hold through this area and draw large numbers of spring and fall anglers. We have taken nice browns, a couple over 20 inches, in early spring when steelheading. It's fun to go back in warmer weather to these same holds and see if one of those released will repay you by coming to a dry. Even if nothing shows, it's more *exciting* to cover water where you know a big guy could be skulking. And while we don't mark fish, Bob purports to have caught the same 16-inch North Branch brown in April and again in June, basing said claim on a distinctive hump in the fish's dorsal area; "apparently a genetic defect or an accident of youth," he declaimed. My ingenuous query about how much of his mistempered youth was spent in abusing fish and calling it an accident was taken with admirable aplomb.

Most of the land below Bear Creek is public and can be accessed via two-track off 142nd Avenue on the west and from 160th Avenue on the east. Caution: Logging in recent years has made it a bit of a jigsaw puzzle hereabouts, particularly on the west side, so if you get to rambling, keep a compass handy.

But if you have a mind to fish near where the North Branch empties into the main stem, give it a shot. I know I have always liked to sample any branch right at and just up from its junction with another river. I have it in my head that the big cannibals from the main river may take a sojourn up a branch (other than to spawn), but they want the larger water close at hand. Not particularly logical, but I keep finding good fish in those locales, and who doesn't like to fish the edges, swirls, and tails of major current convergences?

One way to get to the mouth of the North Branch is to take Fruitvale Road (aka B 86, Skeels Road, or County Line Road) to its crossing of the White River at County Line Bridge by the Happy Mohawk Canoe Livery. Go west about 200 yards to Sand Road (142nd Street), then turn right and go north 2.3 miles. Take a right on the two-track here. (There are several spokes at this juncture, but the main trail goes east toward the river; metal Boy Scout insignia on trees are further landmarks.) Stay on this two-track for 0.6 mile—don't take the first right fork, which is only a bit over 100 yards from Sand Road—and when you come to the next major fork (0.6 mile), take the right-hand trail and you will arrive at a turnaround campsite clearing. A northerly trail from this spot takes you the remaining brief distance to the confluence of the North Branch with the main White River.

Attractor dries can perform quite well in the North Branch. The Royal Wulff, Lime Trude, and the egg-sac version of the Irresistible are good searching patterns. Hex nymphs and the Gold-Ribbed Hare's Ear are smart choices for subsurface probing. Remember that the North Branch gets a sizable steelhead run and that trout eggs are a common food source. Try a small egg-fly dropper on your nymph rig and you may be rewarded with a lusty encounter. Muddler Minnows, Woolly Buggers, and the Light Spruce Fly are favored streamers for the North Branch. Fish them slowly through the deepest holds and undercut banks. It may take several casts, but you should make contact with a big brown if you have the required patience.

Notes:

- While we generally do our own camp cooking or opt for sandwiches from a cooler, when near the upper White at least one stop at "What'ta Pizza" in White Cloud is on the list. Four of us once got three meals from a deluxe model there; talk about *good*. At the north end of town Sally's restaurant with homemade bread and a varied menu is also recommended.

- Rental cottages and resorts abound in the White Cloud and Hesperia vicinities and especially in the White Lake area near Lake Michigan. One can also find beaches, state parks, dune rides, tours of all sorts, canoe liveries, museums, charter boats—you name it. A helpful visitor's guide to Newaygo County can be picked up at most stores and restaurants, and the White Lake Area Chamber of Commerce (231-893-4585) can be most helpful.

- The White River environs—from the headwaters on down—offer good mushrooming, and not just for the famous morel in the spring; stumpers, oysters, and other edible varieties can be found in season (happily during trout time) so keep an eye peeled as you hike to and from fishing spots. It is an enjoyable family activity too. Remember, however, to check with an expert if you are in *any* doubt about identifying edible versus poisonous mushrooms.

- If you're canoeing or just poking around the lower White River's marsh area, evidence of early lumbering skullduggery can occasionally be found in the form of legends with company "brands" stamped on them. Thieves would cut off a log end, discard it in the river, and restamp the log with their own marks. The well-preserved remnants are an interesting historical conversation piece.

- The White River is rich in Indian lore. Tales of ancient battles are chronicled, and Burying Ground Point near Whitehall has an interesting story of an Ottawa chief whose son disappeared while canoeing. The chief is said to have watched for his son faithfully from this point; his body was found much later under a collapsed bank nearby where he had apparently taken refuge from a storm.

ROGUE RIVER
Newaygo County, Kent County

This metropolitan stream is one of those rare jewels that seems to shine brighter with passing time. Despite the rapid population growth of the greater Grand Rapids area and the ever increasing popularity of fly-fishing, the Rogue is fishing better than ever. There is a lot of caring and stewardship to be credited, but the river's natural features contribute mightily to the thriving trout population. I have personal experience with only one other river in the United States that so consistently provides quality angling so close to a major city—and that is the Kinnikinnic in western Wisconsin just 30 minutes from St. Paul, Minnesota.

For this book, the Rogue was a given from day one. It is a quality trout stream of good size, something most southern Michigan streams don't have. For most of its 40-mile flow it is wadable water, so the pressure it gets from being adjacent to Grand Rapids gets spread out nicely. You don't have to feel that since someone may have fished the stretch ahead of you, the fish will be down. And various publications have praised it for having a diversity of insect species rivaling the hallowed Au Sable.

Where to fish this sleeper? An angler new to the Rogue might look at a map and key on the large Rogue River State Game Area through which flow

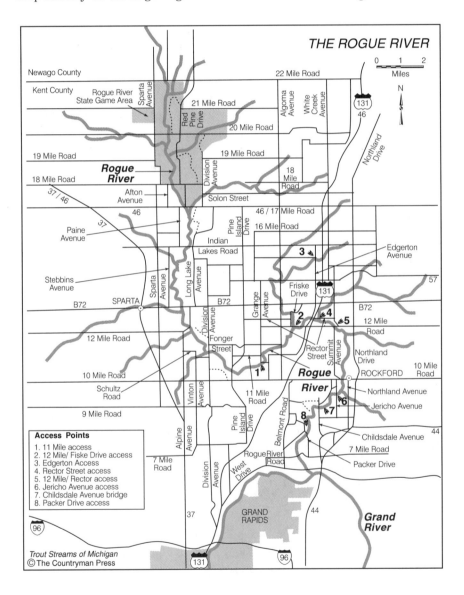

the headwaters. True, it is a bit more primitive there, and access is no concern, but it probably isn't the best choice for quality fishing.

If, however, you do happen to find yourself in the northeast corner of Kent County, and the urge to lay out some line is pressing, the water here is worth a try. In fact, a recent tip that some big fish were being taken up there during the Hex hatch sent us onto the Rogue in the state game area to see what we could find.

We didn't find any big fish—no hatch was on—but a couple of medium browns were snookered by the ever-productive Woolly Bugger, a logical choice in the somewhat swampy, silty environs of the upper Rogue. One stretch that we liked can be reached by taking Red Pine Road to the second public-access trail you come to, which lies 1.5 miles north of Eighteen Mile Road. This trail cuts west to the river and leaves you above a slow, meandering flow running mostly through oozy, timbered low ground. It is 20 to 30 feet in width and 1 to 3 feet deep.

The main virtue here is the abundance of sunken and protruding log cover. We all know how browns love logs, and these old timbers have caused the current to carve out good holes in the sand and silt bottom and against the banks. It does indeed look like good Hex water. If you are just prospecting, you will find that the sluggish current makes you work to get the realistic action you want from a streamer, but of course dead-drifted nymphs and attractor dries require no special effects.

Now let's jump all the way down the mouth of the Rogue and work up through the best water to the east and west of US 131.

Like so many Michigan rivers, the lower Rogue gets a lot of play in salmon and steelhead season as runs move up from its confluence with the Grand River toward the dam at Rockford. It is fast, rocky, and attractive water in these reaches, and anadromous fish find it to their liking, but they do not get all the attention. Resident rainbows and browns have their holds behind the many large rocks and in the deep pools, waiting for the right fly. The fishing below the dam is very good.

Take a look at its wide expanse where it crosses Rogue River Road just up from the mouth and also a bit higher up along Packer Drive; shoulder parking and a couple of small pull-offs give you access to varied and picturesque water. Broad gravel stretches give way to sand, then more gravel appears. Fast riffles tail into deep holds at the bends. You can unleash your casting through here, as room is no problem, nor is wading in most spots. Felts are helpful due to the abundance of slippery rocks.

The water continues to be attractive up by the bridge on Childsdale Avenue. The current is fast, the rocks and boulders form eddies, and slicks and glides invite a dry fly. The water is clear and the fish fairly sophisticated, so light leaders are recommended. We rarely go above 6X, but some of the regulars we have talked with advocate 7X and 8X when fish are fussy and light conditions work against the angler. You can expect numerous fish in the 10-inch range and fair numbers in the 12- to 15-inch category.

Upstream from the Childsdale Avenue access you will find a bridge on Jericho Avenue with adjacent parking. There is a very nice riffle upstream, and below the bridge you will find a repeating series of riffle-run pool configurations. These continue downstream to the "Powerline Pool" which many regard as one of the best spots on the river.

The river has nearly every hatch a person could want, but get in on the White Fly *(leukon)* in September if you can. Blanket hatches have been coming off in recent seasons, down here in the lower stretches as well as in the more popular trout water above Rockford. It is a great hatch that doesn't get the attention that the more traditional Hendrickson, Brown Drake, and Hex hatches do earlier in the year.

Just 2 miles north of Rockford's city center, Summit Avenue intersects Twelve Mile Road and a right turn (eastward) on Twelve Mile will quickly bring you to a parking area near the bridge over the Rogue.

The streambed in this area averages 45 feet in width with a sand- and fine-gravel-based bottom and mud-edged banks. The current is moderate and the nonthreatening flow ranges from 1 to 3 feet in depth. A repeating pool-and-riffle condition is particularly pleasant and conducive to a variety of fly-angling methods. You will notice rather large rocks at midstream, and these should be fished carefully. Both the up- and downstream current breaks, and eddies formed by these rocks are often occupied by feeding trout.

Upstream from the Twelve Mile bridge, there is a long flat of 100-plus yards that bends sharply to the left at the edge of Rector Street. This flat stretch can be very productive even during periods when there is no obvious caddis or mayfly activity. At the outside of the bend (the right bank) near Rector Street the fish can usually be seduced by a small black ant or Secret Rubber Bug. Throughout this run, and in fact throughout the area near Twelve Mile and Rector Roads, terrestrials will almost always produce if fished carefully under the overhanging brush near the banks. Rector Street (which runs west from Summit just north of Twelve Mile Road) parallels the Rogue up to the point where the river flows westerly under US 131, and the fishing in the immediate proximity of the expressway is quite good if you don't mind the rumble and roar of traffic.

Stegman Creek enters the Rogue about 0.5 mile downstream from the bridge on US 131 at the foot of Rector Street. The Stegman's flow is very clean and cold and will drop the temperature of the Rogue as much as 6 degrees F in the warm summer months. Obviously, this is good for the trout in this stretch of the river. In the bitter cold of winter, Stegman's effect is the

BOB LINSENMAN

Steve casts a streamer on the upper Rogue.

opposite; its constant temperature inflow warms the Rogue to a more comfortable range for trout and makes for productive water angling. This nearly 1 mile stretch of river is excellent and a favorite of noted angler and author Bob Braendle.

Upstream from Rector Street, Edgarton Road parallels the highway. Follow Edgarton Road to a bridge over the Rogue. This bridge area has parking room for a couple of cars. This stretch of river has superb Brown Drake and sculpin hatches and is kept cool during the summer by the cold water influx from Cedar Creek.

The Rogue crosses Twelve Mile Road again about 1.5 miles west of Summit. Here the stream is a bit wider, reaching 50-plus feet in some spots. The mild current carries a bit more color in this section, but the light mocha tinge does not seem to adversely affect the ability of the trout to see and take small midges and terrestrial patterns. The streambed is mostly fine gravel and sand with a few large rocks providing likely feeding stations at midriver.

There is a parking space for one automobile at the bridge on Twelve Mile, and just west of the bridge and north on Friske Drive you will find several streamside parking spots (one with a thoughtfully, strategically placed trash receptacle and canoe launch). Just downstream from the first parking spot there is a nice riffle that will often give up a healthy brown in the 12-inch class to a darting Muddler Minnow. This riffle also should be fished with dry flies, and a small Henryville Caddis is an excellent choice for a searching pattern. This area is heavily forested with mature mixed hardwoods that often overhang the stream, providing cooling shade and cover, and only rarely interfere with the length or placement of your back cast.

Algoma Avenue runs north and south about 0.3 mile west of Friske Drive. Approximately 0.75 mile south of Twelve Mile on Algoma Avenue there is a bridge with ample parking on both sides of the river. This access is only 1 river mile up from the Friske Drive area, but the stream at the Algoma bridge has little of the lively spirit or attractive scenery described earlier. Near Algoma Road the Rogue is narrower, perhaps 40 feet, and deeper with a sand and silt bottom, marshy banks, dense cattails, and a slow, sullen current. There are trout in this stretch, however, and some of them reach into the high teens. Try a slow, deep retrieve with a weighted Marabou Muddler, or a dead drift with an olive-shaded Hare's Ear.

Just south of the bridge Algoma Avenue is intersected by Eleven Mile Road. Turn west (right) on Eleven Mile Road, which turns sharply south and becomes Jewell Road. After 0.3 mile you will notice a paved road (marked as Eleven Mile Road) off to the right. This road dead-ends at the beautiful old (closed to vehicular traffic) bridge over the Rogue. There is parking for several cars at this footbridge.

Downstream from the bridge there is an attractive and productive streamwide riffle that has a firm gravel, sand, and rock bottom, shaded banks, and a fair population of brown trout with a few rainbows thrown in for spice. These fish respond well to Pheasant Tail and Hare's Ear nymphs, Woolly Buggers and Muddler Minnow streamers, and terrestrials and Henryville Caddis dry patterns—most of the time.

During an emergence or spinner fall, the prevailing insect must be matched closely for optimum results. We have had good success with parachute ties and Compara Dun patterns when the fish are honed in tight to a specific bug. If you do not tie your own you may obtain all you need, as well as timely, friendly, and accurate information on stream conditions, hatches, and whathaveyou, at the Great Lakes Fly Fishing Company in Rockford..

Upstream from this bridge there is a long, slow flat with aquatic grasses, large rocks, undercut banks, and some superselective fish of above-average size. This slow, smooth water necessitates long leaders, fine tippets, and a delicate delivery. Cress bug imitations, midge pupae, ants, the Griffith's Gnat, and small, soft-hackle wets are effective offerings in this upstream stretch.

On a recent visit to this section I talked to a Grand Rapids angler who had just taken three chunky browns on Hare's Ears from the riffle, so I waded slowly upstream and managed a few nice fish (one a 13-inch rainbow) on foam ants. This is one of the most pleasant and productive reaches of the Rogue and it is highly recommended.

There are easy access points at Nestor Road (where Pine Island Road enters from the northwest) and at Division Avenue near the Sparta Airport, but the river is slow, silty, warmer, and less productive than the downstream run from Eleven Mile Road to Twelve Mile Road at Summit Avenue.

The Rogue fishery is a happy tribute to the fruits of cooperation among concerned citizens. Trout Unlimited, the West Michigan Environmental Action Council, landowners, and other conservationists have joined forces to vastly improve the angling quality of this scenic, metropolitan river.

Notes:

- Grand Rapids has nearly every amenity conceivable to a large city, including lodging, shopping malls, restaurants, and quality public golf courses.
- The John Ball Park Zoo is worth the trip, as is the Gerald Ford Museum.
- Nearby Holland, to the southwest, is famous for its tulips, and this beautiful lakeshore town has many other points of interest including the Netherlands Museum, windmills, and wooden-shoe factories.
- The White Pine Trail is a scenic bike and hiking trail that runs from Comstock all the way to Cadillac.

COLDWATER RIVER
Barry County

When I first started searching for fly-fishable streams in Southwest Michigan back in the early 1970s, the Coldwater River in northern Barry County was recommended. It was receiving a heavy stocking of brown trout back then, whose growth rate was said to be excellent, but was subject to periodic chemical reclamation.

After some desultory dabbles, my endeavors switched to other rivers and it wasn't until the summer of 2000 that I once more waded this veiled treasure. "Habitat improvement with half logs and a change to the Gilchrist strain of browns have greatly improved this fishery," MDNR agent Jim Dexter assured me.

My vague recollections of its roomy width for fly casting were rewarded on a recent visit. The main highway (MI 43) going north out of Hastings, Michigan, hits Broadway, which becomes Hastings Road and crosses a pleas-

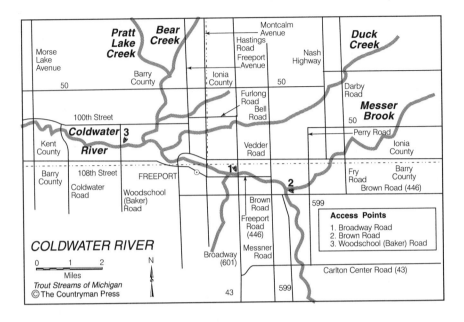

ant stretch of the Coldwater past the Freeport Road intersection. A check with the landowners just south of the stream resulted in a pleasant conversation and a "no problem" permission for access. Cautions against parking along this highway are well founded. Shoulders are narrow and the blacktop pretty busy for an out-in-the-country road. Be careful.

Like many Southwest Michigan streams, the high banks cradling long, straight stretches of "channeled" water gave testimony to dredging and straightening in past years. The silt and sediment also typical of this area's streams added high color to the water, since (as often seems to be the case when stream prospecting) frog-strangling rains had hit the region just prior to arrival.

Even with this, wading was easy against the brisk current as I plied various search patterns. Casting was no problem in the 25-foot width. The abundant cobble and gravel under my boots bespoke the wisdom of felt soles, and prompted the fishing of a favorite crayfish pattern. Even though it would be difficult to see them, it was easy to picture the little crustaceans scurrying away as their rocky crevices were disturbed.

The straight stretches are occasionally broken up with patches of riffle water, caddis havens by their look. Conversations since held with other anglers reinforced this impression; a size 14–18 Elk-Hair Caddis can put you into fish for much of the season.

Large-growing tree trunks standing partially in the water are in abundance here, the current piling against their submerged root systems to form the hideouts browns so love. Overhanging vegetation shades the water giving terrestrials places to clamber about—and fall into waiting jaws.

A later chat with the Fisheries Division revealed that this Broadway crossing area is one section where they conduct electro-shocking surveys. The most recent of these showed good numbers of 16-inch fish and an overall increase in trout numbers.

Conditions being as they were (muddy), the logical move was upstream in search of clearer water. The river makes a bit of a turn south by Brown Road and bends and curves were more in evidence, particularly north of this crossing. A couple of good-sized feeders empty in here also, but the water was still clearer—and trouty looking. A mix of sand, gravel, fallen timber and those long, waving underwater fronds got my senses pricked for action. A Henryville Special shortly produced a prime 12-inch brown—vindication at last.

I have already programmed a late August trip into my schedule to see if some hopper patterns won't spark up a few more browns. The hay and grain fields adjoining the stream hereabouts make one think such an approach could be dynamite.

The whole stretch below Brown Road to Carleton Center Road (MI 43) and even farther down is reputedly good, fly-fishable water. If one's roll casting, tight-quarter skills are in form, it wouldn't hurt to test a couple of

A "channeled" tree-lined stretch, overgrown enough to be picturesque

STEVE NEVALA

the tributaries that feed the Coldwater in this vicinity. Jim Bedford, one of this state's premier trout wizards, speaks well of them in his various articles, Tyler Creek being high on his list.

A later trip found me on the bigger downstream water at the Coldwater Road Crossing a couple of miles west of Freeport. Once again impeccable timing resulted in runoff conditions, but clarity was sufficient to fish. Wading cautions are in order here in this heavier 30- to 40-foot-wide section, and farther on down. Of course, big trout cover is here. Lots of large fallen trees form current breaks and deep swirls. It has the look of Hex water, but learned friends who have done the late-night bank patrol here a time or two report the big bug a no-show.

Having heard that the West Michigan Chapter of TU had provided some access near the Wood School Road crossing (aka. Baker Road), a stop there was in order. It certainly is heartwarming to see a sign reading FISHERMEN WELCOME as opposed to the more commonly seen KEEP OUT sign. This TU group has established a pathway called the Dolan Trail on the north side of the river, so getting into and out of this prime bit of trout water is further facilitated.

As might be expected, habitat improvement has been done along the stretch, and there is a good mix of sand, silt, and gravel. Moderate current and an average 30-foot width make fly-fishing most enjoyable.

It was on this jaunt that I collared Pete Schantz at his sports shop (Al & Pete's Sports) in Hastings to see if any "local expert" input was available. A fortuitous meeting it was, for he was eager to tout the virtues of his local stream.

"The Hendrickson hatches in early spring are pretty dependable," he said, "and Sulphurs go through mid-June. If nothing's in real evidence, you can usually interest fish on parachute Adams, size 14, and smaller Royal Wulff patterns have worked well for me."

He concurred with my favorable impression of the water above and below Brown Road. "Great stretch. We've picked up some good fish there—on dries—and farther down too, working streamers after dark. And that bigger water below Coldwater Road has been known to hold some brook trout where colder feeders empty in, though browns predominate."

Twenty-inch rainbows have occasionally surprised a lucky angler in this river. Jim Dexter has since told me of naturally reproducing rainbows generated from a past "on a whim" planting of leftover steelhead fingerlings. Good things do happen.

The Coldwater was last rotenoned in 1992, and according to the area MDNR, it is unlikely that this will be done again. The current MDNR administration favors habitat improvement and supplemental stocking when need be, finding this approach to show better results than does chemical reclamation.

Give it a try. It is a pretty little river in its farm country environs, and unlikely to disappoint.

A reminder: One of the landowners from whom I had earlier gained entry had cautioned me to be sure to park clear of his farm vehicle lanes. Mentioning this in passing to Pete Schantz elicited an affirmative nod and remarks to the effect that in all these years he had fished the Coldwater, the only negative landowner ever encountered had been one who couldn't get haying apparatus into his field due to some dunderhead parked smack in the center of the only entry lane. Hard to imagine, but it would appear some people shut off their brains right with the car ignition.

Notes:

- Charlton Park in Hastings has a re-created early rural Michigan village on the site of an old Potawatomi Indian landing along the Thornapple River.
- Nearby Gun Lake offers a glass-bottom boat ride on the Gun Lake Princess (616-672-7822).
- "The Devil's Soup Bowl" isn't far away and provides an overview of the Yankee Springs area.

THE GUN RIVER
Allegan County

The Gun River north of Kalamazoo is a down-to-earth sort—she inspires no poetry, she can't even be called pretty . . . but she will, on occasion, treat you right. Every season I hear of someone who has charmed her with the right offering and been rewarded handsomely. Most recently it was a student of a local fly-tying instructor who took lessons to heart and came away with a 6-pound Gun River brown taken on a nymph below US 131.

The Gun, a designated trout stream, empties into the Kalamazoo River near Plainwell after flowing out of Gun Lake about a dozen miles to the northeast. Years ago it was dredged to drain the Gun Plain farms of this fertile area, resulting in some long, straight stretches and the usual negatives inherent in this type of "progress." Fortunately the many springs in this low-ground agricultural belt infused enough cooling water to maintain a viable trout population. The state stocks 8,000 browns each year, and since pressure is light, many trout mature to impressive proportions.

A glance at the map shows the upper river paralleling 2nd Street for quite a way as it flows south toward the tiny farming community of Hooper. This makes access very convenient just about anywhere along this stretch. One can, for instance, park where 114th Avenue crosses 2nd Street, walk up or down however far you care to, step the few feet from the blacktop into the stream, and fish back to your vehicle. The high brush-lined banks screen you from passing traffic, the wading is knee-deep over a firm, sandy bottom, and the 25- to 30-foot width is plenty wide for casting. It is a good spot for a spur-of-the-moment quick fish to see what is happening, and while you aren't likely to hit a large hatch here on the Gun, there is usually enough insect activity to bring out a fish or two. Small dries on a light leader are fun to experiment with.

As you move south, there is a rustic and pretty area above and below the 110th Street bridge. I have fished around here to good effect with soft-hackle wets and nymphs with some flash. But when the urge strikes to go after a serious fish, I will move farther down, get in at the 7th Street bridge east of Plainwell and north of 106th Avenue, and fish upstream.

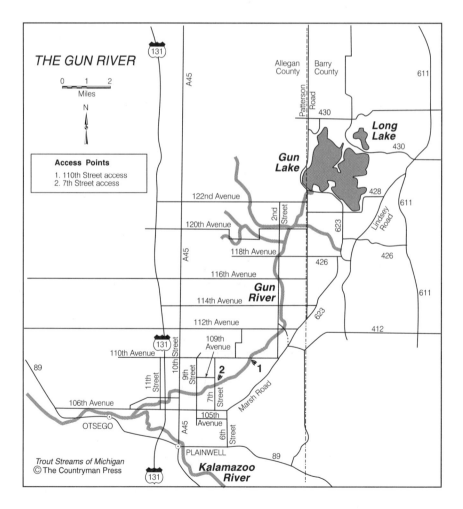

This stretch resembles a pristine river. You will find yourself fishing through sparsely populated farm country with lots of large maples bordering the river. The width is uniform at about 30 feet and the current is lazy. Grapevine tangles and other vegetation clump out over the water to provide plenty of shrouded holds, even in the straight stretches. There is a fair amount of cress and waving aquatic grasses growing in the water for good cover. What is really nice through here is the abundance of logs breaking the current at regular intervals, the larger jams forming those deep, off-current pockets worth a concerted attack.

As in the upper reaches, the bottom is firm, a kind of sand and clay-muck mix, and one rarely has to wade even waist-deep. However, watch your step after a good rain. The water, incidentally, usually carries that tan-gray hue associated with runoff, even during dry spells. The low-lying muck farms it drains explain this. In spite of the coloration, stream visibility is usually fine.

As is my tendency, I will fish smaller dries up through here, often my dark-shaded, bastardized Adams patterns when nothing is popping. Doing so on a recent June excursion, I hooked three or four smallish browns, then switched to a brownish gray, mohair-bodied marabou leech to fish back down. Minutes later a yard-long form detached itself from a submerged log-jam to look more closely at the undulating leech. Momentary heart stoppage, then expulsion of pent breath as he came into better view, turned in a roil of sand, and went to cover. The occasional Gun River whistle-trout (carp) does give one pause, because it is not at all beyond the pale of possibility that a brown of similar dimensions could be the next to inspect your fly.

A couple of other likely lower stretches to try would be in the vicinity of the 9th Street bridge crossing north of 106th Street, or down below US 131 around the Gun River Conservation Club just west of the expressway off 106th Street.

As there are some large trout in these and other areas of the Gun River, experiment with large, wavy fur-strip patterns. The more successful of these is a simple mink-fur leech, basically just a strip of dark brown mink fur tied Matuka-style over a mixed brown and creamy yellow dubbed body. The deeper protected pockets can be probed with other flies that suggest a real mouthful, such as a tan or dark olive crayfish, olive or tan Woolly Buggers, and various marabou streamers. If the color is up, try the latter tied over a Diamond Braid body.

If fishing solitude is one of your major concerns, you can pretty much count on having the Gun River to yourself. Other southwestern streams are more popular, and perhaps the "drain" label has put some off this river. It is unfortunate, but I got that impression recently when I stopped in the hardware store in a small nearby town and began talking with the proprietor. I steered the conversation to local trout fishing, inspiring him to relate his story of a 26½-inch Gun River brown he took many years back, "before the #@*!@ county dredged it and ruined it."

My mild "yeah, buts . . ." regarding very recent (that morning) pleasant and productive excursions didn't impress, and I left thinking that if his attitude reflects the general, it explains the lack of pressure on a river that currently holds some awfully nice browns with more than a couple of wall-hangers lurking in dark, undisturbed pools.

Notes:

- When fishing the lower Gun River, you are virtually in the backyard of the district MDNR office east of Plainwell (612 10th Street, Plainwell, MI, 616-681-6851). It is a good source of information for all sorts of outdoor pursuits, and if the right fisheries personnel are in, you can't do better for up-to-date trout-fishing reports.
- Accommodations and restaurants are plentiful in the Plainwell-Otsego area. Golf courses abound.
- Gun Lake has a public beach and campground, and you are on the southern end of the vast Yankee Springs Recreation Area and its miles of public land, lakes, streams, and camping facilities. Get maps and brochures at the MDNR office.

AUGUSTA CREEK
Barry County, Kalamazoo County

In the Kalamazoo vicinity of southwest lower Michigan, you can't help but take note of the city's namesake, the Kalamazoo River. If you are after trout, the main river, albeit beautiful along many stretches, is not the best choice. It is big water of dubious quality (considerably cleaner now than in the past) and has never been much of a trout producer, though runs of anadromous fish come up as far as the dam in Allegan. *However*—and this is a big however—many of the smaller streams that feed it have superb trout fishing. Of these, the one best suited for an all-around enjoyable fly-fishing experience has to be Augusta Creek.

Augusta Creek flows from the north out of Barry County into Kalamazoo County and empties into the Kalamazoo River at the small town of Augusta, just north of the sprawling Fort Custer Recreation Area. Its approximately 5 miles of fly-fishable water have to be among the most studied and monitored in the state. Michigan State University oversees the Kellogg Forest parcel below MI 89 (all open to trout fishing), and this prestigious school often has professors and graduate students working in the area on various

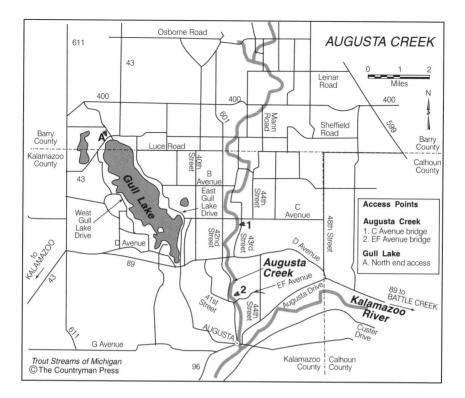

stream-related studies. The Kalamazoo Chapter of Trout Unlimited has put in sediment basins, worked on narrowing the flow in places, generally improving and beautifying the stream, with much more in the offing. The MDNR keeps an ear tuned to angler feedback and formulates much of its management practice from such surveys. Unlike several other area streams, chemical reclamation has not been necessary here.

This close attention, the natural beauty of the stream, the wide variety and proliferation of insects, the ease of access, close proximity to Kalamazoo and Battle Creek, the good numbers of trout—all these factors result in considerable pressure. Most of it is in the early days of the new season when winter doldrums have heightened that opener itch; more rods are in evidence again in early fall when exceptionally good hatches come off. The bulk of the season is uncrowded.

"It's a great place to play match-the-hatch," according to local fish biologist Jim Dexter, "and there are lots of fish, just not a lot of large fish." Not a lot of big ones perhaps, but the occasional 17- to 20-incher can be attested to, and that keeps one's head in the game. Augusta Creek also gets a large yearly stocking of brown trout. This, along with the resident fish, makes for action just about any time of day or season.

As for convenient access to likely stretches, let's start at Augusta and move upstream. Take 42nd Street north from Augusta on the west side of the creek and you will see a power line over the highway just past the village-limits sign. There is plenty of room to park on the east side of 42nd Street, and it is less than 100 yards down the power line right-of-way to the water. A few backyards and homes adjoin the stream down here, so use a little discretion entering and leaving. It is easy to stay in the stream; wading is knee- to thigh-deep along its 20- to 25-foot width and current flow is moderate. The occasional large rock or other obstruction presents some deeper broken-water eddies. When insects are active, as they often are, fish materialize from the varied cover and are remarkably bold about taking up stations in unlikely shallows, so wade and watch carefully.

About a mile north of the power line, EF Avenue crosses Augusta Creek just east of 42nd Street. I like to park at the bridge, walk the streambanks down whatever distance I have time to enjoy, and fish back up to my car. The stream here has mostly waist- to shoulder-high brush edges, giving it a semi-open, meadowy appearance. But don't get careless; this spiky growth gobbles up low back casts and holds on to tippets and flies as tenaciously as Velcro.

Yet it is pretty water below this bridge as it perks along over a darkish bottom with lots of fine to egg-sized gravel. Cut banks with their topknots of grass stems dipping down in the swirls provide plenty of targets when fishing blind. Of course there are always those couple of stems growing just contrary enough to keep you from making the perfect inch-from-the-spot presentation. (Occasionally I break them off for the next guy through . . . well, once I did.)

Above EF Avenue things tighten up a bit as woods predominate. A comfortable 1- to 2-hour fish up through the UpJohn Company holdings puts you at the Kellogg Forest boundary. It is easy to walk out to 42nd Street and walk back to EF Avenue—or fish your way back down.

These lower sections are typical of most of Augusta Creek in that the fish, while sensitized to careless wading and clumsy casting by angling pressure, are not overly critical or selective when it comes down to eating. They will respond to a broad range of attractor dries including the Adams, Irresistible, and Lime Trude. Ants and small beetle imitations are productive along with the Griffith's Gnat. The "standards" should be your first choice in nymphs and streamers as well. Small Pheasant Tails, Hare's Ears, and Fox Squirrel nymphs, and caddis imitations in dark green, tan, and cream will earn strikes. The Light Spruce Fly, Llama, Muddler, and a small (size 10 or 12) Black Ghost or Beaman's Ghost will suffice for the streamer category.

The insects are varied and prolific on Augusta Creek. Carry a selection of Blue-Winged Olives in sizes 16 through 22, Sulphur and Hendrickson patterns (in season), Henryville Caddis, ants, beetles, and a sampler box with Dun and Cream Variants in sizes 16–18. The Green Oak Worm (a very simple-to-tie fly) will often take fish from under the shade near the banks, and a cream-bodied micro-caddis, size 20, is a last-resort insurance policy. (Either Doc's Custom Fly Tackle or Fishing Memories in Portage can supply up-to-date information on stream conditions; both have a complete stock of patterns for Augusta Creek.)

There is nice variety in the EF Avenue area. Brushy little islands occasionally divide the flow, and bends and small pools create that trouty atmosphere we all seek. While there is more human activity as you get farther into Kellogg Forest with its driving loops, hiking trails, and picnic grounds, trees and other foliage shield you, and fishing is pleasant all the way up to MI 89.

There is some private land just above MI 89 so permission should be obtained. And if tighter, more challenging water holds no qualms for you, drive north of 42nd Street to C Avenue. The state owns extensive parcels both above and below this bridge, giving the fisherman access to several thousand feet of fine cold-water trout habitat. Jim Dexter recently told me that mark-and-recapture surveys showed four times the fish below MI 89, but there sure are some nice browns in the higher section.

When I was younger and more ambitious, I would frequently hike and bushwhack until about midway between C Avenue and MI 89. I took nice fish through there, mostly on dries, and it wasn't due to any particular skill. Maybe these harder-to-access fish aren't pestered as often as those in the more popular forest water down below.

The water above C Avenue on up toward B Avenue is where a lot of spawners head in the fall, mostly after the season has closed. During the season, this small water plays host to more chubs than one would expect in the higher reaches of a stream. It is also a bit close for fly-fishing, so I usually curtail activities at C Avenue.

Notes:

- The Fort Custer Recreation Area just east of Augusta has lakes, beaches, trails, and assorted sights to see.
- The Kellogg Forest has a visitor center off 42nd Street just south of MI 89 where you can get current information on programs ranging from day camps to bird watching.

DOWAGIAC CREEK
Cass County

One of the best things to come out of working on this book, besides doing even more trout fishing than our normally excessive amount, was that we were forced to explore water we had always meant to fish, but never seemed to get to. Some of these streams turned out just so-so—too brushy perhaps or sterile or heavy on rough fish, and we would slog away muttering.

But after a couple of trips down to Dowagiac Creek in Cass County, a stream that friends had mentioned many times, the only muttering done was on the phone to get Bob here to sample this enticing and personable little piece of water. This stream and parts of the Dowagiac River proper offer a lot of varied opportunity for the wading fly-fisherman. The creek in particular is a scaled-down version of some of the more vaunted prime northern Michigan water.

After fishing it up and down, asking around regarding seasonal quirks, and getting some very helpful information from the district MDNR personnel, we concluded that this system is, in fact, one of the better trout facilities in lower southwestern Michigan.

Dowagiac Creek was chemically reclaimed in 1971 and 1980 to get rid of competing species, and trout fishing improved dramatically each time. (Only brown trout have been stocked since 1964.) It is unlikely, however, that future rotenone treatments will occur. "Habitat improvement gives a much better return, costs less, and lasts longer," according to fisheries biologist Jim Dexter, who refers to Dowagiac Creek as "one of the better-managed trout streams in southwest Michigan." Jim, who has done comprehensive status reports on several area streams, is very high on the productivity of this fishery, citing its 15 orders of aquatic invertebrates representing 42 separate species, large infusion of groundwater, and good array of habitat.

It is generally agreed in area trout-angler lore, and we found it to be the case, that the better stretches of trout water lie between Bunker Lake to the north down to the rough-fish barrier upstream from Lake LaGrange. There are some rough fish mixed in through here too, but the trout fishing is still superior. The first time I gazed at Dowagiac Creek was from the Gards Prairie Road bridge just north of Volinia. With some misgivings I noted the rather narrow 15-foot casting channel complemented by thick, overhanging vegetation. However, I had earlier that morning talked with a local bait-fisherman who assured me there were some good holes above this spot, and that it was fly-fishable up from there and in the Brown Road area. I found both tips to be true. The current is slow to moderate, the depth averages 2 feet, and the bottom is pretty firm, a mix of sand and silt. While no behemoth was dredged from the occasional hole plumbed with sculpin imitations, the potential for a 20-incher was certainly there. A couple of creek chubs blipped my dry after I switched to a small attractor, but they didn't appear often enough to be overly disturbing. The one decent brown that I brought to hand was a solid, nicely colored, and healthy-looking 13 inches. I commanded him to go forth and eat more chubs.

Trout Streams of Michigan
© The Countryman Press

DOWAGIAC CREEK & THE DOWAGIAC RIVER

Access Points

Dowagiac Creek
1. Marcellus Highway bridge
2. Decatur Road access
3. Kelsey Lake Street access

Dowagiac River
1. Crossing Street bridge
2. Sink Road access
3. Dodd Park access

The stream looks even better in the Russ Forest Area where it crosses Marcellus Highway. Michigan State University owns the property, there is plenty of parking, and paths and bridges bespeak greater human competition. However, the casting is easy due to wide sections, and there is more gravel than downstream. Turning some stream rocks revealed scurrying crayfish, a few stonefly nymphs, and a fair representation of cased caddis larvae.

Bob had a good morning here on a later trip, taking three worth-mentioning browns on small nymphs using his bread-and-butter tandem rig of a size-10 stonefly as the point with a size-14 spiky olive Hare's Ear as the dropper. He confessed to several missed opportunities as well as the three brought to bay and released.

Our helpful fisheries advisor had referred to Dowagiac Creek below Marcellus Highway down to Kelsey Lake Street as the heart of the trout water, with good hatches and lots of wild fish. We tried it in several places through here, and were particularly taken with the creek above and below Decatur Road. Bob spoke warmly of the upstream stretch, open and meadowy environs eliciting "Pennsylvania spring creek aesthetics" and similar name-dropping platitudes with which he is wont to chafe companions. The stream varies from 15 to 30 feet here with lots of cress and grasses breaking the flow and providing cover. Fish hold in these channels and against the banks. It is shallow and clear, but a 12-foot leader terminating in 5X didn't spook the flock, even when the sun was on the water. Dead-drift some scud patterns next to the weeds and through the cress channels. These fish are on the prod for the little freshwater shrimp and sow bugs, and tan, cream, or light olive imitations can be effective. Try tying in one thin strip of pearl Krystal Flash under the plastic shell (back) to add a bit of subdued flash; it can make a positive difference.

The water below the Decatur Road bridge bends and twists its way through a patchwork of woodlots and farm fields, creating promising pools, riffles, jams, eddies, and long glides. I found myself changing flies a lot so I could run some weighted buggy creation through a long pool; then a few feet farther on I would want to dance an attractor Adams variation along the border of a perky riffle. About that time a couple of caddis would appear and require experimentation with a little Trude . . . Lime? . . . no, Royal. And so it would go.

The alternating wide-to-narrow configurations of the stream require a fair amount of roll casting, but about the time that gets old, 50-yard stretches appear, open enough for that full back cast that lets you drop the fly lightly on the mark.

The Griffis Road crossing west of Decatur Road puts you on nice water also, and there is less vehicle traffic along this dirt road. Some fairly large pools call for muddlers, leech patterns, and other meaty depth charges when hatches are quiet. Dowagiac Creek also has a good reputation between Dutch Settlement Street and Kelsey Lake Road to the south. Parking on Dutch Settlement Street is tight, and posted land exists at the Kelsey Lake Road bridge, but permission can generally be obtained, another MDNR assurance we found to be true.

I had heard that fly-fishermen from Indiana often came up to fish these stretches of Dowagiac Creek. "The Sulphur hatch beginning in early May can be spectacular," enthused Jim Gillis of the Cortland Fly Shop in South Bend. "All the traditional Michigan hatches come off well, barring inclement weather. Caddis are active all season." Jim gave a nod to the sparkle pupa, but added that most emerging and low-water dry caddis patterns are effective. He also applauded the reproductive capacities of Dowagiac Creek, noting that he and his group have recently caught 2- and 3-inch trout. Browns

BOB LINSENMAN

You'll often be near or on private property when fishing streams in this area.

are still regularly stocked, and habitat improvement and a switch to the Gilchrist strain (instead of Seaforellen) has led to a high survival rate and greatly improved fishing.

Our other various angler inquiries and readings on the area before our trips revealed a consensus that the creek is not good trout water below Lake LaGrange down to its confluence with the Dowagiac River. This sort of analysis usually piques our interest and we have, on occasion, had a modicum of success in similar scenarios.

We did find the creek to be pretty marshy and silty above and below MI 62, and warm-water species were more in evidence. However, not all was in vain; Dowagiac Creek crosses California Road a few hundred yards north of MI 62 about 3 miles west of the town of Dowagiac, so we hit it there. The high-piled banks and regular channel tell of past dredging and straightening, but time and nature have healed the scars. The brush- and tree-lined high banks make for that tunnel effect common to this form of development, but the water is very clear, the bottom a firm mix of sand and fine gravel with stream vegetation interspersed. Fallen trees and logjams provide holding water, and it was against such a jam that a small brown I watched feeding on little emerging mayflies eventually took the size-18 floating nymph I put over him. I found and tussled with one more active trout by walking the high banks, just looking for rises. Bob had similar luck, taking a couple of fish below the bridge, and we left commenting that we have done a whole lot worse on highly touted stretches. It never hurts to check things out.

THE DOWAGIAC RIVER
Cass County

While Dowagiac Creek has the better reputation in this river system, we have heard tell of anglers who now forgo blue-ribbon rivers to the north such as the Pere Marquette and Manistee in favor of certain areas of the Dowagiac River when the big hatches kick in. We are not sure (yet) we can endorse it that heartily (hatches down here start a little earlier—probably these enthusiasts are getting the best of both worlds) but our explorations and inquiries were encouraging.

The river begins way up in Van Buren County where we first poked around, not much taken with the looks of things after temperature readings and rough-fish encounters. But as we moved south into Cass County the water cooled and the general appearance of the river improved. The stream is quite handsome in the Crossing Street area northwest of Dowagiac. Both up and down from this bridge the water has excellent habitat for caddis, mayflies, dragonflies, and assorted caloric goodies from terra firma. The stream's casting channel is wide enough so that only the rare roll cast is required, and the bottom is firm, allowing easy wading. Try a fat, weighted, brown dragonfly nymph in the slow, deep holes and near the banks or a crayfish pattern similarly offered during periods when insects are not active enough to bring the fish to the surface.

Another appealing area, this below the juncture of Dowagiac Creek, can be fished from a MDNR access site located where the river crosses Sink Road near the road's intersection with Reynolds Road. The more twisting jaunt upstream toward Peavine Road is quite attractive. This is fairly big water, averaging 25 to 40 feet in width and 1 to 3 in depth but can be waded and fly-fished comfortably under normal conditions. The bottom is sand and silt mixed with gravel. It is wooded along the river, with open farmland close to Peavine, so even on those hot summer days the water is shaded and cool.

These two stretches—the Crossing Road area and the Sink Road area—along with other sections in a 3-mile range above and below the Dowagiac Creek confluence seemed particularly suited to terrestrial fishing. Fish we moved were looking for what was falling from leaves, grasses, and banks. The usual assortment of ants (black and cinnamon), small beetles, crickets, hoppers, and jassids are recommended if other insect activity isn't apparent. Bob speculated that if there had been more color in the water, a larger rubber-legged pattern like the Girdle Bug or June Wiggler would be effective in the deep holds and runs.

Just west of the town of Sumnerville, Dodd Park borders the west bank of the Dowagiac River. It can be easily reached about 1 mile south of Pokagon Road (aka Crystal Springs Road) on Indian Lake Road and is a convenient parking and access point to some sizable water known for its sizable brown trout. The river can be waded here, but caution is advised as the current clips along at a pretty fair rate through the predominantly straight channel. The average depth is 3 feet, deeper in many places, and the width runs from 35 to about 50 feet. There is a lot of gravel, cobble, large rock, and some fallen timber cover. If the water is high, one can still walk the banks looking for insect and fish activity. Foot trails parallel the flow up and down for considerable distances, giving a good view of the river and the best spots to enter and go to work.

One of Michigan's many environmentally active groups, the MEANDRS (Meeting Ecological and Agricultural Needs of the Dowagiac River System), has been doing restoration work along this stretch, so things are sure to get even better. Applause.

Our area fisheries biologist Jim Dexter said that the most recent rotenone survey in this and other nearby stretches revealed "a big brown in every piece of habitat where you would expect to find one." It is encouraging to see that the 8,500 browns planted yearly here above the Niles dam are resulting in larger holdover fish. Maybe it was one of these guys at the upper end of Dodd Park who stopped my retrieve, rolled, surged, and broke off. I was disconsolate at losing the fish *and* the size-8 tan crayfish (which takes forever to tie) but consoled somewhat by the fact that I had covertly borrowed the fly from Bob.

Other patterns worth trying here are the Light Spruce and various colors of Marabou Muddlers (weighted) and large spiky nymphs tied with a translucent fur, such as the antron-blended hare's mask. Work them with an erratic strip-and-drop back technique.

The Dowagiac River empties into the *big* waters of the St. Joseph River north of Niles in Berrien County. The St. Joe has become one of Michigan's top steelhead rivers, and their runs come up the Dowagiac River, which then sees a marked increase in angler numbers in spring and fall. But if you are trout fishing in June or July, don't be surprised if a *hefty* summer run of Skamania tears up your terminal tackle and leaves you big-eyed and shaking.

However, this same water has been gaining an additional reputation, one for excellent early spring and summer hatches bringing up big, active brown trout. (Around 7,000 a year are stocked in the lower reaches.) The Brown Drake hatch in particular is eagerly awaited, coming when steelheading has tailed off. Caddis are dependable after early spring, and most other Michigan insect hatches are reputedly in evidence.

A handy access point is Losensky Park on the southwest side of the old dam site off Pucker Street northwest of Niles. A wooden footbridge beyond the parking area gives access for as far down as one cares to wade.

There are lots of rocks and gravel through this stretch of big, deep, cold water. Pick a likely spot, wade gingerly, work what can be safely reached, and regroup when necessary. The dam by Putker Street and MI 51 is no longer operational, so rising water and warning sirens are not concerns as in the past.

We fished this area later in the season, well after the good mayfly hatches. Caddis weren't very active so we sniped away with terrestrials. One that paid off was a foam-bodied ant fished as a dropper off a large deer-hair beetle with a high-visibility dot tied in—strike indicator and tracking aid par excellence. We also used this double dry rig in the slower water down by US 31 near the mouth of the Dowagiac. Fished close to overhanging vegetation, it is an effective, easily worked arrangement.

If you can escape from your obligations for a few hours, drive down to Dowagiac Creek or to the river. Bring an 8- or 9-foot rod balanced to a 4-weight line, some terrestrials, a few caddis (Henryville), some Hare's Ears, Pheasant Tails, scuds, and a streamer or two. You will have a lot of fun.

Notes:

- The Kalamazoo Institute of Arts has five galleries with ever-changing exhibits.
- Restored aircraft and more can be viewed at the Kalamazoo Aviation History Museum.
- Golf courses are abundant in the area.
- West of Dowagiac near Berrien Springs are the Lemon Creek and Tabor Hill vineyards. Both offer tours and wine tasting.

BRANDYWINE CREEK
Cass County, Berrien County

While it is rated a top-quality trout stream in the MDNR's most recent status study, Brandywine Creek is not usually thought of as a "destination" stream. Yet I find myself drawn to it. Portions of its 8-mile length, particularly the lower reaches in southeast Berrien County, have a certain aesthetic appeal due to the many bends, pools, shadowed runs, and fly-munching browns.

The upper section in Cass County goes through loamy agricultural land and is impractical for fly angling. However, its undercut banks and deep runs provide havens for bigger trout which are known to slide down to the more fishable lower water. Browns more than 25 inches are not unheard of.

There are a couple of very accessible stretches not far above Brandywine Creek's confluence with the St. Joe River. Niles Township Community Park just to the northeast from where the creek crosses Bond Street makes for a most convenient place to park and get in a quick hour or two of fishing. Cut to the right of the playground from the parking lot, pass the John C. Owicki memorial stone, and a hiking trail will lead you quickly to an eye-appealing variety of trout water. I usually go in the morning during the week and have yet to see another soul around. The park closes at dark.

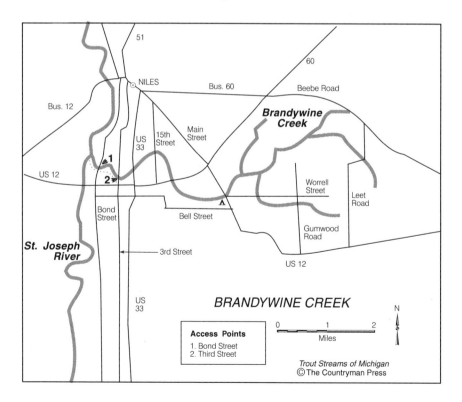

Speaking of when to go, it is wiser to hit this creek during dry, low-water periods if possible. It always carries quite a high tinge of color, which presents the old good news/bad news scenario. The bad is, of course, high, muddy-colored, near-unfishable roaring runoff during rainy times; the good is that if you can hit it in low water periods, the residual "brandywine" color lets you read water and work close to small pools without spooking fish. It had been rain-free for 2 weeks on my most recent excursion yet browns hit dead-drifted nymphs 3 feet from my toes.

There are many small pools in the park waters where such close-in tactics can be used, but the stream has a lot of variety. Current breaks formed by man-made rock placement result in series of wider "stepped" segments of more placid water that allow for longer, delicate presentation of dry flies. Various mayfly and caddis hatches can provide good surface activity in these areas.

While the stream width averages 15 feet, it often narrows to 6 feet, boils through a tight chute, then widens farther on to 25 feet or more. Be prepared to vary techniques to match the constantly changing topography. (Your roll-casting skills will come in handy.)

Another accessible and productive stretch can be quickly reached just to the east where Third Street crosses the creek. There is room to safely park a couple of vehicles a few yards north of the metal guard rails that mark the stream, and the MDNR owns the land on both sides upstream to the railroad bridge.

This is also an attractive stretch with many loops and turns marking a natural "unstraightened" creek, rare in the farming areas of southern Michigan. This was almost lost back in the early 1980s when a bridge washout prompted plans to fill in the old channel and tame the Brandywine. Fortunately, the Fisheries Division was able to step in and prevent this, saving an extensive amount of spawning and rearing habitat.

Like the previously discussed water by the park, those upstream reaches above Third Street provide lots of variety. There is about an even balance between areas of gravel and cobble to sand and silt, and cover abounds in the form of logs, overhanging vegetation, and large rocks. This stretch flows through a forested area, and when the trees are fully leafed out it is like fishing at dusk even in midday. Suburb-dwelling deer bed down in the thick brush and may test your heart rate when they blow out a few yards away.

I have had success here by bank-walking above good holding water and using a downstream drift with little S-mends to present nymphs, scuds, and small Woolly Buggers. Tight casting venues make such an approach more sensible. This would be a good area to test something a western guide once mentioned on a TV production: Use a short fiberglass rod when not much more than the leader and 1 or 2 feet of fly line can be cast. He claims the action of fiberglass superior to graphite for this short-line casting. Maybe someday I'll test this when the charms of branch-shaking and tree-climbing to retrieve a hung-up back cast totally palls—like tomorrow.

Yet even through this portion and some of the water above, there are enough open passages to cast 30 to 50 feet and keep the tight-loopers happy. Freshwater shrimp are abundant where watercress grows, and mayflies, stoneflies, and caddis inhabit the reaches of Brandywine Creek, making it a pleasant place to cast a line when more glorious northern streams won't fit one's schedule.

Notes:

- The Ft. St. Joseph Historical Museum in Niles has some intriguing exhibits featuring early fur trade and military items (616-683-4702).

14 | Mackinac District

The Mackinac (pronounced Mackinaw) district is in the eastern end of a pure peninsula, bound by Lake Superior to the north, Lake Huron to the east, and Lake Michigan on the south. Alger, Delta, Luce, Schoolcraft, Mackinac, and Chippewa Counties segment a region with rugged coastlines, sandy beaches, thundering waterfalls, beautiful islands, and friendly, self-sufficient citizens. St. Ignace, Sault Ste. Marie, Manistique, Escanaba, Munising, and Newberry are the largest population centers. Lumbering and tourism are the region's major revenue producers, but most visitors seem to stick to the southern, Lake Michigan shore along US 2 and less frequently journey to the interior or the northern crags and islands of Lake Superior. Tahquamenon Falls north of Newberry, the Pictured Rocks northeast of Munising along the Lake Superior shore, Whitefish Point north of Paradise, and the Seney National Wildlife Refuge near Seney all are worth the time to visit. These are scenic and high interest side-trip destinations for the non-angling members of your party as well as highly worthy of consideration as a respite from the pursuit of brook trout.

As with all off-highway travel in the Upper Peninsula, good maps, a compass, and a citizen's-band radio are good insurance. A good camera with high-resolution color film should be listed as part of your most essential gear.

THE FOX
Schoolcraft County, Luce County

Nick Adams caught his big trout on the Big Two-Hearted, but Ernest Hemingway fished the Fox. The Big Two-Hearted is the sweetheart of the literati; it is as well known in Moscow, Russia, as it is in Moscow, Idaho. The less widely revered Fox is ardently fished by those who share in one of the world's most widely known "secrets," as well as those more interested in the ebullient native brook trout than the affairs of fiction and critic.

The Fox is generally regarded as the better trout fishery of the two rivers. It rises north of the old lumbering town of Seney in eastern Alger County, crosses into northern Schoolcraft County, and becomes a highly productive and fly-fishable stream near the Old Wagner Dam site off Taylor Dam Road. This spot is easily reached from the town of Seney, which is the only logical base for operations on the Fox River. Seney is located near the northeastern corner of the Seney National Wildlife Refuge at the intersection of highways MI 77 and MI 28 in northern Schoolcraft County.

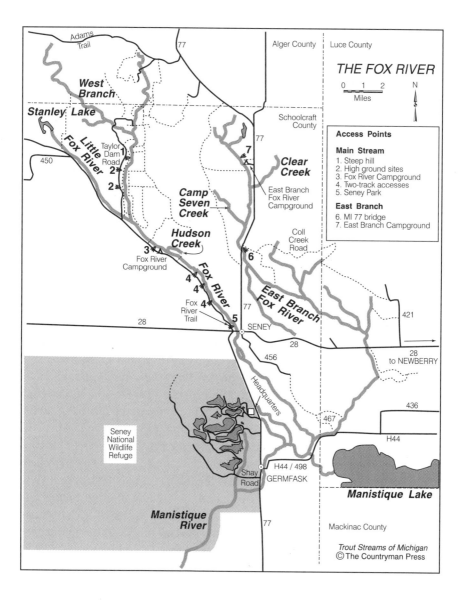

THE FOX RIVER

Access Points

Main Stream
1. Steep hill
2. High ground sites
3. Fox River Campground
4. Two-track accesses
5. Seney Park

East Branch
6. MI 77 bridge
7. East Branch Campground

Trout Streams of Michigan
© The Countryman Press

From the intersection of MI 28 and School Street (School Street changes to Third Street and then to Fox River Road) in Seney, it is a 7.5-mile drive northwest on Fox River Road (CR 450) to Taylor Dam Road. Take Taylor Dam Road to the right (north) for 3.4 miles to a sand two-track headed east. Keep to the left for 0.2 mile and you will arrive at a parking area at the top of a 150-foot hill. Be careful descending the hill; it is probably wise to side-step due to the steep angle and sand base.

This upper section of the Fox is 25 to 35 feet wide and 1 to 4 feet deep with a sand and fine-gravel bottom. The water is relatively clear with only a light iron tinge. Overhanging shrubbery, cedars, and majestic, gnarled white pines shade the stream (on a recent hot, mid-September day the temperature gauge read 52 degrees F at 3 PM). This is beautiful, classic brook trout water. Deep in the Superior State Forest, the visitor is enveloped in the sights, sounds, and smells of the wild. Downed trees and overhanging alders shelter the bankside cuts and riffles, and the smooth, steady flow in the holes and pools parades a steady diet of insects to the *fontinalis* clan. Additionally, man-made stream-improvement structures unobtrusively provide harbor and, whether planned or by happy circumstance, their subtle evidence is appreciated.

The egg-sac version of the Irresistible is a very effective dry fly for the upper reaches of the Fox. Trude patterns, the Renegade, Borcher's Drake, and Rusty's Spinner, in sizes 12 through 18, will adequately cover surface-feeding requirements unless there is a major hatch in progress. Because of the heavy vegetation, a large variety of terrestrials find their way into the Fox, and cricket and black ant patterns are often in order.

Bright streamers are, surprisingly, not as effective as one might ordinarily think on this brook trout stream. A simple, brown and yellow Clouser Minnow, a black Marabou Muddler, or an Olive Leech will generally attract more strikes than a Mickey Finn or Light Spruce. Nymphs need to be suggestive or spiky rather than slim or streamlined, and various shades of the reliable Hare's Ear, in sizes 10 through 14, will be all that is required.

The two-track road that leads to the "high hill" parking spot has a southward spur that parallels the river all the way back to the intersection of CR 450 and Taylor Dam Road, near the bridge over the Little Fox River. There are several high-ground pull-offs along this trail and, after the descent, the fishing and the river's characteristics are pretty much the same as just described. It is certainly worth your time to sample the Fox in at least three points (of your choosing) along this short, convenient access trail. Each spot is similar, yet unique. Deep, dark holes slide into long pools and then a riffle and, at a bend, again into a deep hold crisscrossed with logs and edged by a deep, shrouded cut. These are special places to be approached cautiously and slowly, and fished patiently. Some large brook trout live in this stretch, but their seduction is not an easy matter.

Downstream from the intersection of Taylor Dam Road and CR 450, you will find several lovely, easy access points at the Fox River Campground. This camping area is 5.0 miles north of town on CR 450 (Fox River Road). It is a small campground, but each site is on the river and it is only a very short walk to the water's edge. There is a well-worn trail along the streambank on the campground side of the river and, wonder of wonders, the fishing is quite good here despite the close proximity of the campground.

From this campground the peripatetic angler can roam the hiking trail upstream 10 miles to the old Stanley Lake camp (closed) or downstream for 6 miles to Seney Park, the campground in town. The river is clean, clear, cold, and productive throughout this stretch. The bottom is still sand and fine gravel and the banks continue their cooling shelter with stands of white pine, cedar, and spruce. The high sand banks provide great picnic opportunities with cooling breezes, scented shade from the cedars and pines, and serene vistas of a wild river in wild country.

In addition to the hiking trail there are several Fox River access points reached via short trails off CR 450 between the Fox River Campground and the town of Seney. Just about every two-track that heads east wanders only a few yards before settling in at a parking spot or turnaround at the river's edge. The Fox carries a bit more water in this downstream run, having been fed by the Little Fox, Hudson, Gronden, and Two Mile Creeks. Still, it is wadable for the most part and rarely demands an exit to circumnavigate a snag or large hole.

Downstream from Seney, the Fox makes its way along the eastern edge of the wildlife refuge (east side of MI 77) to its junction with the Manistique River east of Germfask. There are some very large fish, brooks and browns, in the lower river, but access and wading are difficult and it is best fished from a boat with a knowledgeable oarsman.

The East Branch of the Fox is a respectable stream with a population of wild, free-rising brown trout as a complement to the native brookies. The "spreads" area, three miles north of Seney and just a bit east of MI 77, regularly produces quality fishing for those who are willing and able to make the trip and who have enough mosquito repellent to survive.

A better perspective on the East Branch for the visitor can be obtained, with only minor loss of blood, at the MI 77 bridge 4 miles north of Seney and, again, at the East Branch Campground 8 miles north of Seney, just off MI 77.

Along the Fox, local folks will offer to show you where good old Ernest hung his hat by the creek and rested and thought up some nifty adventures for young Nick. You owe it to yourself to go take a look.

Notes:

See end of section on the Big Two-Hearted.

DRIGGS RIVER AND ROSS CREEK
Schoolcraft County

The Driggs crosses MI 28 about 6 miles west of Seney. It doesn't look like much at this crossing but don't pass it by. Just a few yards east of the bridge a narrow dirt road heads north and parallels the Driggs for several miles all the way to its connection to CR 450 near Driggs Lake.

For most of its course from the lake to MI 28, the Driggs ranges from 20 to 25 feet in width with uncountable tight S-curves, overhanging trees, undercut banks, and a mixed bottom ranging from pure sand to gravel to muck.

This little river has wonderful hatches and I once spent a euphoric 2 days on it and its fine tributary Ross Creek, during a prolific Brown Drake hatch. Those 2 days were warm and muggy with overcast skies and little breeze. The bugs began to emerge about 2 PM and were still hatching when the spinners began to fall around 8 PM. It seemed that every brook trout in the stream wanted to gorge on the big flies, and I caught more than many. Some approached 14 inches and resisted as fiercely as any 1-pound fish anywhere.

This is an easy stream to approach. The dirt road follows the Driggs closely for many miles and it is a simple matter to spot beckoning water, park the car, fish, and repeat. As you proceed north the road veers away from the water near Driggs Lake and comes to its intersection with CR 450. Turn left and follow CR 450 westward. You will cross a bridge over the Driggs; the uppermost section of the river can be fished from this access. Continuing west about 2 miles from this spot will put you at a bridge over Ross Creek. Ross Creek will be flowing from west to east. It enters the Driggs about 1 mile downstream.

Ross Creek is a fine brook trout fishery in its own right. During the Brown Drake hatch mentioned above, I caught many brookies (within 200 yards of the bridge) more than 12 inches. The hatch faded for about an hour on the second day and I switched to a small Muddler, then a black Woolly Bugger as an experiment. I cast upstream and twitched my retrieve back. Brookies swarmed out from the banks and swirled around both patterns but would not eat them. I switched to a small Mickey Finn and caught several fish quickly. Then the hatch resumed and it was back to dry-fly heaven.

Both the Driggs and the Ross are small, delicate waterways. Wade carefully and move slowly. A light rod is all that is necessary. I used an 8½-foot 4-weight, which seemed perfect for short, quick casts.

You might consider exploring the Driggs downstream from MI 28. It has a long wilderness flow through the northern section of the Seney National Wildlife Refuge before its confluence with the Manistique River west of MI 77. The map shows Driggs River Road paralleling the stream for several miles southward but the last time I tried this approach, the road was closed (blocked off) just a few hundred yards into the refuge. I suspect the fishing pressure downstream is nearly zero.

Notes:

- The Michigan gray wolf reintroduction is a real success story. The population is strong and growing in the Seney area. Listen for their songs. They are unmistakable. You will not confuse them for coyotes.
- This is wild country with few roads. Carry water and lots of bug repellent.
- Consider exploring Stutz Creek to the west along a series of rough roads, off MI 94. It is full of wild brook trout that rarely, if ever, see an artificial fly. Fill up your fuel tank, take extra water, lots of film, and double your supply of mosquito repellent.

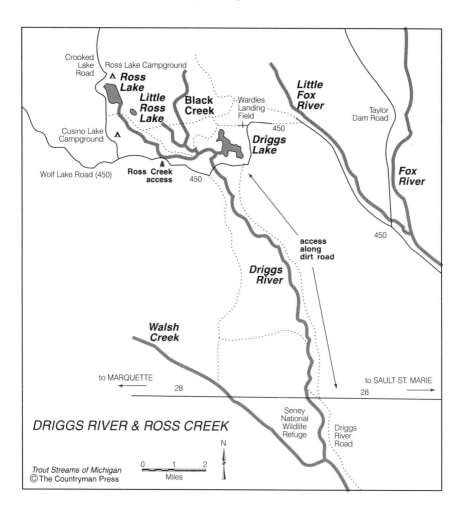

DRIGGS RIVER & ROSS CREEK

Trout Streams of Michigan
© The Countryman Press

THE BIG TWO-HEARTED
Luce County

The Big Two-Hearted is smack dab in the middle of the deep woods of northern Luce County on the shores of "the big one," Lake Superior. The main river is fed by the West Branch and Dawston Creek, joining forces downstream from the High Bridge Forest Campground on CR 407, 5 miles south of Lake Superior. From this point, the river flows on a northeasterly persuasion to its junction with the East Branch downstream from Red and Green Bridge and then, continuing its northeasterly course, it enters Lake Superior at the shoreside Two-Hearted Campground on CR 423.

The West Branch provides the best fly-fishing on the Big Two-Hearted, with the reach of river from Hunter Dam (upstream from High Bridge) to just below High Bridge presenting pleasant, rugged scenery, relatively easy wading and casting, and healthy populations of brook and rainbow trout.

The High Bridge—the Big Two-Hearted for that matter—really isn't close to anything that serves as a convenient reference point for automobile travel. Newberry is the closest town of substance so it will be the focal point. Newberry is located in the southern part of Luce County just north of the intersection of MI 28 and MI 123. Approximately 4 miles north of town, MI 123 is intersected from the west by CR 407. Take CR 407 west for approximately 4 miles and continue on through the hard right-hand curve, due north, for 14 miles to High Bridge. If you intend to reach High Bridge from any other location be sure you have a compass, good maps, and a full tank of gasoline.

The very first trail to the left after crossing High Bridge is CR 418. Take CR 418, stay to the left and after 0.4 mile, you will come to a parking area at the top of a hill 60 feet over the river. There is a path that leads approximately 100 yards down the hill and through the woods to streamside. At the end of this path the river ranges from 35 to 40 feet in width and from 1 to 5 feet in depth. There is a strong current and the tea-colored water flows over a bottom of sand with occasional, very slippery, patches of clay. Despite the width of the stream proper, the casting channel is often much smaller, sometimes as narrow as 10 feet. This is caused by the very heavy brush and bankside timber, and roll casts are often necessary to present a fly without a hang-up in the brush.

Deep, midstream runs hold quite a few fish. The undercut banks, especially those canopied with alders, stumps, or logs, conceal the feeding action of vigorous rainbows and brooks. The dark, quiet holes are the sanctuary of the largest trout and, during the appropriate months, the temporary resting and staging areas for migrating steelhead and salmon.

Proceeding west (upstream) on CR 418 will take you to several parking

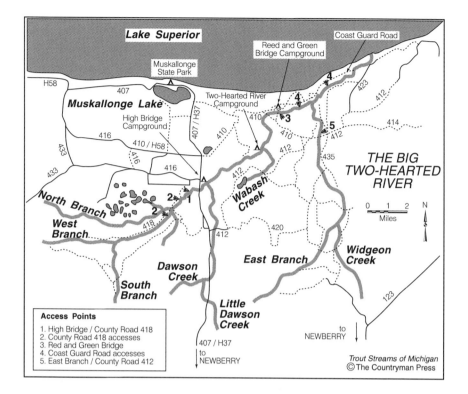

Trout Streams of Michigan
© The Countryman Press

areas within easy walking distance of the West Branch. The river slowly is becoming narrower and congested by brush as you follow the upstream course toward Old Hunter Dam, but it is still fly-fishable and productive for the cautious wader with moderate casting skill. An 8- or 8½-foot rod balanced to a 4- or 5-weight line is about right for the West Branch, and 9-foot leaders with 4X tippet are fine enough for all but the most critical conditions.

The Spruce Fly (light) is one of the top streamer patterns for the Big Two-Hearted system. The flash of peacock and scarlet topped with a pulsing badger hackle wing excites the brookies and rainbows and has been known to earn the heavy smack of a steelhead or salmon. Sculpin imitations produce a fair share of strikes as do representatives of the Thunder Creek little-trout series. The olive Woolly Bugger, for some unexplained reason, will bring flashes and swirls and an occasional nip at the tail, but does not produce solid takes on the Big Two-Hearted.

Brown Drakes, Sulphurs, and Olives are reliable hatches on the Big Two-Hearted. Caddis appear all season long and a large stonefly dry will bring solid nocturnal strikes from heavy fish. As always the Adams is a prerequisite dry fly, and wherever there are rainbows and brook trout in cohabitation, the Royal Wulff and Lime Trude will perform well. Marabou or philoplume dragonfly nymphs in olive, gray, and brown will earn trout when fished in the deep holes. Hare's Ears, Pheasant Tails, and Woolly Worms are good, all-around probing nymphs for the West Branch.

One mile north of High Bridge, CR 410 intersects CR 407 at Perch Lake and heads north by northeast for 5.0 miles to the Red and Green Bridge and the campground of the same name. This campground sits high on the north bank of the river, its seven spacious sites all overlook the stream, and several paths lead directly to the water's edge. The river at the Red and Green site is 60 feet wide, a bit narrower in a few spots and wider in some. Its bottom is sand with silt edges and scattered runs of coarse gravel. Under low-water conditions the stream's depth ranges from 1 to 4 feet and considerably more, but the light tea color and firm footing provide stable and generally safe circumstances for the cautious wader. There are, however, some very deep holes and even deeper, semihidden, midstream pockets that demand a watchful eye and wary step.

Downstream from the campground the river runs through a series of tight S-curves. There is a convenient and well-worn path that follows the river's course for a considerable distance. This path, luckily, takes the angler to several spots that afford wide-open areas for longer casts to the deep water at the outside of the curves. Both brook and rainbow trout are present in good numbers throughout the season and this area has been known to produce decent results for those in pursuit of steelhead on the fly.

County Road 410 turns into Coast Guard Line Road at the campground and continues between Lake Superior's south shore and the Big Two-Hearted for several miles. This is a rough and tumble two-track under the best of conditions and may be impassable on any given day. It does, however, present a great opportunity for a hike with a lunch, camera, and pack rod. If you take this route be sure to budget more time than you would for a neighborhood stroll of a similar distance. You will want to fish at the junction of the East Branch and the main river, and you will probably want to spend some extra time taking photographs.

The East Branch is accessible from Pine Camp Road, Shamrock Road, and at the East Branch Bridge on CR 412. It is more difficult to fish than the mainstream or the West Branch due to a narrower flow and the ever-repeating tangles of jackstrawed timbers. It supports a healthy population of wild, stream-born brook trout and dynamic and aggressive concentrations of immature steelhead. It would be great fun on a hot day to leave the waders in the car and navigate the water and logjams in shorts and wading shoes. Attractor patterns, streamer and dry, would do the trick. These fish are rarely bothered by fly-rod addicts.

The Big Two-Hearted is a long system; its different branches and feeder streams drain impenetrable swamps and rolling sandy hills. Deer, moose, bear, bobcat, coyotes, and wolves are present. Loons cry on the lakes and ponds and eagles and osprey are seen regularly. Ruffed grouse and spruce hens thunder out from under your feet. The river shimmers and slides through a bend. It's a beautiful place to visit and fish.

Notes:

- The National Wildlife Refuge at Seney is approximately 100,000 acres of wilderness. Visitors will see herons, eagles, cranes, deer, geese, and perhaps a bear or moose. There is a population of timber wolves in the refuge.
- The Fox River Campground is within the territory of a pack of very vocal coyotes. Their singing is a real treat.
- The cinnamon rolls at the Poor Boy Cafe in McMillan are worth a side trip.
- There are many abandoned, but undisturbed logging ghost towns in the area that are worth seeking out for a journey into the past.
- The book *Daylight in the Swamp* (1978, Doubleday: Garden City, NY), by Robert W. Wells, is a colorful, factual, and humorous account of the old logging days in northern Michigan and, in particular, the Seney area. It's a good read.
- Newberry, Germfask, and Seney have good restaurants, accommodations, and friendly citizens.
- Both the Fox and the Two-Hearted have received "Wild Scenic River" designation from the State of Michigan.

THE CARP RIVER
Mackinac County

Frenchman Lake, Wegwaas Lake, and Carp Lake are tightly clustered near the small town of Trout Lake in extreme southern Chippewa County about 2 miles north of the Mackinac county line. The outlet of Carp Lake takes a southerly direction into Mackinac County and closely follows Carp River Road (also known as Ozark Road) for about 3 miles, angling to the southeast. For much of its journey the Carp River is surrounded by public lands, either the Lake Superior State Forest or the Hiawatha National Forest.

This is a great stream for fly-rodders. It receives only moderate pressure throughout the summer months, it has relatively easy access (by Upper Peninsula standards), a healthy trout population, plenty of room for casting, and last, wading is generally easy if not totally carefree. Because the Carp River is paralleled by several roads and is approached by many smaller trails, it is easy to explore. Highlighted here are a few favorite spots that are easy to find and will serve as a starting point for a successful exploration of the Carp River system.

Just downstream from the junction of the Carp and the South Branch of the Carp there is easy access to very productive water at the bridge on FS 3458. This is best reached from MI 123 (Tahquamenon Trail) about 9 miles northwest of the US 75 and MI 123 junction north of St. Ignace. As you approach the noted mileage you will cross Forest Highway 2. At this point you are 2.0 miles from the westward turnoff at Burma Road (FS 3124). Follow Burma Road west for 3.5 miles to FS 3458 and turn right. Proceed north for 1.5 miles to the bridge over the Carp River. There is no room to park right at the bridge, but you can safely leave your vehicle at a parking area about 40 yards south.

The river is usually very clear in this area. It has a pale sand bottom with abundant trout cover formed by bankside cuts, downed timber, and the protection of overhanging tag alders. The downstream side ranges from 20 to 35 feet in width with depths ranging to a bit more than 2 feet. The upstream journey will take you into slightly deeper, calm water with most of the fish found tight to the banks. Fishing in either direction is rewarding and provides a good measure of solitude. Canoes and other anglers are a rare sight.

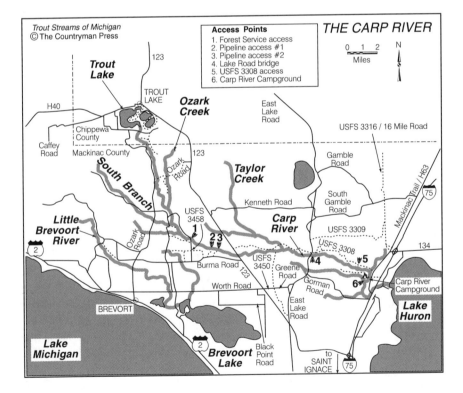

There are two more relatively easy access points off Burma Road between FS 3458 and MI 123. Driving east from FS 3458 toward MI 123 on Burma Road, you will come to a two-track lane after 1.5 miles. This lane heads north to the Carp and is easily identified by the sign indicating the location of the North County Hiking Trail. Just 0.3 mile farther east you will cross another gas-line trail that slashes through some soupy ground to the river. Take your vehicle on this trail only when it is very dry. A four-wheel drive will make it, but a normal passenger automobile will not. Both of these points of entry have very good fishing for a mixture of native brook trout and rainbows, and occasionally you will encounter a pool of immature steelhead that will take just about anything. Do you want to catch a steelhead on a dry fly? Do you want to catch two at a time? Tie on a Lime Trude with a Royal Wulff on the dropper and make your own personal angling history. As long as you don't say exactly how big those steelhead were, you can swagger a bit. I usually size these little dynamos by saying something like "Oh, they were all under 8 pounds, nothing to get excited about." A 4-ounce fish is, after all, under 8 pounds.

Back at the intersection of Burma Road and MI 123 you will want to drive southeast for about 2 miles to FS 3458. Turn left and drive eastward to Lake Road, also known as FS 3119, and follow FS 3119 north to the bridge. There is ample parking south of this bridge very close to the river.

This is an extremely lovely stretch of trout river. Both upstream and downstream directions show a flow averaging 40 feet in width. The weak-tea-colored water is of moderate current and its depth varies from 1 to 4 feet. The bottom is sand with silt edges. Logs, deep holes in the curves, bankside cuts, and some nice riffle water shelter the trout. There is plenty of room to punch out a long cast when it is (rarely) required and just about any rod you favor will work nicely.

The classic Mickey Finn pattern is a favorite on the Carp River. Fish it with a quick, erratic retrieve and you will get results. The Pass Lake, Woolly Bugger, and Grizzly Spruce will round out an effective streamer selection. Hare's Ear, Pheasant Tail, Zug Bug, and Sparkle Caddis emergers all produce fish. Favorite dry patterns include the Adams, Rusty's Spinner, Royal Wulff, Lime Trude, and Griffith's Gnat.

From the bridge on FS 3119 drive north for 1.0 mile to FS 3309 and turn right. Follow FS 3309 to the east for 5.0 miles to the intersection with FS 3316 and turn right. Follow FS 3316 for 0.7 mile to its termination at Mackinac Trail. Turn right on Mackinac Trail and drive south for 1.5 miles to FS 3308. If you pass the road to the Carp River Campground you have gone too far. Take FS 3308 for 1.1 miles to its dead end at the river and the large circular parking area. This is a favorite spot for local and downstate anglers in pursuit of steelhead and salmon and it does feel some pressure at certain times of the year. It is also an area with splendid grouse and woodcock covers and you can expect to hear a shot or two on crisp fall days.

The river at the foot of FS 3308 is about 40 feet wide with a quick current flowing clear over gravel, ledgerock, boulders, and sand. There are mud banks around the rotting stumps and old logs for burrowing nymphs, and overhanging cedars, white pine, birch, and alders drop a full menu of terrestrials into the streams.

There are some large trout in this section of the river and it pays to be prepared for a fish you would weigh rather than measure. Marabou Muddlers, Woolly Buggers, Clouser Minnows, and the Light Spruce are your best bets in streamer patterns. Large nymphs are effective and rubber-legged critters such as the June Wiggler and Yuk Bug can be very good. Large attractor dry patterns such as the Stimulator will bring fish topside. A dead-drift in the dark runs and deep holes with a black Yuk Bug or June Wiggler and a Micro-Egg dropper can provide a hook-up to a Lake Huron monster. Use a rod with some power and a reel with a good drag on the lower Carp.

The Carp River Campground is just a short distance downstream from the water at the foot of FS 3308. The next road south of FS 3308 (off Mackinac Trail) is FS 3445 and this is, basically, the campground service road. Immediately adjacent to the campground you will find an old trestle bridge with a wooden stairway leading down a short hill to the river and a quite deep hole with a lovely pool tailing out into a handsome riffle. This is very fancy water and a real delight to fish despite its proximity to the campground. The bottom is sand, gravel, and rock with mud edges. Excepting the deep hole, the depth ranges from 1 to 4 feet and the average width is about 40 feet. Salmon and steelhead rest in this deep hole and there are numerous nonmigratory trout present as well. The campground is spacious and clean with several sites at the river's edge. Hiking paths lead upstream and downstream and it is an easy matter to explore the river and surrounding countryside.

The Carp is a lovely, productive river and a great experience for the fly-fisher. You will enjoy the fishing and exploring, be it for only a few hours or for several days.

Notes:

- St. Ignace has something of interest for everyone. The town has a wide variety of events scheduled throughout the year: antique-car shows, boat races, you name it. There is a casino in town, golf with a view, and boat service to Mackinac Island.
- For a lengthy side trip take the drive to Whitefish Point and visit the Shipwreck Museum, lighthouse, theater, and bird observatory. Follow this with a visit to Sault Ste. Marie, the Soo Locks, and a visit to Canada.

BOB LINSENMAN

Michigan streams present a wide variation on water types. This stretch of rapids is typical of brook trout water.

- The view from North Huron Shore Drive (MI 134) is really wonderful. Numerous islands and sheltered bays are a photographer's dream. North Huron Shore Drive intersects I-75 just north of the Carp River Campground. Drive east to Cedarville and load up on high-resolution color film.

STURGEON RIVER
Delta County, Alger County

This lovely stream comes to life in western Alger County about 10 miles north of the Delta county line and about 12 miles south of Lake Superior. Like its larger western neighbors, the Whitefish and the Escanaba, it favors a southerly course and directs its flow into eastern Delta County and on to Lake Michigan at Stony Point on Big Bay De Noc.

The Sturgeon is lightly fished by touring anglers. Most of the little pres-

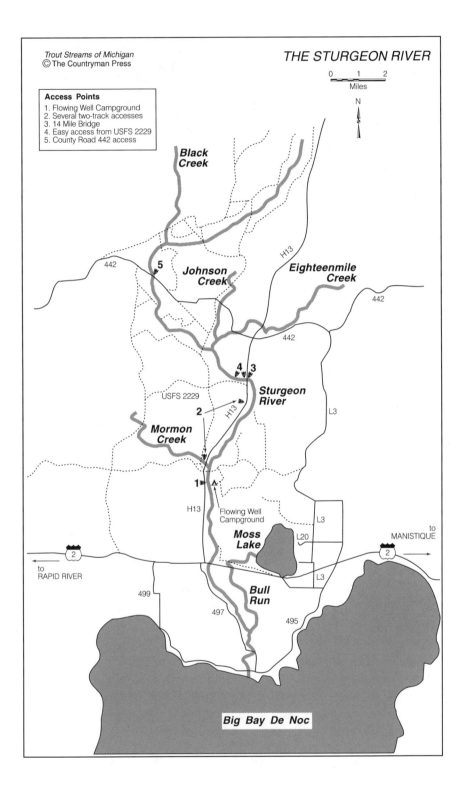

THE STURGEON RIVER

Trout Streams of Michigan
© The Countryman Press

0   1   2
Miles

N

Access Points
1. Flowing Well Campground
2. Several two-track accesses
3. 14 Mile Bridge
4. Easy access from USFS 2229
5. County Road 442 access

Black Creek

Johnson Creek

442

5

H13

Eighteenmile Creek

442

442

4 **3**

Sturgeon River

USFS 2229

2

H13

L3

Mormon Creek

1

Flowing Well Campground

H13

Moss Lake

L3

L20

L3

to MANISTIQUE

2

to RAPID RIVER

2

499

497

Bull Run

495

Big Bay De Noc

sure on the system comes from knowledgeable local residents and a few campers in the close proximity of campgrounds or bridges. Even so, the concentrated pressure at the obvious locations has not diminished the quality of the experience.

US 2 bridges the Sturgeon about 5 miles west of the village of Isabella and at Nahma Junction where Forest Highway 13 intersects from the north. Slightly west of Forest Highway 13, CR 497 turns south and parallels the Sturgeon for 4.0 miles to its mouth. FH 13 northbound is the better selection and it is just 3.0 miles to the handsome Flowing Well Forest Service Campground.

At Flowing Well the Sturgeon is 25 to 30 feet wide and flows from 1 to 3 feet deep over a shale, rock, and sand bottom. The pale-tea-colored water (it is actually more the color of a very lightly dressed scotch and soda) is quickly paced and swirls through deadfalls and cedar sweepers, under banks, and into some impressive pocket water in the riffles.

Brook trout and rainbows coexist handsomely in this happy scene. Both are aggressive in pursuit of prey and will show themselves without hesitation if a decently presented fly is within range. Brightly colored attractors seem to be more effective than more somber patterns. The Royal Wulff, perhaps a Lime Trude, are the only dry patterns needed on a warm, sunny day. The Zug Bug and Prince Nymph have been consistent strike producers and a small (size 10 or 12) Light Spruce seems to work just about anytime.

Just north of the campground you will find several trail roads that head directly to the Sturgeon from FH 13. A fair example of these trails is FS 2231, which heads east for 0.1 mile to a bridge over the river. Forest Highway 13 parallels the Sturgeon, with more solid-based, two-track trails running right to the river, up to Fourteen Mile Bridge, which is just north of the point where FS 2229 enters FH 13 from the west.

The stream at Fourteen Mile is wider and more shallow than at Flowing Well Campground. It approaches 45 feet in width and its depth rarely exceeds 2 feet. Still, there are trout to be found in this stretch. Fish the midstream depressions, ahead and behind larger rocks, and tight against the shaded bank. This is an area that allows wide-open casting, and a 9-foot rod for a 4-weight line is a good choice. Light tippets and small ant patterns are an effective combination.

From the Fourteen Mile Bridge area, take FS 2229 west. This road closely follows the stream for nearly a mile before the Sturgeon's course comes from the north and FS 2229 continues due west. Access to the river from FS 2229 is easy—just park and stroll. This is a beautiful stretch of the Sturgeon. The bottom is sand and fine-to-medium gravel. The stream averages 35 feet in width and 1 to 2-plus feet in depth. There are numerous runs of productive pocket water and some very attractive riffles in this area.

Many bends have deep holes and undercut banks to shelter the fish. One recent early July day the fish ate Irresistibles, Wulffs, and Light Spruce streamers like kids nailing cookies. It did not seem to matter if the fly was wet or dry; as long as it came through the trout's hot zone without drag, it was eaten.

After the Sturgeon and FS 2229 separate, you can leapfrog to another convenient, upstream access by driving west on FS 2229 for about 3.4 miles to FS 2233. Turn right on FS 2233 and drive north, past Ramsey Lake on your right, for about 4.5 miles to CR 442. Turn right on CR 442 and you will arrive at a bridge over the Sturgeon after 1.5 miles. Here the stream is about 30 feet wide with a very nice riffle on the downstream side of the bridge. Farther downstream there are some productive bends, stretches of calmer, placid flow, and then more deep bends and undercut banks. The patterns mentioned earlier will work here as well, but it's worth noting that some undulating marabou is stimulating in slow water and an olive Woolly Bugger is a good selection for this area.

You are now deep in the Hiawatha National Forest, and farther upstream access is largely achieved via remote logging trails. The truly adventuresome angler will want to backtrack on CR 442 (west) to northbound FS 2252 and drive north past Little Black Creek to the immediate turnoff to the right. This road is FS 2440 and it roughly follows the upstream course of the Sturgeon for several miles. There are several crude two-tracks that meander in a southerly direction from FS 2440 to within walking distance of the river. A compass is recommended.

Notes:

- A short scenic side trip along Big Bay De Noc is worth a few minutes of your time. Take CR 499 south from US 2 at St. Jacques. Follow CR 499 past Indian Point to Nahma and take CR 495 past Stony Point, Poplar Point, and Porcupine Point back up to US 2.
- Another very scenic drive is found along MI 183 east of Isabella. Take MI 183 south to Fairport and be sure to have film in your camera.
- Just west of the Sturgeon River lies Little Bay De Noc and the urban services of Gladstone and Escanaba. There are fine restaurants, hotels, and resorts with splendid views throughout the area.
- The town of Bark River, just west of Escanaba on US 2 and US 41, has a large casino operation.
- The town of Manistique, to the east on US 2, has a photogenic shoreline and lighthouse. You can usually find the lowest gasoline prices in the Upper Peninsula near Manistique.

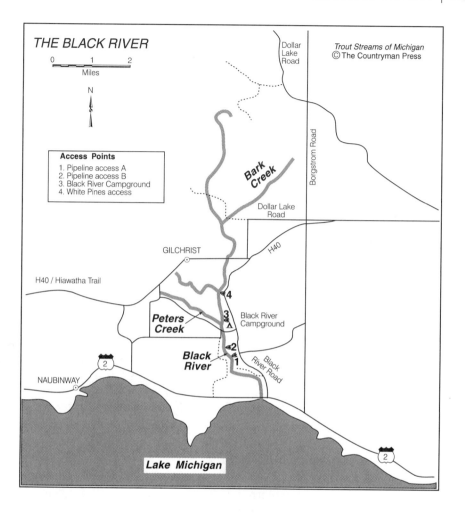

THE BLACK RIVER

0 1 2
Miles

N

Trout Streams of Michigan
© The Countryman Press

Dollar Lake Road

Access Points
1. Pipeline access A
2. Pipeline access B
3. Black River Campground
4. White Pines access

Bark Creek

Borgstrom Road

Dollar Lake Road

GILCHRIST

H40

H40 / Hiawatha Trail

Peters Creek

Black River Campground

Black River

Black River Road

NAUBINWAY

Lake Michigan

BLACK RIVER
Mackinac County

This is a short fishery with only about 12 miles of flow from the headwaters in west-central Mackinac County to its mouth at Lake Michigan, just yards from US 2 and 5 miles east of the town of Naubinway.

At the mouth, the Black River is wide and slow with a flat, calm surface and a heavy dark tea stain to the water. The lower reach is composed of a sandy bottom littered with intertwined logs, stumps, and assorted other ankle busters. Excepting periods of high runoff, it has little current and one gets the sensation of fishing a slowly migrating pond rather than a vibrant, living stream.

Disregard any initial impressions presented by the view from US 2. Instead, drive north on CR 832 (Black River Road) for 1.3 miles to a two-track trail headed west. This gas-line trail will bring you to the crest of a small, but steep, sandy hill after 0.1 mile. If you have four-wheel drive you can descend the hill, with care, and proceed another 0.2 mile to an open parking area. Do not drive farther. The next 200 yards or so to the river is swampy and slippery, tough going even on foot.

The narrow swath cut by the gas-line crews is surrounded by tough, rocky ground and thick forest with abundant deer, grouse, and woodcock. The river at the base of the slope is 14 to 20 feet wide and 1 to 3 feet deep. Its dark, tea-colored water dances over granite boulders and a mixed sand-and-gravel bottom. The banks are thick with cedar, pine, alders, and birch. Undercut banks, eddies behind larger rocks and boulders, and midstream pockets hold aggressive, brilliantly hued brook trout that will eagerly make a snatch at a fly.

Downstream from your first view of the river there is a boisterous rapids, and you will hear it before you see it. This is a short, raucous stretch of water. It runs only 40 yards before dumping its oxygen- and food-rich bounty into a large, inky, deep hole with several swirls and back flows. If you can roll cast a weighted streamer or nymph and mend line to swim the fly properly you have a good chance of hooking a large brook trout or, at proper times of the year, a Lake Michigan steelhead or brown trout.

In both upstream and downstream venues, the pipeline access presents similar characteristics of the Black. Alternating pools and riffles, undercut banks, midstream boulders, and quiet back eddies at the outside of the bends harbor hungry fish. The trick is to roll cast, mend, and be ready. Short rods, not more than 8 feet, and leaders in the 7- to 9-foot range are the recommended tools for this part of the Black.

The next upstream access of note is only 0.3 mile farther north on CR 832. At this spot there is another trail forged by the gas-line people. Take this trail west for 0.25 mile to the top of a steep hill, and park. The Black is only 150 yards to the west and a trail of sorts will lead you right to the bank.

At the spot where you reach the river you will notice that the flow has split and circles a small island directly in front of you. Some fine brook trout have pounced on Mickey Finn and Royal Coachman streamers on the west side of the island. Just upstream from the island there is a nice pool with a moderate current and deeply sheltered banks. This pool supports a number of resident fish and an occasional holdover spawner, so be prepared at any point in the season. Farther upstream there is a productive, lively stretch of rapids. This area has excellent pocket fishing, but requires a rapid-fire technique to avoid a dragging fly. Quick casts, short floats, and repetition excite the brookies.

Gaudy streamers and sparkle-fur nymphs are effective in the Black

River. The Pass Lake, Mickey Finn, Royal Coachman, Light Spruce, and white Marabou Muddler all take fish. Woolly Buggers, particularly if they have some flash in the tail, are equally productive. Standard nymphs, with the addition of some sparkle or light-gathering material, are the order of the day. The Hare's Ear, Prince, Zug Bug, and Fox Squirrel nymph are all strike producers. The Black River brook trout eat dry patterns as well and the Royal Trude, Lime Trude, and Adams will cover your needs.

Continuing north on CR 832 takes you to the Black River Campground. This is a well-maintained camp and is a good choice for a spot to picnic and relax. A well-marked path, complete with wooden steps, leads from campsite 11 down a short hill to the river. The stream averages 15 feet wide and 1 to 2 feet deep in the campground area. It has some very productive riffles and attendant pocket water with logs, rocks, and heavy brush providing necessary cover and shade. The banks are thick with assorted fly-grabbing bushes, and roll casts are required. A 7½- or 8-foot rod for a 3- or 4-weight line is about right for the Black. Leaders need not be long or particularly fine; a 7- or 8-footer with a 4X tippet will do nicely near the campground area.

As you leave the campground you will notice a fork in the road. The right fork takes you back to CR 832, but the left fork takes a downhill mosey for 0.25 mile to a dead-end, circular parking area at the river. There is a wooden footbridge over the Black at this spot. A very large hole at the downstream side of the bridge hosts some significant seasonal visitors and is home to healthy resident trout. This hole is nearly 45 feet wide, deep and dark. There is room enough for back casts that will allow coverage of the entire area. Bright flies that will sink to fishing depth quickly are needed to induce strikes. The Clouser Minnow patterns, particularly the Mickey Finn style, are representative of the type of fly necessary for success.

Downstream from this hole it is still possible, but a tad difficult, to place a fly on the water in the vicinity of an excitable trout. Roll casts with short rods, short leaders, and bright flies are required. Upstream from the footbridge it is too brushy for fly-fishing for 50 or so yards. The stream opens a bit beyond this point, but is still insistent on tight-quarter tactics.

Exactly 1.0 mile north of the campground turnoff you will notice a small clearing on the left of CR 832. This clearing is centered by a majestic, multibeamed white pine. At the foot of the tree there is a path that descends a steep hill to the stream below. At this spot the Black is 10 to 15 feet wide and 1 to 3 feet deep. Its bottom is made up of sand, gravel, and forest rubble. Undercut banks hold most of the fish. Due to the tight channel created by a very heavy growth of tag alders, the fishing is difficult. Just 0.1 mile north there is another two-track parking area on the left that presents virtually the same stream conditions. Very difficult casting, lots of wild fish—what to do?

The uppermost limit for fly-fishing the Black has been reached with one exception. There is a bridge over the Black on Barber Road just 0.4 mile west of the intersection with CR 832. Upstream from this bridge the river is not fly-fishable unless you enjoy dapping. Downstream from the bridge limited fly-fishing is possible with roll-cast techniques and a large measure of patience.

Notes:

- Naubinway and Epoufette, both on US 2, have good restaurants and motel accommodations.
- The Hog Island Point Campground on Lake Michigan is outstanding.
- The Lake Michigan beach in this area is a great place for a stroll, picnic, or swim.
- St. Ignace, to the east, is the closest city of any size, but it has everything including a well-run casino.

EAST BRANCH OF THE TAHQUAMENON RIVER
Chippewa County

With Strongs Corner on MI 28 as the upstream limit, the Michigan Department of Natural Resources has designated 19 miles of the East Branch of the Tahquamenon as a blue-ribbon trout stream.

The East Branch meets all of the blue-ribbon criteria and adds a wilderness solitude to the mix. At Strongs Corner the stream is 12 to 17 feet in width with a fairly narrow casting channel. It ranges from 1 to 3 feet deep, with a sandy bottom and heavily brushed banks. Where it crosses Strongs Road, just north of Strongs Corner, it breaks into several channels and forms deeply undercut banks along the tag alder, cedar, and pine. These are the hiding places of the native brook trout and they will respond to nearly any well-fished streamer or nymph. Eagerness and bright color in the fish is the good news. The bad news is that this is not easy water to ply with a fly rod. Roll casts are necessary a majority of the time and although there is a nice, fairly open hole downstream from the culvert, the river quickly closes in again and demands a creep-and-crawl and roll-cast approach.

Access to the East Branch, at least the upper reaches between Strongs Corner and Eckerman, is difficult. There are some faint trails leading through the Hiawatha National Forest south from North Road that will take you close, but you will need a compass, four-wheel drive, and CB radio to sanely consider the voyage without a guide. The east-west railroad track from Strongs to Eckerman closely parallels and even crosses the East Branch, and if you are fit enough for a hike this is the wiser approach.

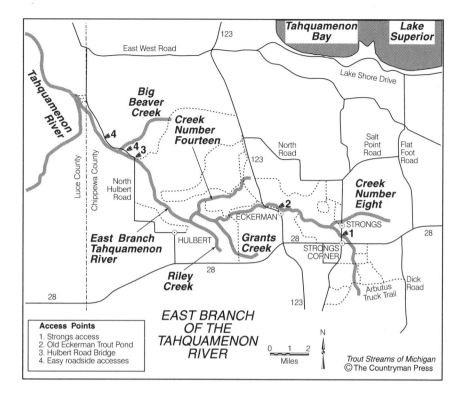

East West Road

123

Tahquamenon Bay

Lake Superior

Lake Shore Drive

Tahquamenon River

Big Beaver Creek

Creek Number Fourteen

North Road

Salt Point Road

Flat Foot Road

123

Luce County

Chippewa County

North Hulbert Road

ECKERMAN

Creek Number Eight

STRONGS

1

28

East Branch Tahquamenon River

HULBERT

Grants Creek

28

STRONGS CORNER

STRONGS

Riley Creek

28

28

123

Dick Road

Arbutus Truck Trail

28

Access Points
1. Strongs access
2. Old Eckerman Trout Pond
3. Hulbert Road Bridge
4. Easy roadside accesses

EAST BRANCH OF THE TAHQUAMENON RIVER

N

0 1 2
Miles

Trout Streams of Michigan
© The Countryman Press

The water between Strongs and Eckerman is very lightly fished by any means and hardly touched by fly-rod purists. It ranges from 15 to 20-plus feet wide and 1 to 4 feet deep. The brush is thick and the insects are ravenous, but if you are looking for a trophy, stream-bred brook trout, this is the place for you. Carry weighted, colorful streamers and a healthy supply of fast-sinking nymphs. The Mickey Finn, Light Spruce, and assorted Clouser Minnows will bring hard, no-nonsense strikes. Rubber-leg wets such as the Girdle Bug, June Wiggler, and Yuk Bug should be tried along with Hare's Ears and the Fox Squirrel nymph.

The village of Eckerman is 2.0 miles north of MI 28 on MI 123. At Eckerman there is a sign on MI 123 indicating the direction to a public access on the East Branch. Follow this gravel road for 0.25 mile to a well-marked, groomed parking and picnic area at the site of the "Old Eckerman Trout Pond." This is a lovely setting and a great place for lounging and picnicking as well as fishing. There is a picturesque footbridge, very old stonework (including an old stone service shed of some kind), a flowing well, and, of course, the river.

At the footbridge the river is about 18 feet wide with a slow to moderate current and a flat, smooth surface. Heavy bankside cuts and overhanging shrubs shelter the fish, which are considerably wiser than their upstream relatives. There is a stretch of gorgeous riffle water downstream from the footbridge and a two-track trail follows the river's course up to a parcel of private property near the bridge on MI 123. This is lovely water to fish. It is highly oxygenated and food-rich. The pockets behind the rocks and the deep swirls by the banks hold trout that will quickly smack any reasonable offering. Soft-hackled wets, particularly the Grouse and Peacock, are very effective. An 8- or 8½-foot rod balanced to a 4-weight line is about right in the Eckerman area. Seven- to 9-foot leaders with a 4X tippet will be satisfactory. You should probably quit fishing and leave the stream before crossing under the bridge on MI 123. The downstream side of this bridge is private property and is heavily, argumentatively posted.

Between Eckerman and the village of Hulbert, the East Branch of the Tahquamenon is joined by Grant's Creek, Riley's Creek, and several smaller unnamed tributaries. This swells the flow considerably and wading is a serious matter from Hulbert downstream to the junction of the East Branch and the mainstream at Slater's Landing in extreme western Luce County.

There are some old fire and logging trails that lead to the river in the Hulbert area but they are not for casual, worry-free travel. Rather than risk an unwelcome overnight in the big woods, take Hulbert Road north from town for 4.5 miles to a bridge over the river. The East Branch ranges from 40 to 50 feet wide in this area and its stained water covers depths to 4 feet and more. The dark water and flat surface give, under certain light conditions, the impression of a highly reflective ink that can assist in the composition of some stunning photographs.

To repeat a wading caution is necessary. Watch your feet and look ahead several steps to be sure of firm footing. The sand bottom fades quickly in the dark water and the darker logs and stumps can topple you quickly. Fish are found throughout the width of the river, but seem to be most numerous and active close to the banks. Marabou leeches, Woolly Buggers, and yellow Marabou Muddlers work well when fish are not actively rising. If the fish are feeding on top near the banks and no hatch is in evidence, try a size-16 black ant, a cricket pattern, or the Griffith's Gnat. At dawn or dusk, a large Deer-Hair Mouse plopped near the stumps and logs can be very productive for larger trout.

Proceeding north from the bridge (the road turns from pavement to gravel), you will notice that the river flows very near the road after about 0.5 mile and continues to parallel the road closely for another 1.3 miles. All the same river characteristics apply to this reach of the East Branch. It is slow, flat, and deep with some very deep holes at the outside bends of the serpentine, lazy turns. This stretch could be fished very effectively with a float tube for safe navigation and a stealthy approach to the best lies.

BOB LINSENMAN

An old stone shed near the Eckerman Trout Pond on the East Branch of the Tahquamenon River

Downstream from the entrance of Big Beaver Creek (this is very near the Chippewa-Luce county line), the East Branch is marginally warm for trout, although some very large fish are taken all the way to the mainstream junction. This area is better explored as a hiker, naturalist, or photographer than as a fly-rodder, but enjoy it; it is beautiful and very wild.

Notes:

- Eckerman has several wood-carvers and rock shops that have real bargains.
- Freighter's Restaurant in Sault Ste. Marie has good food and live entertainment. Sault St. Marie is the major city in the area—complete with casino.

- The Tahquamenon Hotel in Hulbert is an elegant, old-style oasis with a full bar, fine dining, and comfortable rooms.
- The Toonerville Trolley and Hiawatha boat cruise to Tahquamenon Falls is a daily adventure that is well worth the time. The train and boat trip begins at Soo Junction about 8 miles west of Hulbert.

15 | Copper Country

The western Upper Peninsula, for purposes of this book, comprises Gogebic, Ontonagon, Houghton, Keweenaw, Baraga, Iron, Marquette, Dickinson, and Menominee Counties. Bordered by Lake Superior to the north and Wisconsin to the south and west, it features a rugged and picturesque coastline, majestic waterfalls, ghost towns, vast forests, and, for the adventurous angler, an almost endless cascade of cold and pure trout waters.

Copper and iron mining and the wealth in timber opened the territory to the ravages of unchecked exploitation in the late 19th century. Communities boomed, sputtered, and died, and with the increased costs of mining and the end of the vast white pine forests, the western Upper Peninsula has returned, more or less, to a near-wilderness condition with tourism as a major contributor to the region's economy.

Despite the very real requirements of serious backcountry travel (such as careful planning, a reliable vehicle with four-wheel drive, maps, compass, and emergency overnight equipment), the western Upper Peninsula has several cities with a broad range of services and very warm hospitality. Iron River, Iron Mountain, Ironwood, Ontonagon, L'Anse and Baraga, Marquette, and others have fine restaurants, comfortable accommodations, medical and dental facilities, tennis and golf, and a wide range of scenic and historical attractions for the interested traveler.

BLACK RIVER
Gogebic County

This is a big waterway. The river originates in southern Gogebic County at Black River Lake just a few hundred yards from the Wisconsin state line. From the lake it flows almost due north to US Hwy 2 east of Bessemer, then loops back westward for several miles before lunging straight north again to

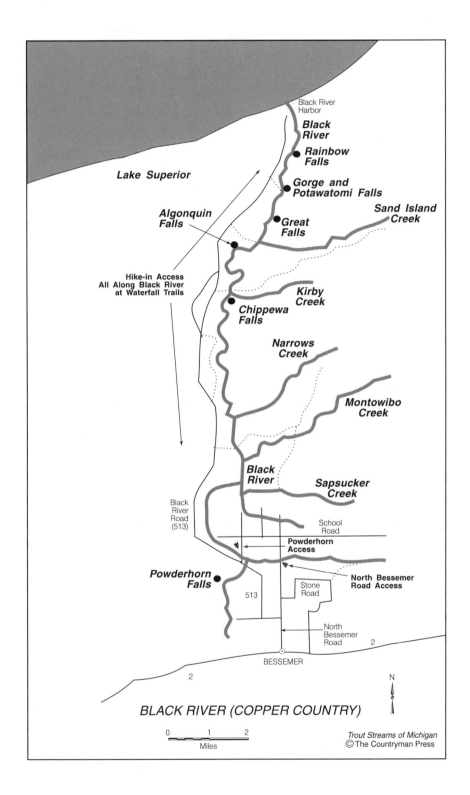

Black River
Harbor

**Black
River**

**Rainbow
Falls**

**Gorge and
Potawatomi Falls**

**Sand Island
Creek**

Lake Superior

**Algonquin
Falls**

**Great
Falls**

**Hike-in Access
All Along Black River
at Waterfall Trails**

**Chippewa
Falls**

**Kirby
Creek**

**Narrows
Creek**

**Montowibo
Creek**

**Black
River**

**Sapsucker
Creek**

Black
River
Road
(513)

School
Road

**Powderhorn
Access**

**Powderhorn
Falls**

**North Bessemer
Road Access**

Stone
Road

513

North
Bessemer
Road

2

BESSEMER

2

N

BLACK RIVER (COPPER COUNTRY)

0   1   2
Miles

Trout Streams of Michigan
© The Countryman Press

Lake Superior. Along this last reach before the big lake, the Black is paralleled by Black River Road which, along with several turnouts, trails, and side roads, provides access to incredible wild scenery and first-class angling.

First-time visitors to the Black River will wonder why they waited so long. The overall impression is of a backward leap in time. The wild, lush vegetation is almost "rain forest" in density and variety. There is old growth timber of unimaginable magnificence—white pines that easily measure 8 feet in diameter, hemlocks nearing 80 feet in height, spruce, fir, gnarled cedar, ancient hardwoods, and more. The river's course from Bessemer to Lake Superior is blessed with clear, bubbling springs, brookie-laden tributary creeks, and thunderous, awesome, death-dealing waterfalls. This river valley is paradise primordial. Bear, moose, lynx, and wolves walk with anglers here.

Throughout its course the Black nurtures brilliantly colored wild brook trout, some of which grow to a size more expected in remote Canada. Smallmouth bass are also present and these too reach substantial proportion. Below Rainbow Falls, the upstream barrier to migratory fish, a fly-angler can reasonably expect steelhead, brown trout, coho and king salmon, and (rarely) coaster brookies. At the "tidal pool," inside the breakwater where the Black blends into Superior, anything goes. All of the salmonid species are present as well as walleyes and northern pike. It pays to pack several matched outfits for the Black if you are interested in variety.

For me, the wild brook trout and the spectacular scenery are the main attractions. A fly rod, a camera and the company of my good friend, John Ramsay, makes a complete package of pure joy. John is the premier fly-fishing guide in the western Upper Peninsula, and the Black River is his home. Literally. His neat cabin (he calls it "camp") is perched on a bluff high over the river. The Black sings him to sleep and awakens him every night and day. It is no wonder at all that he left the competitive world of music (piano and vocals—Blues and Boogie) in Chicago for the rough-and-tumble comforts of the rugged Ottawa National Forest and the Black River. He is no longer John Ramsay, the piano player; he is Black River John, but he is still very entertaining.

My most recent visit to the Black was in late June 2000. My nephew—godson and namesake Rob—had the gall to schedule his wedding during the Hex hatch! And not even close to home, but in Rice Lake, Wisconsin! On the way home I took a couple of days to unwind, hang out with Black River John and fish for brookies.

It had rained hard for two days and the river was high and stained when I arrived. John suggested a warm-up at the mouth of the river. "We'll throw streamers and see what we pick up. Maybe a steelhead, a brown, perhaps a northern." We hopped in John's van and drove north about a mile to the

BOB LINSENMAN

The Black River near Lake Superior

Black River Recreation Area and the "tidal pool." I was tired and stiff from the drive and cast poorly but managed a northern of about 2 feet in length. John caught a twin and we retooled for brook trout above Rainbow Falls on the main river and a couple of its sparkling tributaries.

Between Bessemer and Lake Superior there are more than a dozen feeder streams and seven waterfalls on the Black. Numerous white-capped rapids, stark, vertical ledgerock walls, and northern rain-forest lushness make this rugged fishery a photographer's dream come true. Be sure to carry your camera (and several rolls of color film) along with your fishing gear no matter how inconvenient it might seem. A small waterproof backpack with a light lunch and a bottle of water will keep the camera and film safe.

The brook trout of the Black and its tributaries are lovely and simple, as is the way of brook trout. But they are not foolish. They demand and deserve the respect accorded more pressured trout. Wade and cast carefully. Mend for a drag-free drift and you will be more than pleased.

Black River John keeps his fly selection pretty much to the basics. He likes sparsely tied streamers, specifically the Royal Coachman, Muddler, and an Orange and White in sizes 6–10. Similarly, his dry-fly box carries specifics for each hatch (we saw quite a few Sulphurs on June 24 and 25) and some classic attractors such as the Adams and Royal Wulff. His dry-fly rod is a 4-weight (a gift from an appreciative client), and a rugged 7-weight serves as his choice for streamers. He also swings some "old fashioned" wets in the classic manner. "They all work," he said.

Notes:

- Copper Peak is the world's tallest "ski-flying" jump. It can be seen from Black River Road. You will want to take a quick side trip for a close-up view. It is an awesome, spine-tingling sight.
- Be sure to take some of the scenic pathways to the various falls.
- Black River Recreation Area has mowed lawns, a boat launch, and picnic tables. The Lake Superior beach has wondrous rocks, driftwood formations and a view that goes forever.
- Nearby Bessemer, Wakefield, Ironwood, and Hurley (in Wisconsin) have all the necessities and amenities of modern life.

COOK'S RUN
Iron County

Cook's Run flows west to east in southwestern Iron County. Its flow turns northeasterly near the bridge on US 2, about 10 miles west of the town of Iron River, and continues in this direction beneath FH 16 for another 3-plus miles to its junction with the South Branch of the Paint River near Basswood.

About 1 mile upstream from US 2, Cook's Run is home to the Iron County Trout Rearing Station and fishing is vigorously discouraged in this area. Downstream from the rearing station, the creek is fly-fishable (with patience and a short rod) to its merger with the Paint.

The stream at US 2 is about 20 feet wide. It is smooth, serpentine, and spring creek–like in its appearance and fishability. There is abundant aquatic growth, including watercress and various grasses, and the resident brook trout seem to favor channels in the vegetation as a source for both cover and food. The bottom in this area is sand and fine gravel and the depth ranges from 1 to 3 feet. Downstream from US 2 (looking north) heavy vegetation, overhanging brush with undercut banks, provides most of the trout cover. The brook trout are in the obvious places and respond very well to Woolly Buggers and small Spruce Fly streamers, Hare's Ear and Fox Squirrel nymphs, and Royal Trude and Adams dry-fly patterns. These fish are not fussy at all.

Just a few yards downstream from US 2 there is a bridge with easy access at FH 16 just south of Golden Lake Campground. There is a nice, deep hole on the downstream side of this bridge, and although fished moderately hard, the trout seem always willing to oblige. A small marabou Mickey Finn pulsed slowly through the pool's tail-out is very productive.

Farther downstream, Cook's Run averages 20 to 25 feet wide with a sand and gravel bottom, muck edges, and downed trees. The fish are exactly where it appears they should be and will take wet patterns with slow twitches or a skittering Irresistible or Humpy with equal enthusiasm.

Cook's Run
Access Points
1. US 2 bridge
2. FH 16 bridge
3. Junction access

South Branch, Paint River
Access Points

A. FH 149 access
B. County Road 436 access
C. FH 151 access
D. Gold Mine access
E. Paint River Forks Campground

COOK'S RUN &
SOUTH BRANCH OF
THE PAINT RIVER

Trout Streams of Michigan
© The Countryman Press

Proceeding downstream toward the South Branch of the Paint, all vestiges of streamside paths disappear. Walking the bank is much more difficult than in-stream navigation, and in some spots very deep muck holes can make the venture problematic. By staying in the stream the angler can proceed safely and cast to wild fish that rarely see an artificial fly.

As you continue downstream you will notice more gravel and grass with a sampling of sizable rocks. The stream is quite shallow in this area, but the limited sweeps and pocket water all hold trout, and careful roll casting will put you in contact with them.

Cook's Run is an enjoyable, rewarding stream to explore. It requires patience, above-average casting skill, and a generous supply of insect repellent, but the brook trout are more than eager and very beautiful.

SOUTH BRANCH PAINT RIVER
Iron County

The South Branch of the Paint River traverses west-central Iron County, and from the bridge at FH 149 to its junction with the North Branch at Gibbs City, it is ranked by the Department of Natural Resources as a blue-ribbon trout stream. It has sand, gravel, muck, rocks, boulders, aquatic grasses, logs, stumps, overhanging brush, and a high density of wild trout.

Approximately 10 miles west of the town of Iron River, FH16 runs northerly toward the Houghton county line from US 2. Just 4.0 miles north of US 2, FH 16 takes a 90-degree jog to the left (west) and at this turn FH 149 goes off to the right (east). About 1.5 miles east, FH 149 crosses the South Branch of the Paint River. There is room to park your car here, and since this is the uppermost section of the Paint that is designated as blue-ribbon trout water, it is a reasonable place to start.

A railroad bed parallels the river on the west side and it is a good technique to follow the railroad south (downstream) for a few hundred yards, then fish back upstream to your automobile. Paint River is narrow and brushy in this sector and, except for the early season bait-angler, very lightly fished. The stream is 15 to 20 feet wide in most places with a sand, rock, and gravel bottom. Overhanging brush makes casting difficult and the mosquitoes can be murder. But the good news is that moderate roll-casting skill, a light, short rod, and a supply of bug juice will put you comfortably in contact with lively, very wild brook and brown trout. On a recent early June day, there was a very sizable hatch of Sulphurs on this section of the Paint, and a size-16 parachute pattern produced fish up to 13 inches.

The next reasonable downstream access to the Paint is at Basswood on CR 436 just east of Golden Lake. Do not be misled. Basswood is only a spot on the county map, it is not a town. Two miles south of FH 149, FH 16 crosses CR 436 (if you pass Golden Lake Campground you have gone too far) and both the railroad bed and the South Branch of the Paint River closely parallel the road on the north side about 1.5 miles east of FH 16. An easier (to find) access is just 1.0 mile east, where Cook's Run crosses the gravel road a few yards before its juncture with the Paint. The railroad bed is clearly visible here and there is plenty of parking room off to the side.

The river in this area is 20 to 30 feet wide with very slippery rocks ranging from baseball to bowling-ball size. There is also an ample mix of sand and gravel with some muck on the edges. The vegetation is thick, and casting, though generally easy, sometimes requires a studied delivery.

There is a good population of native brook and naturally reproducing brown trout in this area and they are in all the obvious holding spots. They are not stupid but neither are they overly selective. The Adams, Royal Wulff,

BOB LINSENMAN

A wild brookie from a small stream in the Upper Peninsula

and Lime Trude are effective top-water patterns in sizes 12–16. The Hare's Ear, Grouse and Peacock Soft Hackle, and olive Woolly Bugger are all the subsurface patterns you are likely to need for a successful outing.

Approximately 2 miles downstream (east) FH 151 enters from the left, and about 100 yards up (north) from this junction the Paint crosses FH 151. This is another good fishing access and the stream's characteristics are identical to those just described. Proceeding northeasterly, the Paint recrosses FH 151 after 2.0 miles and near the site of an abandoned gold mine. This too is a productive stretch. Both of these access points are easy to reach and put the angler in touch with beautiful sections of the river. In addition to the flies mentioned earlier, a small yellow Marabou Muddler seems to work very well on cloudy days.

The next easy downstream access is at the small USFS Campground just west of Gibbs City on CR 657. Proceed northeast from the "gold mine" access about 3.5 miles to CR 657, then turn left for 0.5 mile to the campground. This is where the South Branch meets the North Branch of the Paint River. Here, the North Branch is slower moving, with warmer water and, although there are trout downstream from the campground, the Paint has lost its happy character and handsome, lively riffles. Upstream from the junction with the North Branch the South Branch remains a productive, easy-to-fish stream. A poor dirt road just west of the campground will lead you to some beautiful water that is lightly fly-fished. Caddis are prevalent and the Elk-Hair patterns with tan or olive bodies in sizes 14 and 16 are excellent producers. Small streamers including the Mickey Finn and Pass Lake will bring respectable fish out from the deeper lies, and the Hare's Ear is probably the only nymph you will need.

The Paint is one of the prettiest small streams in the Upper Peninsula. It supports an abundance of wild trout, is easy to find, and is relatively easy to fish. It is well worth a full day on your itinerary.

Notes:

- Golden Lake Campground near US 2 is quite scenic and just a few minutes' drive from the town of Iron River. Golden Lake has nesting loons.
- The Happy Italian Roma Cafe in Iron River has reasonable prices, good service, and excellent food.
- The Iron County Museum in Iron River features displays and exhibits on lumbering, mining, farming, and transportation.

BRULE RIVER
Iron County

The Brule River defines the Michigan-Wisconsin state border from its birth at Brule Lake in extreme southwestern Iron County to its merger with the Michigamme River near the Dickinson county line.

The Brule supports trout throughout its flow but the premier cold-water fishery is generally regarded as that stretch bounded by MI 73 at the upstream limit and MI 189 south of Iron River on the downstream side. The Brule in this stretch is cold, clear with a light tea stain, has varied rates of flow over sand, gravel, muck, and rock bottom, and supports a strong, naturally reproducing stock of trout.

From Nelma (Wisconsin side) downstream to MI 73 and beyond, the river is about 45 feet wide and 1 to 4 feet in depth. The Brule at the MI 73 bridge has a moderate to slow current with a smooth, flat surface. It flows over sand, fine gravel, and silt and has excellent mayfly and caddis populations. Most of the trout in this section will be found along the banks and under the cooling shelter of overhanging trees and shrubs.

On a recent June evening, Brown Drakes *(simulans)* began emerging at 8:30 PM just downstream from the USFS Campground on the Wisconsin side near Nelma. By 9 PM both emerging duns and spinners were luring trout to the surface for an easy meal. The hatch was also in progress near Rudolph Road, which enters MI 73 just north (Michigan side) of the bridge. There are several parking spots along Rudolph Road and all are within a short, easy walk to the river.

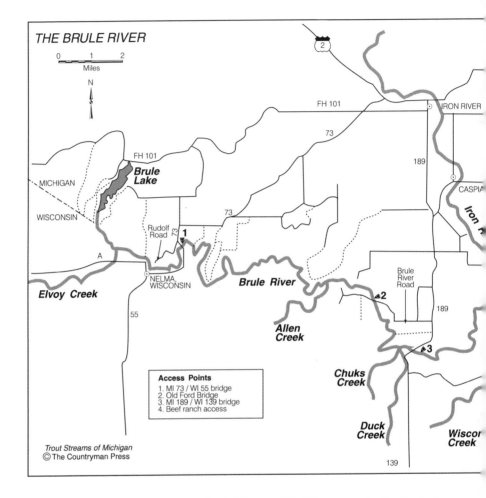

THE BRULE RIVER

Access Points
1. MI 73 / WI 55 bridge
2. Old Ford Bridge
3. MI 189 / WI 139 bridge
4. Beef ranch access

Trout Streams of Michigan
© The Countryman Press

From MI 73 downstream to the bridge on MI 189, access to the Brule is a bit tricky. Several roads that show on county and regional maps dead-end into private, heavily posted property very close to the river, and this is extremely frustrating. Two examples of such seeming "access" points are the dirt roads proceeding south to the river from Bass Lake and Camp Lake. Both go to the river but only through tightly controlled private lands.

An excellent, easily located access can be reached via Brule River Road, which is about 1.5 miles north on MI 189 from the bridge at the state line. Drive west on Brule River Road about 1.5 miles to where the main road dead-ends at private property. Take the right turn on a seasonal two-track and drive 1.0 mile to a parking spot at the river near the remnants of the old Ford Bridge. The Brule at this location is about 40 to 45 feet wide with an interesting array of water types. It has deep, swirling holes, fast riffles, long pools and glides with undercut banks, and jackstrawed lumber snags. Its

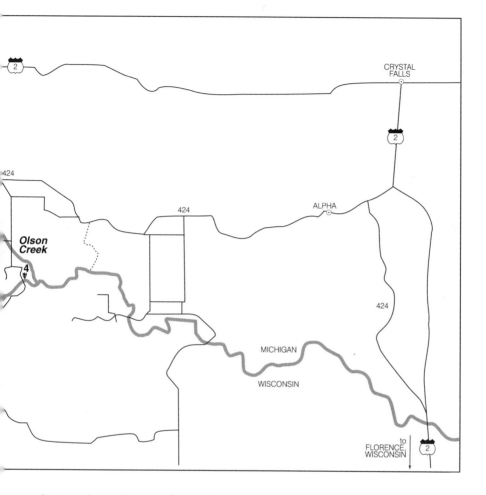

bottom is a mixture of gravel, sand, large rocks, rotting timber, and silt. There are aquatic grasses, abundant mayfly and caddis populations, and large trout in residence.

An 8- to 9-foot rod balanced with a 5- or 6-weight line is a good choice in this stretch. Throughout the course of a day, or several hours, it is likely that the fly-rodder will want to switch from small nymphs to dry patterns to weighted streamers, and the more versatile the rod the better.

Elk-Hair Caddis and Henryville Caddis, Adams, Dun Variant, Light Cahill, and Royal Wulff are good general searching patterns for this area. The Hare's Ear, Pheasant Tail, Caddis Creeper, and dragonfly nymphs will produce, and a streamer selection should include Marabou Muddlers, Clouser Minnows, and weighted crayfish.

The bridge area on MI 189 is another surprisingly good area to fish, and the area just downstream from the bridge, and extending for several hundred yards, has very good hatches and a population of free-rising trout. North of the bridge (0.4 mile) there is a narrow dirt road that follows a power line to the right (east). This road dead-ends at the river about 0.5 mile downstream from the bridge next to private property. This section of the Brule has some nice riffle water and some deep, placid runs that hold respectable brook and brown trout. Any reasonable hatch, emergence, or spinner fall will bring them topside and the fishing can be very good. This area is easy to wade and the better holding water is easy to locate. Directly across from the end of the road there is a good riffle that turns into a long, deep run on the far bank. This particular run is home to some nice brook trout.

General attractor patterns work on all but the brightest days for the brook trout, but the browns seem to require a more precise imitation of the current hatch in either dry, nymph, or soft-hackle emerger versions. Streamers are effective if fished deeply and slowly and the Clouser Minnow, white Zonker, and crayfish are good choices.

Another good access point within striking distance of MI 189 is in the Scott Lake area southeast of the village of Gaastra. County Road 424 winds eastward through Gaastra to Scott Lake Road. Drive south on Scott Lake Road through a very large (by midwestern standards) beef ranch to where the road swings left and turns into a two-track. Follow the trail down a hill to the parking area at the river. There is a small island in the center of the river at this spot, and the remains of an old bridge, combined with the deep and heavy downstream run, provide excellent cover for large fish. This is excellent stonefly habitat, and Brown or Black Stonefly nymphs in sizes 6 through 12 work well.

Upstream from the island there is a wide (60-plus feet), slow flat with good fish throughout. This stretch has some deep pockets and requires very careful wading to reach the trout that typically stay tight to the banks and under the cover provided by the overhanging vegetation. This is an excellent stretch of water for burrowing mayflies, certain caddis, and terrestrials, and provides very good dry-fly fishing when conditions are right. The slow downstream, classic wet-fly method will work when the fish are not surface feeding, but it is a more enjoyable and productive venture to nymph-fish the big, weighted stonefly patterns in the heavier water downstream from the island. Woolly Buggers, Clouser, and crayfish patterns are effective throughout this stretch and particularly so on cloudy or overcast days and at dawn or dusk. A Deer-Hair Mouse with a marabou or chamois tail is worth casting close to the banks. Hold on!

The Brule is a highly regarded river. It is a favorite of trout anglers and canoeists throughout its length. Its banks teem with woodcock and grouse and the larger valley is home to trophy-sized white-tailed deer. Nearby Iron River has all the necessities and most of the amenities for a well-balanced family vacation. Once visited and fairly tried, the Brule will bring you back time and time again.

Notes:

- There are many beautiful campgrounds in the area. Both Wisconsin and Michigan sides of the river have state and federal facilities.
- This is one of the few areas of Michigan where ticks can be a problem. Be mindful of both wood ticks and the smaller deer ticks and take appropriate precautions.
- There are several good restaurants and motels in the vicinity. Iron River, Michigan, and Florence, Wisconsin, are full-service communities. Golf, boating, hiking, and scenic exploration are in order. The area is rich in history. Lumber and mining attractions are close by.
- Visit Horse Race Rapids 6.0 miles south of Crystal Falls on US 2.

FENCE RIVER
Iron County

The Fence River flows through Michigan's moose country north of Michigamme Reservoir in northeastern Iron County. Bordered by a mixture of private and public lands and lying generally in the Copper Country State Forest near the Marquette county line, the Fence is a wilderness river with the attendant joys and sorrows. A competing angler is rarely seen, but the same is true for a rescue vehicle if one is stuck on the roadside. The mosquitoes and blackflies are voracious and it is a long drive for a cold beer or soft drink, but the sight of a moose with her calf, or the yipping of a coyote pack at dawn, is long-remembered compensation.

Michigan 95 runs north and south in southwest Marquette County through the village of Republic and the tourist community of Witch Lake near the Iron county line. At Witch Lake there is a paved road heading west. This is Fence River Road and it remains paved, though hilly with tight curves, for approximately 5 miles. The following 8 miles are typically narrow, rocky gravel and sand, twisting through an active timbering area; heavy logging trucks are a regular navigational hazard.

There are resorts on Fence Lake and the county maps show easy road access to the river in this immediate vicinity, but these roads end at posted, private property. It is wise to continue westward past Mitchigon Creek about 4 miles to the wooden bridge on the Fence before attempting to fish.

The Fence River at the bridge is 40 to 50 feet wide and 1 to 4 feet in depth with a sand, gravel, and muck bottom throughout. The water is a dark tea color and wading should be undertaken only during daylight hours and

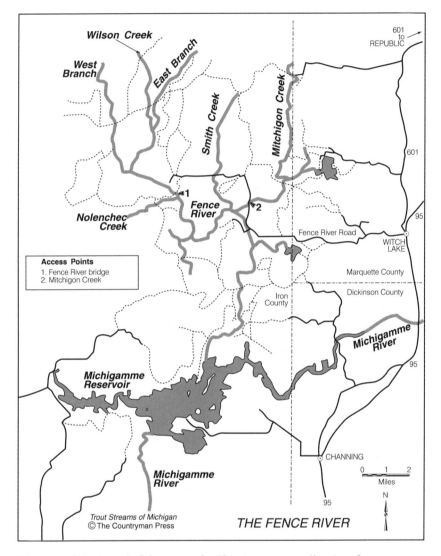

Access Points
1. Fence River bridge
2. Mitchigon Creek

Trout Streams of Michigan
© The Countryman Press

THE FENCE RIVER

with a careful, thoughtful approach. This is an area allowing for very easy casting and the rod length is inconsequential to success.

Brook trout up to and often exceeding 12 inches are regularly taken from the Fence on a variety of surface and subsurface patterns. Your selection should include the Lime Trude, Royal Wulff, Adams, and Elk-Hair Caddis dry patterns. Hare's Ear and caddis pupae are effective nymphs, and leech imitations along with the Mickey Finn will cover streamer requirements.

The Fence is a long way from anywhere and a difficult approach for anything but a stout vehicle (with four-wheel drive recommended) and a careful driver. It is lightly fished, however, and not surprisingly the fish grow quite large. A short, carefully planned float trip would be an ideal way to further explore this fishery.

Mitchigon Creek, a major tributary, is worth fishing. It has solid, scrappy brook trout up to 12 inches that readily take attractor dries and small streamers. This creek crosses Fence River Road about 8 miles east of Witch Lake. It is 20 to 25 feet wide with a fine gravel and sand bottom. It has a lively current downstream from the bridge and the crisscrossed timbers provide excellent brook trout habitat.

Notes:

- Maps, a compass, and a full tank of gas provide some psychological insurance for Fence River excursion.
- Wild game abounds and even moose have been sighted in the area. Be sure to carry a camera.

LITTLE CARP RIVER
Porcupine Mountains Wilderness State Park
Ontonagon County, Gogebic County

Porcupine Mountains State Park lies on Lake Superior's shore about 15 miles west of the city of Ontonagon. Its 63,000 acres comprise a true wilderness with virgin timber, rugged terrain, abundant wildlife, and pure, cascading streams with spectacular waterfalls.

Automobile traffic in the park is restricted to the South Boundary Road and MI 107. Access to the park's wonders, including the best trout fishing, is by foot. Ninety miles of hiking trails traverse the park and many follow the path of the park's best trout streams.

The Little Carp River is one of the most accessible of the park's waters. It is easily reached via the South Boundary Road and a very short walk from the parking area near Greenstone Falls. The Little Carp River Trail follows the little stream's descent to its mouth at Lake Superior, and the hike from the parking area to the big lake and back is about 11 miles with superb brook trout fishing throughout the journey.

Those not inclined to serious backcountry hiking will find very good fishing close to their automobile. By following the trail downstream for a preselected distance and fishing back up to the parking area, an angler can cover a comfortable distance and fish in truly beautiful, rugged country to eager, opportunistic brook trout.

This angling will be for smallish, delicate fish of vivid color; an 11-inch fish is a large one. But what they lack in size they make up in energy. The Little Carp is 12 to 16 feet wide and 1 to 2½ feet deep. Its bottom is gran-

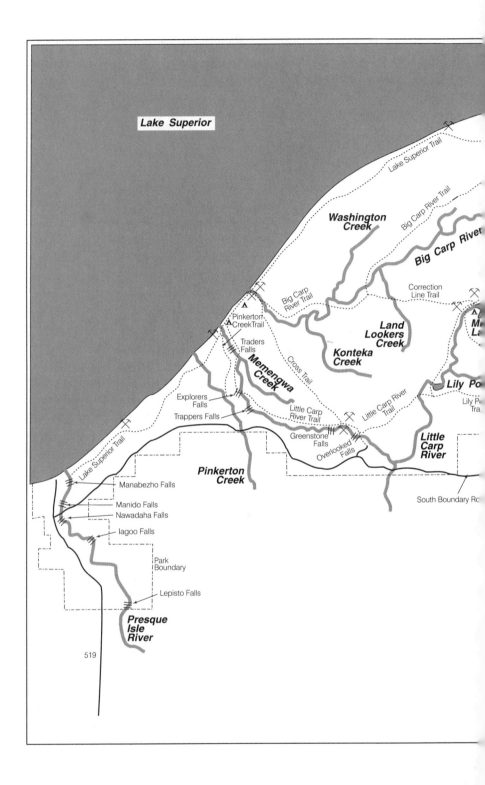

Lake Superior

Lake Superior Trail

Washington Creek

Big Carp River Trail

Big Carp River

Correction Line Trail

Big Carp River Trail

Pinkerton Creek Trail

Traders Falls

Land Lookers Creek

Konteka Creek

M.
La

Memengwa Creek

Cross Trail

Lily Po

Explorers Falls

Little Carp River Trail

Little Carp River Trail

Lily P
Tra

Trappers Falls

Greenstone Falls

Overlooked Falls

Little Carp River

Pinkerton Creek

South Boundary Rc

Lake Superior Trail

Manabezho Falls

Manido Falls
Nawadaha Falls

Iagoo Falls

Park Boundary

Lepisto Falls

Presque Isle River

519

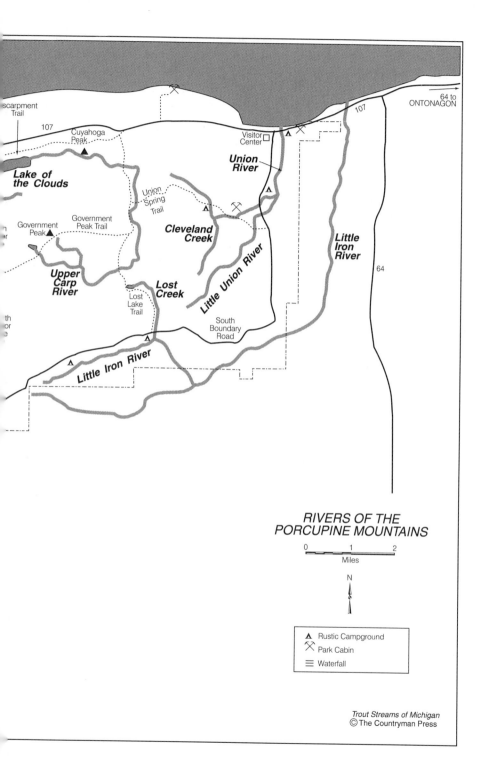

scarpment
Trail

107

Cuyahoga
Peak

Lake of
the Clouds

Government
Peak Trail

Government
Peak

Union
Spring
Trail

Upper
Carp
River

Lost
Lake
Trail

Lost
Creek

Cleveland
Creek

Little Union River

South
Boundary
Road

Little Iron River

Visitor
Center

Union
River

Little
Iron
River

107

64 to
ONTONAGON

64

**RIVERS OF THE
PORCUPINE MOUNTAINS**

0   1   2
Miles

N

▲ Rustic Campground
✕ Park Cabin
≡ Waterfall

Trout Streams of Michigan
© The Countryman Press

ite ledgerock and all the deep, shaded pockets and pools hold one or more trout. At times the trout seem to be everywhere—behind stumps, in small eddies, beneath banks, in midbrook riffles! Fish all the pockets, cast to every rock. You will love it!

Almost any fly will work, but a small Silver Hilton seems to always bring a strike. The olive Woolly Bugger and Mickey Finn are favorites along with dry patterns such as the Lime Trude, Royal Wulff, and Adams. Pinch down your barbs and try to release the fish without touching them if at all possible. The surroundings—the towering trees, minifalls, and tiny rapids—will make your photography a stunning reminder even without a fish in the picture.

The "Porkies" contain many fine trout streams; the Little Carp is highlighted here only as an appetizer. Fish the Big Carp River from Lake Superior to the junction with Washington Creek. Try the Presque Isle below Manabezho Falls and out into the surf for big rainbows. Check in at the visitor center at the park's east entrance for up-to-date information, and prepare yourself for a magnificent venture.

Notes:

- Do not feed the bears.
- Lake of the Clouds sits high above Lake Superior. The view from Escarpment Trail is breathtaking.
- Nearby Ontonagon has a fine golf course, excellent shopping, and several good restaurants.
- Union Spring pumps out 700 gallons of water a minute. It is only a 2-mile hike from South Boundary Road.

FIRESTEEL RIVER
Ontonagon County

Both the East and West branches of the Firesteel River originate near the Houghton county line in extreme eastern Ontonagon County. The East Branch rises from springs near MI 26 north and east of Greenland, while the West Branch starts its flow at Sudden Lake south of MI 38 and just east of Forest Highway 16.

At the bridge on MI 38 the West Branch can be reached via a two-track road that descends to the river on the south side of the highway. There is ample parking at a level spot in a field of wildflowers and then there is a mild descent by foot to the river. The river at MI 38 is approximately 15 feet wide and has tight fishing to brook and rainbow trout. The West Branch clouds very quickly after a rainfall due to the heavy clay and it is best to leave it alone if there has been any measurable precipitation.

Just a short distance downstream, both the East and West branches of the Firesteel cross MI 26 a few hundred yards apart. The East Branch at MI 26 is approximately 20 feet wide with fine gravel and sand as the predominant bottom characteristic. Ledgerock and some silt complete the picture as the light tea-colored water flows through numerous log tangles and under banks. Streamside wildflowers are abundant, and the undergrowth is cut by numerous deer trails.

Downstream from the highway bridge, the first deep run holds both rainbow and brook trout, and farther down through a deeper hold and slow bend, fish rise regularly to wind-blown terrestrials. Trout up to 12 inches attacked a small Woolly Bugger and then a soft-hackle Hare's Ear in these two spots on a recent excursion.

Upstream from the bridge two very nice brook trout (in the 12-inch class) hammered a size-12 weighted Mickey Finn. The best spot for larger fish, in the immediate vicinity of the parking area at the bridge, is a very large tangle of fallen trees just upstream about 40 yards from the footpath. Fishing throughout this section will require roll casting with a short rod and, depending on water clarity, short leaders tapered to 4X. A selection of small, bright streamers and a few impressionistic dry flies such as the Adams and

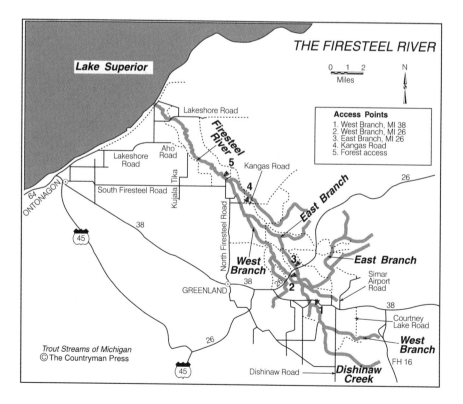

THE FIRESTEEL RIVER

Lake Superior

0   1   2 N
Miles

Access Points
1. West Branch, MI 38
2. West Branch, MI 26
3. East Branch, MI 26
4. Kangas Road
5. Forest access

Lakeshore Road

Firesteel River

Aho Road

Lakeshore Road

Kangas Road

East Branch

South Firesteel Road

Kujala Tika

64 ONTONAGON

45

38

North Firesteel Road

West Branch

38

GREENLAND

East Branch

Simar Airport Road

38

26

Courtney Lake Road

West Branch

FH 16

Trout Streams of Michigan
© The Countryman Press

26

45

Dishinaw Road

Dishinaw Creek

BOB LINSENMAN

Guide John Ramsay fishes pocket water in Copper Country.

Lime Trude will cover the stream's requirements.

Downstream from MI 26 the two branches flow northwesterly for about 4 miles before joining a few hundred yards south of Kangas Road. At Kangas Road the river ranges from 30 to 40 feet wide with a nearly all-sand bottom and deeply undercut banks. It provides easy casting but the sand is soft in spots and cautious wading is advised. Upstream from this bridge the river makes a lazy S-turn through a large field after emerging from the woods at the field's edge. This is an excellent area for grasshopper, beetle, and cricket imitations. The high sand banks and sweeping curves push water deep into holes at the bends and around fallen trees and these are excellent spots to probe with a weighted Woolly Bugger or Clouser Minnow.

Downstream from the bridge the river parallels the road for about 80 yards before turning north toward Lake Superior. The same general conditions are in effect here. Sand bottom, deep holes, downed logs, and brush provide the habitat for rainbow (immature steelhead) and brook trout.

From the junction of North Firesteel Road and Kangas Road (4.8 miles north of Greenland and MI 38) drive 1.0 mile north on Firesteel Road to where the main road (paved) curves to the left and a dirt road proceeds directly north. Follow this dirt road 0.5 mile to the next downstream bridge. The river here averages 25 feet in width and retains all the previously mentioned characteristics. The rainbows and brooks are in the deep holes and under the banks.

For the mountain-man spirit, there are logging roads that cut through the forest and reach to the lower Firesteel before it crosses Lake Shore Road and meets Lake Superior. Even with a full tank of gas in a stout four-wheel drive it is best to give careful thought to such an adventure. The maps may not be current or precise, and if this is attempted on a cloudy day a good compass is mandatory.

The mouth of the Firesteel can be best reached by driving northeast from the city of Ontonagon for about 5 miles. Steelhead, brook trout, and an occasional brown trout are often caught on streamer flies at or near the mouth.

Notes:

- The Bessemer-Ironwood area has many beautiful waterfalls.
- Ontonagon has a fine golf course and its owners are especially proud of the eighth hole.
- The Adventure Mine in Greenland conducts a very interesting tour.
- Prehistoric mines at Rockland are worth visiting.
- Agate hunting and photography along Lake Superior's shore is a peaceful diversion.
- Isle Royale National Park has resident moose and timber wolf populations. It can be reached by boat from Copper Harbor.

JUMBO RIVER
Houghton County

This excellent brook trout stream is a major tributary to the East Branch of the Ontonagon River, entering the larger river just a few yards north of MI 28 about 2 miles west of the town of Kenton (see the map in chapter 9).

At the MI 28 bridge the Jumbo averages 25 feet wide and dances over boulders to provide exciting fast-water pocket fishing for brook trout and rainbows (immature steelhead). It is only a quick downstream trip from the highway to the merger with the East Branch, and it is possible to take quite a few fish roll-casting an olive Woolly Bugger or Silver Hilton to the pockets and eddies behind rocks and logs. Your trip back upstream will produce fish on a Royal Wulff, Adams, or a Lime Trude.

Just west of the bridge Golden Glow Road heads south from MI 28 and leads you to the Jumbo after about 1.5 miles. The river flows through mixed hardwoods with gradually heightened banks as you proceed upstream. There are two convenient parking areas just off Golden Glow Road. The first is visible on your left as you enter a large clearing. The closed bridge at the foot of an overgrown two-track is a good place to park and fish in either direction. The second parking area is about 0.5 mile farther upstream. As you cross the clearing, the road turns into a two-track and climbs a slight hill into a fairly heavy woods. About 200 yards into the woods there is an opening (on both sides of the road) large enough to park a vehicle and turn around. The river is on your immediate left and down a short, steep hill. Both of these parking areas provide convenient access to lively fishing for the stream's wild brook trout.

Throughout this section the Jumbo averages 25 feet wide and is 1 to 3 feet deep. Its bottom is ledgerock and boulder, and the cover is in pockets, rock-ledge pools, and deep, cedar-lined holes. Most of the fish are brook trout from 8 to 12 inches, but occasionally a holdover rainbow of real proportion will emerge from a dark piece of water to intercept a bright streamer. This usually results in some considerable, albeit short-lived, excitement.

The fish in the Jumbo seem particularly fond of an olive Hare's Ear nymph in size 12. Additional nymphs for your box should include the Halfback, Caddis Creeper, and Fox Squirrel patterns. A streamer assortment can be complete with only the Pass Lake, Woolly Bugger, Muddler, and Light Spruce Fly—all in sizes 10 and 12. The Adams and Royal Wulff will, on most days, suffice for top-water efforts, but on breezy summer days a pale yellow–bodied grasshopper in size 10 will bring enthusiastic strikes.

Upstream from the second parking spot (the one in the woods) there is a path that parallels the river. Follow this path for about 80 yards and you will come to the foot of a 4-foot-high waterfall that dumps into a deep hole and broadens into a flat pool and tail-out. A small Light Spruce Fly with a size-12 Hare's Ear dropper will almost always bring solid takes if cast into the base of the falls and allowed to sink before a slow, hand-twist retrieve is begun.

The Jumbo is an ideal stream for a beginning fly-angler or one of only moderate skill. It is easy to wade, the fish are where they should be and not terribly shy, casting is moderately easy, if not carefree, and the overall experience is rewarding. Beautiful surroundings, a lively dancing stream with handsome, eager fish—that is the Jumbo River.

Notes:

- Bond Falls and Agate Falls, both on the Middle Branch of the Ontonagon, are easily accessible and worthy of a side trip. Bring your camera and color film.
- Numerous lighthouses with surrounding panoramic vistas are worth a drive to either Lake Superior or Lake Michigan.
- There are Las Vegas–style casinos at Watersmeet and Bark River.

Appendix A:
Hatches and Fly Patterns

If you ask a Michigan resident or tourist-angler which insect is most important to the fly-rodder, nine times out of ten the answer will be the *Hexagenia limbata*. The tenth answer might be Brown Drake, Hendrickson, or if the respondent is a steelheader, the Black Stonefly (nymph). The "Hex" receives more attention than the other bugs and this is due to the insect's size and predictability. It is one of the largest mayflies in North America. The incredible nighttime spinner falls bring the river's largest trout to the surface, and if a vacation or long weekend is planned around the July Fourth holiday, Hex activity will be found, somewhere. All is not cream and strawberries, however. Like the giant salmonfly circus in the West, the hatch varies in intensity, the hatch moves, and on the more famous rivers, the angling pressure can be unsettling.

One of the goals of this book is to spread the fishing pressure. With that in mind, it is hoped that the following compilation of hatches will facilitate planning and provide high-quality fly-fishing throughout the season. These major hatches are reliable, generally attract less angling pressure (than the Hex), and bring substantial fish topside. This listing is only a general guideline. The rivers you plan to fish may push the edges of the schedules by a few days for a variety of reasons.

Hatches

The emergence schedules use the Roscommon-Grayling-Lovells area as a base point. Hatches on the Black River, in Cheboygan County to the north, will average 7 to 10 days later, and this later emergence is reflective of streams north of Gaylord. Upper Peninsula streams will lag even more with peak activity 10 to 14 days behind the Au Sable at Grayling. Streams that precede the Au Sable's hatches are the White River and Rogue and other rivers in the west-central part of the state.

SOME MAJOR MICHIGAN HATCHES

Common Name	Scientific Name	Peak Dates	Hook Size
Blue-Winged Olive	*Baetis vagans*	April 27–May 10	18
Little Black Caddis	*Chimarra aterrima*	May 1–15	16–18
Mahogany Drake	*Paraleptophlebia adoptiva*	May 5–20	16
Hendrickson	*Ephemerella subvaria and invaria*	May 1–20	12–14
Sulphur	*Ephemerella dorothea*	May 17–June 15	16–18
Popcorn Caddis	*Nectopsyche*	June–August	16
Gray Drake	*Siphlonurus rapidus*	May 20–June 15	12–14
Brown Drake	*Ephemera simulans*	June 1–12	10
Green Oak Worm		June	10–12
Michigan Caddis or Hex	*Hexagenia limbata*	June 15–July 4	6
White-Gloved Howdy	*Isonychia bicolor*	June 12–July 25	10–12
Light Cahill	*Stenonema/Stenacron canadensis*	July 5–July 20	14
Blue-Winged Olive	*Ephemerella lata*	July 15–August 15	16
Tiny Blue–Winged Olive	*Pseudocleon anoka*	August 14–September 25	22
Trico	*Tricorythodes stygiatus*	August–September 15	22–26
White Fly	*Ephoron leukon*	August–September	12–16
Flying Black Ants		August–September	14–16
Grasshoppers		July–September	6–12
Crickets		June–August	8–10
Ants		May–September	14–20

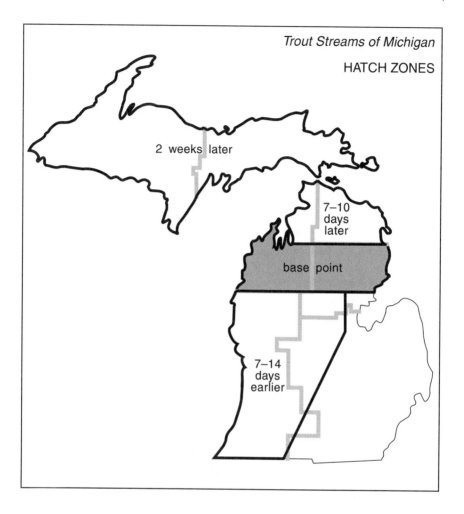

For example, it is possible to chase the Hendricksons from late April to mid-June: Start on the North Branch of the White around April 22, move north to the Pere Marquette, Little Manistee, then east to the Au Sable around May 5, then north to the Sturgeon, Black, Pigeon (or slightly west to the Upper Manistee), and finally, into the Upper Peninsula in mid-June.

The chart on page 296 presents basic information on some of the more significant hatches on Michigan trout streams. It is not a complete listing and regional variations can and should be confirmed through local fly shops. A very thorough and accurate guide to the important trout stream insects of Michigan has been prepared by the Challenge Chapter of Trout Unlimited. Copies can be purchased at many fly shops, or directly from the Challenge Chapter, Trout Unlimited, P.O. Box 63, Bloomfield Hills, MI 48013. And another guide with fishing tips in a size to fit in your vest has recently been published. It was researched and written by John Oberlatz and funded jointly by the Anglers of the Au Sable and the Martuch Chapter of TU with all proceeds going back to cold-water resources. *The Hatch Guide* is available at fly shops throughout Michigan.

This listing is incomplete by design. There is enough stream-to-stream variation in strength and timing of hatches to make any schedule that is presented as anything more than an approximation a disservice to the reader. Additionally, there are local hatches of major significance on certain rivers or sections of rivers. An example of this is the White Fly *(Ephoron leukon)*. It does not appear on all Michigan trout streams, but where it prevails, such as on the Rogue and lower Au Sable in late August and September, it is a true superhatch with very large fish regularly feeding on the surface. Consult any of the fly shops listed in this book for accurate information on hatches, patterns, and stream conditions.

Michigan Fly Patterns

Anglers, fly shops, and guides in each of the state's districts have developed specialized patterns to effectively mimic local hatches, and some of these, over the years, have attained varying degrees of local, national, and worldwide fame.

Listed here are a few Michigan creations that belong in everyone's fly box.

ADAMS AND FEMALE ADAMS IN SIZES 10–20

This is probably the single most productive dry fly ever developed. It successfully imitates a wide variety of mayfly duns and is adequate for certain caddis. When in doubt, start with an Adams.

BORCHER'S DRAKE 10–16

This pheasant-tail or turkey-bodied mayfly utilizes smoky dun wings, moose-mane tail, and grizzly/brown hackle mix to successfully represent a variety of dark mayfly duns including the Mahogany Drake, Hendrickson, and Brown Drake.

RUSTY'S SPINNER 10–18

Grizzly hackle tips tied spent with a mixed grizzly and brown hackle, pheasant or dark brown hackle tail, and a deer-hair body make this pattern a must for dark mayfly hatches.

ROBERT'S YELLOW DRAKE 10–18

This parachute tie is effective in its representation of the light duns such as the Sulphur. A light cream or pale yellow deer-hair body, ginger tail and ginger hackle, with a white deer-hair or calf-tail wing makes a very productive pattern throughout Michigan. Tied in large sizes this fly works very well during the *Hexagenia limbata* riot.

SPRING'S WIGGLER/CLARK LYNN NYMPH 6–10

This nymph is famous as a steelhead fly, but is fished with success throughout the season by knowledgeable anglers. It is a reasonable imitation of the Hex nymph and is very easy to tie. A fox squirrel tail and shell-back pulled forward over a cream or yellow body palmered with ginger or reddish brown hackle is very productive during late May and June. The June Wiggler is tied as above, but sports two pairs of fine, white rubber legs.

BEAMAN'S GHOST 8–12

Hugh Beaman's adaptation of the Black Ghost uses a black wool body with gold tinsel rib, white hackle wing, and either a red or yellow throat (use hackle fibers) tied sparse and lightly weighted. It is a seductive streamer for brook trout throughout the state.

GRIFFITH'S GNAT 16–24

George A. Griffith, founder of Trout Unlimited, popularized this one. It is the most effective general-use midge pattern fished today. A simple peacock herl body with a proportionate grizzly hackle wrapped palmer-style creates a protein illusion that trout find hard to resist.

SRB (SECRET RUBBER BUG) 12–18

This is a souped-up version of the Griffith's Gnat and is very effective as a general search pattern. It represents a housefly, deerfly, or beetle. In addition to the classic Griffith's Gnat recipe, the SRB sports a pair of grizzly hackle tip wings tied in a delta down-wing attitude and a shell-back of black or dark gray evasote.

ZOO COUGAR

This sculpin streamer pattern is now one of North America's top producers of trophy trout. It was developed by Kelly Galloup of Traverse City.

Last, the authors recommend a selection of Dun and Cream Variants in sizes 12–18, cream and brown Bivisibles in sizes 12–14, Royal Wulffs, Royal Trudes and Lime Trudes, and Irresistibles as a thorough collection of attractor dry patterns. Pheasant Tail, Gold-Ribbed Hare's Ear, and caddis nymphs, in a variety of sizes, both weighted and unweighted, are productive throughout Michigan. Clouser Minnows, Muddlers, Woolly Buggers, Light Spruce, and Zoo Cougars were the streamers most often in need of replacement as the research for this book was conducted. The Deer-Hair Mouse and weighted crayfish are two specialty patterns that should be in your fly box.

Appendix B: Fly Shops, Outfitters, and Guides

Although not an all-inclusive list, the businesses listed here are full-service operations. The shops offer a complete selection of patterns, equipment, fly-tying supplies, and accessories. The shops and guides have a thorough knowledge of the hatches and trout streams in their respective areas and can be of invaluable assistance in the planning and execution of any trip to Michigan's trout waters.

Detroit Metro Area

The Benchmark
32715 Grand River Avenue
Farmington, MI 48336
248-477-8116

Orvis Detroit
29500 Woodward Avenue
Royal Oak, MI 48073
248-542-5700

MacGregor's Outdoors
803 North Main
Ann Arbor, MI 48104
734-761-9200

John and Chris Vincent
Flymart
1002 North Main Street
Royal Oak, MI 48067
1-800-573-6335; 248-584-2848

and
31009 Jefferson
St. Clair Shores, MI 48082
810-415-5650

Bueter's Outdoors
120 E. Main Street
Northville, MI 48167
248-349-3677

Westbank Anglers
Bloomfield Plaza
6612 Telegraph Road
Bloomfield Hills, MI 48301
248-538-3474

Paint Creek Outfitters
203 East University
Rochester, MI 48307
248-650-0440

Au Sable Outfitters
17005 Kercheval
Grosse Pointe, MI 48230
313-642-2000

Mid-Michigan
Jay's Sporting Goods
Old US 27
Clare, MI 48617
517-386-3475

Frank's Tackle
Linwood, MI 48634
517-697-5341

M. Chance Fly-Fishing Specialties
5100 Marsh Road
Okemos, MI 48864
517-349-6696
877-359-8937

Jac Ford (guide)
Country Anglers
2030 S. Thomas Road
Saginaw, MI 48609
517-781-0997

John Hunter (guide)
1193 Plains Road
Leslie, MI 49251
231-848-4344

Little Folks Outfitters
143 E. Main Street
Midland, MI 48640
517-832-4100; 877-550-4668

Northern Highlands
Rusty Gates
Gates Au Sable Lodge
471 Stephan Bridge Road

Grayling, MI 49738
517-348-8462

Steve Southard
The Fly Factory
P.O. Box 709
Grayling, MI 49738
517-348-5844

Bob Linsenman (guide)
5875 Loon Lake Road
Rose City, MI 48654
517-685-3161

Gary Nelkie
Nordic Sports
218 West Bay Street
East Tawas, MI 48730
517-362-2001

Kelly Neuman
Streamside Custom Rods & Guide
Service
2085 N. Abbey
Fairview, MI 48621
517-848-5983

Mike Bachelder
Bachelder Spool & Fly
1434 E. State Road
West Branch, MI 48661
517-345-8678

Hartman's
East County Road 612
Lovells, MI 49738
517-348-9679

Fuller's North Branch Outing Club
East County Road 612
Lovells, MI 49738
517-348-7951

Thunder Bay Territory
Alphorn Sport Shop
137 West Main Street
Gaylord, MI 49735
517-732-5616

Mike Moreau (guide)
P.O. Box 342
Onaway, MI 49735
517-733-6050

Sleeping Bear
Backcast Fly Shop
1675 Benzie Highway (Crystal Plaza)
Benzonia, MI 49616
1-800-717-5222

Jeff Bower
Aries Tackle
7567 Michigan Avenue
Thompsonville, MI 49683
231-378-4520

The Troutsman
4386 U.S. 31 North
Traverse City, MI 49686
1-800-30-TROUT

Whippoorwill Fly Shop
305 E. Lake Street
Petoskey, MI 49770
231-348-7061

Jordan River Fly Shop
105 Main Street
East Jordan, MI 49727
231-536-9925

Hawkins Outfitters
17660 E. Oviatt Road
Lake Ann, MI 49650
231-228-7135

Schmidt Outfitters
P.O. Box 211
Wellston, MI 49689
231-848-4191
1-888-221-9056

Streamside Orvis Shop
440 Grand Traverse Village
Williamsburg, MI 49690
231-938-5339

Wine Country
Thornapple Outfitters
1200 East Paris
Grand Rapids, MI 49546
616-975-3800

Pere Marquette River Lodge
MI 37, Route 1
P.O. Box 1290
Baldwin, MI 49304
231-745-3972

John Kluesing (guide)
Northern Lights Guide Service
1141 Wolf Lake Drive
Baldwin, MI 49304
231-745-3792

Bob Nicholson (guide)
1916 Croton Drive
Newaygo, MI 49337
231-652-4016

Merrill Katz
Doc's Custom Fly Tackle
1804 Thrushwood
Portage, MI 49002
616-327-8917

Fishing Memories
8842 Portage Road

Portage, MI 49002
616-329-1803

Al & Pete's Sports
111 S. Jefferson
Hastings, MI 49058
616-945-4417

Steve Fraley
Baldwin Tackle
9331 So. MI-37
Baldwin, MI 49304
231-745-3529

Angler's Edge
218 Washington Street
Grand Haven, MI 49417
616-842-8588

Matt Supinski
The Gray Drake
7176 So. Hazelwood
Newaygo, MI 49337
231-652-2868

Glen Blackwood
Great Lakes Fly-Fishing Co.
2775 10 Mile Road
Rockford, MI
1-800-303-0567
616-866-6060

Walt Grau
7805 Comanche Pass
Branch, MI 49402
231-757-3411

Lunker's
26324 U.S. 12 East
Edwardsburg, MI 49112
616-663-3745

Parsley's Sports Shop
70 State Road
Newaygo, MI 49337
231-652-6986

Phil Cusey
1029 Pinecrest S.E.
Grand Rapids, MI 49506
616-243-9581

Upper Peninsula
Lindquist's Outdoor Sports
131 West Washington
Marquette, MI 49855
906-228-6380

John Ramsay (guide)
15414 N. Black River Road
Ironwood, MI 49938
906-932-4038

Bart Domin
Black Bear Sports
100 W. Cloverland
Ironwood, MI 49938
906-932-5253

Appendix C: Michigan Angler's and Traveler's Information

EMERGENCY:

Natural Resources Law Violations (RAP) 1-800-292-7800
Pollution Emergency Alerting System (PEAS) 1-800-292-4706

Department of Natural Resources:

Fisheries Division, Lansing, 517-373-1280 www.dnr.state.mi.us
Fishing Hotline, 800-ASK-FISH
Weekly Fishing Reports, 517-373-0908
Hearing Impaired, 517-373-1137
Law Division, 517-373-1263
Wildlife Division, 517-373-1263
Travel Michigan, 517-373-0670

Lake Superior Management Unit, 906-293-5131

Alger, Baraga, Chippewa, Gogebic (northern half), Houghton, Keweenaw, Luce, Marquette, Ontonagon (northern half)

Northern Lake Michigan Unit, 906-875-6622

Delta, Dickinson, Iron, Mackinac (western half), Marquette (southern half), Menominee, Schoolcraft

Central Lake Michigan Unit, 231-775-9727

Antrim, Benzie, Charlevoix, Clare (northwest), Emmet, Grand Traverse, Kalkaska, Lake, Leelanau, Manistee, Montcalm (northern half), Muskegon, Newaygo, Oceana, Osceola, Roscommon (western half), Wexford

Southern Lake Michigan Unit, 616-685-6851

Allegan, Barry, Berrien, Branch, Calhoun, Cass, Clinton, Gratiot (southern half), Hillsdale (northwestern half), Ingham, Ionia, Jackson, Kalamazoo, Kent, Montcalm (southern half), Ottawa, Shiawassee (western half), St. Joseph, Van Buren

Northwest Lake Huron Unit, 517-732-3541

Alcona, Alpena, Cheboygan, Chippewa (southern half), Crawford, Mackinac (eastern half), Montmorency, Oscoda, Otsego, Presque Isle, Roscommon (northeast)

Southern Lake Huron Unit, 517-684-9141

Arenac, Bay, Clare (southeast), Genesee, Gladwin, Gratiot (northern half), Huron, Iosco, Isabella, Lapeer, Midland, Ogemaw, Roscommon (southeast), Saginaw, Sanilac, Shiawassee (eastern half), Tuscola

Lake Erie Unit, 734-953-0241

Hillsdale (southeastern half), Lenawee, Livingston, Macomb, Monroe, Oakland, St. Clair, Washtenaw, Wayne

MDNR Forest Management Division	517-373-1275
State Forest Campgrounds	517-335-3338
Hiking Trails/Pathways	517-373-1275
Camping Reservations	800-44-PARKS
Michigan Parks & Recreation	517-373-9900
Michigan State Police	517-336-6161

United States Forest Service:

Ottawa National Forest	906-932-1330
Hiawatha National Forest	906-786-4062
Huron-Manistee National Forest	231-775-2421

APPENDIX D: Suggested Reading

Deubler. *Trout Ponds & Lakes in the Upper Peninsula of Michigan*. Two Rivers, WI: Siskiwit Press.

Linsenman, Bob. *Au Sable River Journal*. Portland, OR: Frank Amato Publications.

Linsenman, Bob, and Kelly Galloup. *Modern Streamers for Trophy Trout*. Woodstock, VT: The Countryman Press.

Linsenman, Bob, and Steve Nevala. *Great Lakes Steelhead*. Woodstock, VT: Backcountry Guides.

Michigan Department of Natural Resources. *Inland Trout and Salmon Guide*.

____. *Michigan's Blue-Ribbon Trout Streams*.

____. *Michigan Fishing Guide*.

____. *Michigan State Parks Guide*.

Midwest Fly-Fishing Magazine. Minneapolis, MN: Midwest Fly-Fishing.

Oberlatz. *The Hatch Guide*. Martuch Trout Unlimited/Anglers of the Au Sable.

Richards-Braendle. *Caddis Super Hatches*. Portland, OR: Frank Amato Publications.

Rulseh. *Michigan Seasons*. Waukesha, WI: The Cabin Bookshelf.

Supinski, Matt. *Pere Marquette River Journal*. Portland, OR: Frank Amato Publications.

Trout Unlimited. *Angler's Guides: Black River; Boardman River; Manistee River; Pere Marquette River; Sturgeon River; Au Sable River*. Challenge Chapter–Trout Unlimited.

Index

C